Libraries and Librarianship
in India

Libraries and Librarianship ❃ in India ❃

Jashu Patel and
Krishan Kumar

Guides to Asian Librarianship
Tze-chung Li, Series Editor

GREENWOOD PRESS
Westport, Connecticut • London

Library of Congress Cataloging-in-Publication Data

Patel, Jashu, 1939–
  Libraries and librarianship in India / Jashu Patel and Krishan Kumar.
    p. cm.—(Guides to Asian librarianship, ISSN 1073–6530)
  Includes bibliographical references and index.
  ISBN 0–313–29423–2 (alk. paper)
  1. Libraries—India. 2. Library science—India. I. Krishan Kumar, 1933– II. Title.
  III. Series.
  Z845.I4 P38 2001
  020′.954—dc21   00–035454

British Library Cataloguing in Publication Data is available.

Library of Congress Catalog Card Number: 00–035454
ISBN: 0–313–29423–2
ISSN: 1073–6530

First published in 2001

Greenwood Press, 88 Post Road West, Westport, CT 06881
An imprint of Greenwood Publishing Group, Inc.
www.greenwood.com

Printed in the United States of America

The paper used in this book complies with the
Permanent Paper Standard issued by the National
Information Standards Organization (Z39.48–1984).

10 9 8 7 6 5 4 3 2 1

Contents

Preface

As a result of development in transportation, communication, and new technology, some universities and other institutions of higher learning worldwide have internationalized their curricula for comparative aspects in different subjects. It is through internationalism that extensive borrowing of ideas, activities, and technology occurs from one country to another. Library science students, faculty, librarians, and persons interested in international and comparative aspects of librarianship have shown a need to study or research libraries and librarianship in India. This book is an attempt to convey to library science students some understanding of how libraries came into existence and the role they play in contemporary Indian society. The authors have used various sources, which were widely scattered and not always conveniently available to students. Suggestions for further research have been provided with examples. This reference book is an informative guide to libraries and librarianship in India, a comprehensive introduction to the field.

India is a republic and comprises twenty-five states and seven union territories. The country is bounded in the northwest by Pakistan; north by China, Tibet, Nepal, and Bhutan; east by Burma; and southeast, south, and southwest by the Indian Ocean. New Delhi is the capital of India. It has a population of 913.07 million (1994) and U.S.$310 gross national product (GNP) per capita (1994). Hindi is the official language. There are eighteen languages including Hindi listed in the eighth schedule of the constitution.

India became independent in 1947. Since 1947 the government has given some recognition to the vital role played by libraries in the national development. As a consequence, during the last fifty years or so, a fairly good infrastructure has been set up, although its full potential has not yet been realized.

The book traces the developments of traditional and modern libraries and librarianship. Accordingly, we have made efforts to describe the development of libraries and related activities in the field of librarianship from ancient through medieval and modern India to the late 1990s. In compiling this survey, we have consulted many English-language books and articles that have been published in the past. We acknowledge the contributions made by other writers of Indian librarianship and take responsibility for any significant omissions that may have occurred during the process of writing this book.

The first chapter ventures into the history of librarianship, followed by the activities and services of various types of libraries, which include the national libraries, academic libraries, public libraries, special libraries, and school libraries. The chapters dealing with each type of library generally include the libraries' organizations, resources, functions, services, and staff.

Subsequent chapters deal with such topics as bibliographical control and services, professional organizations, library education, and library automation. A chapter-by-chapter list of sources consulted appears at the end of each chapter.

We hope that this book will prove useful for library science students and faculty in South Asia and other countries for a library in society, international library resources and services, or comparative study in librarianship type of course. We also hope that the book will also be valuable to scholars in the field of world study in librarianship and comparative library education.

❅ 1 ❅

A History of Librarianship

Libraries are as old as worldwide civilizations. What is to be learned from the study of the history of libraries that can be of value to the profession itself and to librarians? Jesse Shera has stated that history is the "logical starting point for almost every inquiry into the nature and function of the library as a social agency."[1] Learning about the evolution of librarianship allows librarians to understand its present status in society. It can give perspective to the profession of librarianship. Pierce Butler wrote on the topic of historical understanding that "librarianship, as we know it, can be fully apprehended only through an understanding of its historic origins. . . . It is obvious that the librarian's practice will be determined in part by his [her] historical understanding. . . . Unless the librarian has a clear historical consciousness . . . he [she] is quite certain at times to serve his community badly."[2] The relationship between the library and society is a dynamic one, and the history of libraries must be studied in relation to the educational, social, economic, and political institutions of society.

GENERAL BACKGROUND OF INDIA

India is a federal republic in South Asia. The population of the country is increasing every year. In 1981 it was 683.3 million and as of March 1991 it was 846.3 million, one of the most populous countries of the world. In addition to a large population, India exhibits great cultural-linguistic complexity. Although Hindi is the official national language of the country, English predominates in government and academia. Important publishing activities in many fields take place in the regional languages.

India's civilization dates back to 3,000 B.C. To Americans India has often been perceived as a country of romance and oriental mysticism, where the "peacock proudly spreads his colored fan; of elephants, of tigers, the Taj Mahal, and moonlight on the Ganges."[3] Americans and other Westerners generally know India only through Kipling and Nobel Prize winner Rabindranath Tagore. To the average late Victorian or Edwardian Englishman, India was "the jewel in the crown." J. H. Shera, on Indian culture and contribution, wrote, "Not until I began to study philosophy in college did I come to realize the rich tradition of Indian culture and the contribution it has made to Western thought."[4]

There is an urgent need to change the curriculum in Western elementary and secondary schools with respect to Eastern cultures and civilization. India has a long and rich tradition in various fields of knowledge. Significant contributions to human knowledge have been made by India's philosophers, religious leaders, poets, mathematicians, medical experts, and librarians. Some examples of the world's debt to India are:

the decimal system of numeral notation, the invention of an unknown Indian mathematician early in the Christian era. . . . Parallels may be traced between a few passages in the New Testament and the Pali scriptures. . . . Subtler, but more powerful, has been the influence of Mahatma Gandhi. Through the many friends of India in the West who were impressed by his burning sincerity and energy and by the ultimate success of his policy of non-violence in achieving India's independence. Greater than any of these influences, however, has been the influence of ancient Indian religious literature through philosophy.[5]

In Europe, "Goethe and many other writers of the early 19th century read all they could of ancient Indian literature in translation. . . . Goethe borrowed a device of Indian dramaturgy for the prologue to "Faust."[6] In the United States strong Indian influence was apparent in the writings of Emerson, Thoreau, and other New Englanders who studied much Indian religious literature in translation and influenced their contemporaries and successors.[7] The contribution of India to the culture of the world has been extensive. People must consider India's "ancient heritage in its successes and its failures, for it is no longer the heritage of India alone, but of all mankind."[8]

LEARNING AND LIBRARIES IN ANCIENT INDIA (3000 B.C.–A.D. 1206)

Since ancient times Indian has been a country devoted to pursuit of knowledge, where learning and scholarship have been held in high esteem. The Vedas, Upnishads, Suttras, and Epics, coupled with philosophical works of great sages and the considerable body of Buddhist literature, reveal that there was great progress made in learning in ancient India. Primarily religious and the privilege of the priestly class, the vast literature in ancient India existed in oral communication only and was not available in writing. However, with the passage of time and growth of literature and learning, the oral tradition became too much to continue. During the Buddhist period of Indian history, according to one writer, there were more "living manuscripts" than "written manuscripts."[9]

The earliest written and recorded materials found in India are the inscriptions on stone pillars of King Ashoka (300 B.C.); these inscriptions could be called the first outside open libraries. "The great importance of libraries [in ancient India] is demonstrated by the emphasis that is laid on the making of gifts of manuscripts (written materials) to the temple and the fear of incurring sin which is held out to those who destroy, damage or spoil the manuscripts, and this importance is stressed in the scriptures."[10] For example, on stealing a book, it was stated in the Sanskrit-language scripture that "he who steals a book may become blind of one eye, and be visited by troubles. After death he goes not to heaven, but also takes his father to hell."[11] Sanskrit was a scholarly language, which was influential in the development of linguistics. Chinese Buddhist travelers (e.g., Hiuen Tsang, I-taing, and other scholars) visited India at various times between the fourth and seventh centuries for the procurement of authentic texts of Buddhist books on the discipline of monastic life. It is evident from the records mentioned in the travelers' sources and other epigraphic material that there were monastic and university libraries in ancient India.[12] There were also libraries attached to palaces, for example, the King of Harsha Vardhana's palace library.

Of the ancient universities, Nalanda and Taxila were great reputable institutions. About Nalanda, Hiuen Tsang has left a very vivid description. It was one of the most famous of Buddhist institutions of learning. It was the place of birth and death of one of the disciples of Buddha. Nalanda University had a very big library to meet the needs of its thousands of students and hundreds of faculty who were involved in the curriculum of arts and sciences. Its library was located in three beautiful buildings. One of the buildings—Ratna-sagara (sea of gems)—had nine floors. "Both Buddhist and non-Buddhist literatures were available, and . . . one of the travelling scholars, I-tsing, stayed at Nalanda for 10 years to copy about 400 Sanskrit texts mostly on religion, amounting to 500,000 verses."[13] The library flourished until the twelfth century. Taxia, then in northern India, and now near Rawalpindi (Pakistan) flourished for about one thousand years earlier than the fifth century. It became one of the ancient centers of higher education in the Vedic literature, philosophy, and Buddhism. It had its own library and its collections included manuscripts relating to the curriculum in a variety of courses. Libraries in ancient India also developed at other famous centers of learning, such as Vikramshila, Odantapuri. "The monastic center" at Vikramshila "was founded about 810 A.D. and here scholars, who came from distant parts, translated and transcribed books and built up for the institution a valuable library."[14] Evidence also shows that there was a library at Odantapuri.[15] The Gupta period (320–540) saw an increase in compilation and writing of various subjects, including poetry, philosophy, grammar, mathematics, astronomy/science, architecture, painting, music, drama, love-making manuals, codes, and treatises, such as Sidhantas, Samhitas, Shastras.[16] The Gupta period is called "the Classical Age" of Sanskrit literature. The reference books were compiled in Sanskrit. They include dictionaries of Vedic Sanskrit, Vedic indexes, and a scientific encyclopedia on astronomy and astrology. The writer of the famous astronomical treatise, *Aryabhatiya*, was Aryabhatta. Born in A.D. 476, he is known as the father of Indian epicyclic astronomy.[17] He was one of the most original and brilliant scientists. In *Aryabhatiya* he demonstrated his fine grasp of facts and logic. His treatise is a masterpiece on mathematics and astronomy.

The temple (Mandir) libraries existed in the eleventh, twelfth, and thirteenth centuries. They were maintained by royal grants or donations from wealthy people.[18] After the Gupta period, "the library portion of the temple of Lord Jagannath at Puri in Orissa, the Great Temples in South India and the Raghunath Mandir at Jammu in north India became living monuments of the architecture."[19] The ancient Indian temple was open to all members of the community. The people who came to the temple for worship also visited the library to get "medicine for the soul" or food for the mind as "prasad" in the form of sacred books to recite there as a part of daily ritual. The recitation of the Vedas or other sacred texts is still practiced in the temples of South Asia. The library activated the spirit in man, and the devotee would go out of that temple of knowledge spiritually and mentally satisfied.[20] Holy Jains believed in possessing beautiful copies of their religious books. They wrote, encouraged reading, and distributed other items of merit to the recognized centers of Jain learning. Later their interest in reading and writing grew into the practice of Jainism. As a result of this religious practice, they established libraries that were attached to their temples. The famous *Jain Bhandars* (literally, storehouse of knowledge) were located at Jaisalmer, Patan, Khambhat, and other places; they are presently well known for their rich collections.[21] Good books were kept in the families, and daily reading became the ritual as one of the duties of the family. As a result, some learned individuals had at home a sizable collection of the Vedas, Smritis, Shastras, and other books for their own use and reference.

The administrative and organizational aspects of libraries have been dealt with in the only existing work, Bhaskara Samhita, which tells that a library should be located in a finely built stone building. "In shelving, the method . . . was to cover each MS [manuscript] in a piece of cloth, tie it up and place it alongside others on iron stacks. The librarian in charge of the materials had not only to look after the materials and see to its preservation, but also to guide readers in their studies and inquiries."[22]

The administrators of ancient university libraries (e.g., Taxila, Nalanda) knew the system of classification of books, which was developed by the great Sanskrit scholar, Panini. The books were classified by subjects[23] or by form. The writing materials were the palm leaf, silk, silver and copper plates, wood, and leather, metal and stone. "The palm leaf archives of the temple of Jaganath at Puri contain specimens of writings of early history. . . . King Kanishka (78 A.D.) had the sacred writing of the Buddhists engraved on copper plates."[24] In India "the art of writing was known . . . about the 5th or 6th century B.C.—the generally accepted date for the Buddhist canonical literature."[25] Copper plates were strung together. Palm leaf manuscripts were stitched together, and they were stored on wooden shelves or in leather or wooden boxes.

Financial support for libraries, both educational and religious, came from rulers and wealthy men.

It was a common practice of the ruler to give land grants to the priests, the scholarly class of Aryans, who devoted their whole lives to the cause of learning and education. . . . The gifts of land and building and the revenue of a hundred villages had been set apart for meeting the recurring expenditure in maintaining Nalanda University, which was originally founded by the liberal endowments created by 500 traders who after purchasing land with their money had made a gift of it to Buddha.[26]

From the foregoing evidence of financial support for libraries, it can be concluded that "ancient India had so many Carnegies to give huge gifts of property in charity for the cause of education and libraries in India."[27] The library at Vallabhi received a grant to purchase books of "the Holy Faith." The priestly class recorded the religious materials for one class, and these materials were not meant for other classes in the society. This limitation to "one class and the rigid caste organization persisted . . . until the advent of Buddhism."[28]

LIBRARIES IN MEDIEVAL INDIA (1206–1757)

The Mughal emperors of India made remarkable contributions in establishing libraries. However, the ancient library tradition in India continued for a long time. The royal/court libraries existed during the time of kings like Harsha. Even at the present time, valuable collections are available in the court libraries of Bikaner, Mysore, Tanjore, Kashmir, Jaipur, and Nepal. The royal libraries were consulted by scholars from other countries for study and research. The Brahmanical centers of learning flourished from the tenth century onward, through the studies of Vedas and Shastras in the community and educational institutions. The Muslim rulers started making great changes "not only in the social and political fields" but also in education and libraries. During this period, "The personal character of the reigning sovereign was the most important factor affecting education."[29] Sir Abdul Qadir wrote, "The libraries which came into existence in India as a result of the love of learning of many of its Muslim rulers were a great help to the cause of learning."[30] The Muslim rulers opened up new centers of learning. They made great contributions to Indian culture also, and libraries played a significant role in the cultural development of the nation. Firuz Shah and other Muslim rulers of the Tughaluq dynasty supported the establishment of libraries generously.

It was only under the establishment of the Delhi Sultanate (1206–1526) that different types of libraries were founded as a result of the literary and educational activities. Sultan Jalaluddin Khilji (1290) established the Imperial Library and regarded its librarian so highly that he "conferred upon him the honour of wearing a white robe which the members of the Imperial House and Nobles of the highest order alone could wear."[31] Sufi Nizamuddin Auliya, "the great religious Muslim leader of the time, also established a library by raising funds; it contained a large collection of manuscripts and was open to the public."[32] The private collections of Ghazi Khan, an Afghan noble of the Punjab, became notable also. The period of the Mughal is considered as the golden period of Indian history for its educational, literary, and library activities.[33] The Mughal rulers had their palace libraries.

Babur established the first Mughal Imperial Library in 1526. His library consisted of rare manuscripts, which he selected from his forefathers' private collections. He also acquired books during his rule as the emperor of India. Humayun, his son, succeeded Babur in 1530. He built the magnificent Khana-i-Tilism at Agra. "Its main portion, the central one of the three buildings which was known as 'Khana-i-Sadat,' had the library. There were books, gilded pen cases, portfolios, picture books and beautiful works of calligraphy in the library."[34] Akbar (1556–1605), his son, the "Great Mughal" succeeded Humayun in 1356. He administered the Imperial Library by introducing and implementing "reforms into the management, classification and storage of books."[35] He created a separate department for systemizing its management. He died in 1605. It was revealed that the Imperial Library had twenty-four thousand books at the time of his death. Akbar founded colleges in Agra, Delhi, and Fatehpur Sikri. He also established a library only for women at Fatehpur Sikri. Jahangir (1605–1637), another Mughal emperor, increased the Imperial Library collection to about 60,000 books. He also established a picture gallery and acquired miniature paintings. He had his own personal library in addition to the Imperial Library. He purchased "a copy of the Yusuf-Zulaika, a book with paintings and illustrations, for . . . slightly more than £3,000 [British pounds]. Two copies of this are still available in India, one at the Khuda Baksh Library of Patna and the other at Shantiniketan, the University founded by the [Nobel Prize winner] poet Tagore."[36] Jahangir, during his power, made a law that when the wealthy men died heirless, the property should be used for building and repairing schools, monasteries, libraries, and other institutions. Shah Jahan, who built the Taj Mahal, also founded the Imperial College at Delhi. He also encouraged education and learning at Lahore, Ahmedabad, and Kashmir. The Imperial Library and Museum were moved to the new capital at Delhi under his rule. During Shah Jahan's rule, "good libraries had been started by Jesuit Fathers in Agra and Delhi. These libraries contained manuscripts in eastern languages written by Jesuits, as well as oriental religious documents."[37] Aurangzeb established his rule in 1656. His interest in reading Islamic law and theology led him to increase books relating to the subjects. He also "helped in opening schools and libraries in connection with Mohammedan mosques."[38] He was the last of the great Mughal emperors. Even though mosque libraries were founded during this period of the Mughal Empire, the Hindu method of education with the support of libraries continued in educational institutions and temples. Mosque libraries were open to the general public in India.

The learned scholars and wealthy men had private libraries and they contributed to the growth of libraries. Abdul Rahim Khan-i-Khanan had a large personal library. He opened his library to scholars. Shaikh Faizi and Qutbul-Mulk, as well as Mughal princesses, also had their personal libraries, which contained manuscripts and rare books. The first princess who maintained her personal library was Gulbadan Begum, daughter of Babur. The ruler of Mysore, Jaipur, and other places possessed their own libraries. Maharaja Sowai Jai Singh of Jaipur, for example, established a library in 1724, which had a special collection of books on astronomy. There were also libraries and archives of the Maratha rulers. The Peshwas had their personal libraries. They "not only procured manuscripts but got other rare and old manuscripts copied."[39] Madhava Rao, for example, spent Rs. 31.00 every month for copying his library's manuscripts between 1765 and 1766.[40] "Like the Mughuls, Marathas also maintained a big establishment, the imperial secretariat or Hazur Daftar to preserve all state papers, documents, and account books with utmost care and order, employing more than two hundred Karkuns or clerks."[41] The Maratha kings established the Tanjore Saraswati Mahal Library in 1523. It is the only one surviving now and contains 20,000 manuscripts. . . . Out of this collection, 8,000 volumes are on palm leaves."[42] There were also libraries attached to Hindu centers of learning at Benaras, Mithila, Nadia, and elsewhere. These Hindu centers of learning played important roles in the library development of medieval India.[43] "The libraries of these centers contained huge collections of manuscripts on religion and philosophy as well as on other subjects like medicine, science and history."[44] The Christian missionaries also contributed in the development of libraries in medieval India. "Contribution of Christians to the development of libraries in India began with Vasco da Gama in 1498."[45]

In terms of the organization and management of libraries in medieval India, the library personnel had important status through their positions. During the Sultanate period they were known as "Kitabdar" or "Mushaf Burdar." They were scholar-librarians. During the Mughal period, the head librarian was known as "Nizam" and the assistant librarian as "Muhatin" or "Darogha." There were the Nizams of Akbar's Imperial Library. Jahangir had a Nizam, Muktab Khan. Other types of staff during the Mughal period included scribes, book illustrators, calligraphers, copyists, translators, bookbinders, and gilders. With the introduction of the first printing press in India in 1556, book production grew. In the late medieval period, the manuscript collections in Jain Bhandars were preserved in cardboard boxes, each containing ten to fifteen manuscripts.[46]

During the Mughal period, books were classified broadly by subjects. The library of Akbar was classified according to the following subject divisions: (1) astrology, (2) poetry, (3) medicine, (4) music, (5) philology, (6) philosophy, (7) suffism, (8) geometry, (9) theology, (10) commentaries, and (11) traditions. The fixed location system for classification was used by the Jain Jnana Bhandars. Accession numbers were given to the manuscripts and the manuscript boxes.[47] Cataloging was done through indication of the manuscript number, the manuscript title, number of pages, and sometimes the name of the author.

THE BRITISH PERIOD (1757–1947)

British influence spread after the decline of Muslim power in India. A number of academic institutions were established during the British period by the East India Company (the representatives of the British Empire) and by the Christian missions. Warren Hastings, then governor of India, founded the Calcutta Madrasa (college) in 1781. Jonathan Duncan, then British agent, founded the Benaras Sanskrit College in 1792. The Calcutta Fort William College was also established in 1800. Libraries were attached to these academic institutions. Other colleges were also founded as a result of the Charter Act of 1813, to which their libraries were also attached. The present university libraries of India were created by the British rulers during the nineteenth century. The first University of Calcutta was founded in 1857, followed by the University of Bombay, and the University of Madras. These three universities were based on the model of the University of London, which was originally an institution for conducting comprehensive examinations, and they followed a British system of organization and administration. The University of Calcutta opened its university library in 1873, followed by the University of Bombay in 1879 and the University of Madras in 1907. The Indian University Act of 1904 contained specific provisions to build, equip, and maintain university libraries. The place of a library became important in colleges and universities. The Act of 1904 also contained provisions to lend books to students. There were only nineteen universities in India prior to 1947. Improvements were made in Indian academic libraries after consultation with library experts from the United Kingdom and the United States. In this context, C. G. Viswanathan wrote:

The years 1919–1939 witnessed some far reaching changes in university library administration. It was because of closer contacts with Western libraries, mainly British, which had effected certain improvements such as open access, card catalogues, subject bibliographies, reference service and inter-library loans as essential features of library service. Some university librarians from India studied librarianship abroad and brought their experiences to bear on the functioning of Indian university libraries.[48]

In 1913 the first university librarian from India was sent to the United Kingdom for formal training in librarianship. The Panjab University at Lahore was the first university to appoint an American librarian, Asa Don Dickinson, who was trained under Melvil Dewey during 1902 to 1903. His library assignment in 1915 was to organize, catalog and administer the university library and to give a training course in modern library methods.

In the early eighteenth century the first free public library of Bombay was established as the Bombay Branch of the Royal Asiatic Society. Lord Minto was the governor general of India from 1806 to 1813. He wrote a note in 1811, which made "provisions for public access to libraries and status of librarians, which were far ahead of contemporary thinking of these issues worldwide. The roots of free public library movement in South Asia go back to this historical note."[49] Lord Minto proposed the principal rules for the institutions which also included public libraries.

"The expressions used in these rules (i.e., rule 5 and 7) are 'public library' and 'ready access . . . to strangers,' i.e., the general public."[50] According to Mumtaz A. Anwar, "This idea of establishing public libraries attached to colleges providing newly access to the general public coming from the top authority (i.e., Governor) of the country (India) was far ahead of its times. A far more revolutionary proposal was to provide the same status to librarians as that enjoyed by the teachers (Rule 6)."[51] Anwar, on Lord Minto's rules, commented, "It is a great tragedy that those who followed Lord Minto did not see it fit to implement his recommendations. If these rules were implemented then, we would have had no reason to complain about the bureaucratic apathy towards free public libraries today."[52]

The establishment of a library by the Asiatic Society of Bengal in 1784, the Madras Library Society in 1812, the Calcutta Public Library in 1835, and the establishment of libraries in other towns to serve mostly the "chosen few" and also "all ranks and classes without distinction,"[53] laid the foundation of the concept of a public library.

In Bombay the growth and development of libraries was facilitated by the initiation of the proposal by the Bombay government to register libraries, which were to receive free copies of books published from the "Funds for the Encouragement of Literature." The Gujarat Vernacular Society along with a library was established in Ahmedabad in 1848. Two new libraries, the Native (Public) Library in Ahmedabad and the Andrews Library in Surat were established in 1849 and 1850. Other libraries were established in towns like Ahmedabad (1870), Nadiad (1892), Broach (1855), Godhra (1866), Ankiewar (1888), and Jalalpur (1897).[54] Public libraries were established in the state capitals of Saurashtra (now part of Gujarat State). Some such libraries included Lang Library, Rajkot (1856); Government Library, Junagadh (1867); Barton Library, Bhavnagar (1882) and Victoria Jubilee Library.[55]

The story of the National Library starts with the establishment of the Imperial Library at Calcutta in 1891. In 1902, due to the efforts of Lord Curzon, Calcutta Public Library (established in 1835) was merged into the Imperial Library, Calcutta. After independence in 1948, its name was changed to National Library of India. Another public library that was opened to the general public was the Punjab Public Library at Lahore (now in Pakistan), established in 1900. The Press and Registration of Books Act in 1867 proved to be beneficial for the establishment of libraries and the development of the National Library, and Connemara Public Library in Madras in 1896.

Public libraries were also established in Indian states and they were in operation by 1892. For example, states like Baroda established the Baroda State Library in Baroda in 1877; Cochin established the Public Library and Reading Room in Trichur in 1873; Dhar established the Victoria General Library in Dhar in 1856; Indore established the General Library in Indore in 1852; Jaipur established the Maharajah's Public Library in Jaipur in 1866. Other states established such libraries including Jammu and Kashmir in 1879; Kathiawar in 1886; Kolhapur in 1850; Nizam's Dominions in 1891 and Travancore in 1829.[56] Public library development in India also benefited from "Indo-American library co-operation" created by the first American library pioneer in India, William Alanson Borden (1853–1931). He declared: "I determined to introduce into Baroda (India) what we in the United States have recognized as a goal to be ultimately attained, but which we have not yet reached. . . . What America could only dream of, Baroda could do, and in a measure has done."[57] Thus wrote Borden to his fellow U.S. librarians who created a library link between India and the United States. Borden learned his first lessons in library management as a pupil-assistant of Charles Ammi Cutter at the Boston Athenaeum and taught at Columbia School of Library Economy as a colleague of Melvil Dewey.[58] He initiated a free public library system in Baroda, the first of its kind in India, in 1910. As the director of state libraries, he planned a network of free public libraries "constituting a state central library, four district or divisional libraries, forty-five town libraries, and more than a thousand village libraries—all integrated into one chain–a system."[59] As a result of this system, "within two decades 85 percent of the Baroda urban and rural population had access to libraries."[60] Borden also established the first library school in India and trained his own assistants and successors; moreover, he developed a scheme of library classification especially suited to Indian libraries. He was instrumental in the foundation of the Baroda Library Club and its journal called *Library Miscellany* (published quarterly in three languages between 1912 and 1919). Among other notable achievements of Borden in Baroda included an extensive traveling library service, children's library service, and a visual instruction department.[61] What Borden accomplished in Baroda had a tremendous influence on many other parts of India and other South Asian countries. For example, "the Librarian's Club originally comprising librarians of the Baroda libraries had its echo in Punjab where Asa Don Dickinson in 1915 founded the Punjab Library Association."[62] Dickinson published *The Panjab Library Primer* in 1916, which was the second library science publication in India.[63]

Tipu Sultan, the ruler of Mysore, was a great lover and collector of books. The library built by Tipu Sultan was famous for its rich collections of manuscripts, books, and art. A part of the collection of Tipu Sultan found its way to the India Office Library in London (established in 1798) and formed the basis for its growth. During this period, the efforts were made by the government of India in 1868 and thereafter for the development of Sanskrit manuscript libraries in India. Sanskrit manuscripts were collected and preserved. As a result of these efforts, western scholarship benefited through loans, copies, and acquisition.[64] Some notable Indian libraries that included strong manuscript collections were the Sampurnanand Sanskrit University Library in Varanasi; the Saraswati Mahal Library, Tanjore; the Khuda Baksh Library, Patna (1838); the Sanskrit Manuscript Library, Madras; the Rampur Library; and the Bhandarkar Oriental Research Institute Library, Pune. Other notable research and special libraries were the Asiatic Society Library, Calcutta (1784); the Geological Survey of India Library, Calcutta (1851); and the Theosophical Society Library, Madras (1875).

There is still discussion about the professional status of librarianship among both librarians and nonlibrarians. A definition of a *profession* will reveal some of the elements that are used to signify librarianship as a profession. A profession, according to S. R. Ranganathan, is "a set of people, organized people of sufficient ability, who are dedicated to do a particular service in a particular field."[65] Based on the foregoing evidence of the first Baroda Library School and the first library science periodical, the profession of librarianship in India emerged.

In the early twentieth century with the establishment of library associations and commitment of dedicated trained librarians, the development of libraries in the various states became evident. The first state library association was the Andhradesa Library Association (1914). During this period, other library associations were formed in Bengal (1926), Madras (1928), Punjab (1929), Bihar (1936), Assam (1938), and Kerala (1945). The first All-India professional body was the All-India Public Library Association (1918). The first All-India Conference of Librarians was sponsored by the government of India (Lahore, January 4–8, 1918). The first national association was the Indian Library Association (ILA), established in Calcutta in 1933. The founding of the Indian Library Association was achieved through the efforts of Sir A. C. Woolner, M. O. Thomas, Khan Rahadur, K. M. Asadullah, R. C. Manchanda, and S. R. Ranganathan. The Government of India Libraries Association (GILA) was another association established in the same year (1933). The name was changed to Government of India Librarians Association in 1977 and changed again to Association of Government Librarians and Information Specialists (AGLIS) ten years later. However, its membership is limited to those librarians who are employed in the government libraries.

The development of literature of librarianship began with publication of the first journal, *Library Miscellany*, in 1912. Another journal in Telugu, *Granthalaya Sarvaswamu*, started in Andhra by the library employees. Andhra also started another journal in English, the *Indian Library Journal*, in 1924. The *Modern Librarian* journal was published by the Punjab Library Association in 1930. The library periodical the *Pustakalaya* in Hindi was published by the Bihar Library Association. The Indian Library Association started its first journal, *Library Bulletin*, in 1942. S. R. Ranganathan published his *Five Laws of Library Science* in 1931. On the topics of classification and cataloging, he published *Colon Classification* (1933) and *Classified Catalog Code* (1934). The library literature emerged through the writings of many professional leaders. As a result of foreign library experts, some changes were made for the improvement of libraries. Some of these foreign library experts included J. A. Chapman, John Macfarlane, W. A. Borden, Asa Don Dickinson, John Sargent, A. C. Burnell, and A. M. R. Montague.

Many Indian library leaders of this era also contributed to the development of libraries and librarianship. Some, among others, included Asadullah Khan, M. O. Thomas, Lala Babu Ram, Wali Mohammed, and N. R. Ray.

As indicated earlier, the first formal library training program in India was conducted by Borden in Baroda in 1911. Another professional training program at the university level was started in 1915 at Punjab University, Lahore, by Asa Don

Dickinson. In 1937 the University of Madras was the first to offer a one-year full-time program, leading to a postgraduate diploma in library science. Benaras Hindu University started a yearlong postgraduate diploma program in 1941; a yearlong diploma program also started at Bombay University in 1946 and at the University of Delhi in 1947.

POSTINDEPENDENCE DEVELOPMENT

With the achievement of independence in 1947, India made rapid progress in librarianship. S. R. Ranganathan was very much in the forefront of the development of librarianship in India. Before independence he published *The National Library System: A Plan for India* (1946); in 1947 he published *Post-War Reconstruction of Libraries in India* and in 1950 he published *Library Development Plan With a Thirty Year Program for India*. Sir John Sargent, then education adviser to the government of India, appointed a National Library Committee in 1947 with Ranganathan as one of its members. Various other committees and commissions were also appointed to examine libraries in India. The appointment of the University Education Commission in 1948 was the first major event after independence, with S. Radhakrishnan (later vice president and then president of India) as its chairman. The University Grants Commission (UGC) was appointed in 1953 for the development of the university libraries. Later the Education Commission was appointed (1964–1966) for the benefit of university libraries. The Secondary Education Commission, also known as the Mudaliar Commission, was appointed in 1953 for the development of school libraries. The government appointed the Advisory Committee for Libraries in 1957, which strengthened the development of public libraries in India. These foregoing committees and commissions made recommendations that changed finances, services, and working conditions of different types of libraries and their staff. In 1951 the U.S. government, through Public Law 480 Plan and a Wheat Loan Program of Educational Exchange assisted the eighty-eight university and research libraries in collection development. Another benefit derived from the Wheat Loan Exchange Program was the provision of grants to thirty-five university librarians for study and travel in the United States and grants for five American librarians to work in India.

The development of public libraries began with independence in 1947 to the credit of Ranganathan and other library leaders. The Madras Public Library Act of 1948 was the first library legislation to be enacted in independent India for providing public library service. Ranganathan showed the way that effective library development could be achieved through passing library acts in various states. The government of the various states became aware of the utility of library acts. After Madras, Hyderabad followed suit in 1955, Andhra Pradesh in 1960, Mysore in 1965, and Maharashtra in 1967. Others to follow were West Bengal in 1979, Manipur in 1988, Kerala in 1989, Harayana in 1989, and Goa and Mizoram in 1993. A significant development of the postindependence era was that in 1948 the Imperial Library in Calcutta became the National Library of India. The Delivery of

Books (Public Libraries) Act of 1954, as amended in 1956, laid the foundation for the four national depository centers. They included the National Library in Calcutta, Asiatic Society in Bombay, Connemara Public Library in Madras, and Delhi Public Library in Delhi. The Delhi Public Library, a joint government of India and UNESCO pilot project, was founded in 1951. It was the first UNESCO library project. Within four years the library had a membership of over twenty-seven thousand registered borrowers and a collection of sixty-five thousand books. Its open access system was appreciated. It provided "all modern techniques"[66] to the Indian situation and served the people of Delhi and the suburbs.

The significant developments in providing documentation service first took place in special libraries. The development of special librarianship in India has been to a large extent sponsored by the government. During the postindependence period, the scientific and technological progress has been the main concern of India for the development of the industrial sector. The setting up of National Information System for Science and Technology (NISSAT) in 1977 is a landmark in India's science and technology information system. Documentation service is a postindependence activity. According to Ranganathan, "The credit of having started a systematic continued large-scale documentation work, for the first time in India, goes to the Forest Research Institute, Dehra Dun."[67] However, the most significant development in the area of documentation was the founding of the Indian National Scientific Documentation Center (INSDOC) at New Delhi in 1952 under the sponsorship of the Government of India and UNESCO. Since 1954 its library journal, Annals of Library Science and Documentation, had played an important role for research in library science and documentation. In 1964, INSDOC started advanced training in documentation. The Documentation Research and Training Center was established at Bangalore in 1962 under the directorship of S. R. Ranganathan for providing advanced training in documentation. The Indian Association of Special Libraries and Information Center was established in 1955.

The development of library science literature became apparent in 1912. "Between 1912 and 1987 Indian library professionals published 84 periodicals, 17 newsletters, and many annual reports. Of these only 40 periodical titles have survived to 1990."[68]

During this period, India's contribution in librarianship has been recognized in the West, particularly the work of both Ranganathan and Kaula. Writing about a basic contribution in methods of formation of knowledge, Shera said:

When Ranganathan set forth his morphology of the growth of knowledge-denudation, dissection, lamination, and loose assemblage—he opened, for me, and I am sure for many others, a completely new insight into the philosophical foundations of what librarianship is. Apart from the development of a book, or information, classification scheme that relegated Dewey to the bottom shelf, the work of the Indian scholars was far more than the formulation of a system of schedules, however intelligently done. Their thinking was far more extensive than devising a new method of "marking and parking". . . . It was a restatement of the relationship of the librarian's art to the bonds that unite user and graphic record.[69]

On contributions made by Kaula, Shera commented:

The great contribution that Kaula and his associates have made to librarianship is . . . more than the development of classification as a science: it is a way of looking at the world of librarianship, the "image," . . . of the library world, what it is and what it should be. . . . We are over concerned (in library schools) about teaching the techniques of the profession, and the "research" that emerges from it. We know very well how to do things, but we do not stop to ask why we do them, or even if we should be doing them at all.[70]

Other Indian library leaders who made contributions include D. N. Marshall, Jagdish S. Sharma, B. S. Kesavan, N. N. Gidwani, Sant Ram Bhatia, S. Bashiruddin, S. Das Gupta, and Girja Kumar.

Tremendous progress has been made in librarianship (particularly in science and technology) and in library education in India since the years following independence. Drawing upon both his U.S. and Indian experiences, L. J. Kipp, Ford Foundation consultant at the University of Delhi in 1966, concluded: "Indian librarianship is moving very rapidly. It will continue to move if it can be demonstrated that the library and the librarian contribute something of value. Administrators need to be convinced that the library is worth what it costs. Librarians cannot demonstrate this unless they are able to examine their work objectively."[71]

NOTES

1. Jesse Shera, "On the Value of Library History," *Library Quarterly* 22 (July 1952), 240–251.

2. Pierce Butler, *An Introduction to Library Science* (Chicago: University of Chicago Press, 1933), 81.

3. J. H. Shera, "Of Peacocks, Elephants, and the Philosophy of Librarianship," in V. Venkatappaiah, ed., in *March of Library Science: Kaula Festschrift* (New Delhi: Vikas, 1979), 19.

4. Ibid.

5. A. L. Basham, *The Wonder That Was India* (London: Sidgwick & Jackson, 1967), 3d rev. ed., 487–488.

6. Ibid., 488–489.

7. Ibid., 489.

8. Ibid.

9. D. N. Marshall, *History of Libraries: Ancient and Medieval* (New Delhi: Oxford & IBH, 1983), 110.

10. Om Prakash Sharma, "Forces behind the Indian Public Library Movement, 1858–1892," unpublished Ph.D. dissertation, Graduate Library School, University of Chicago, 1970, 3.

11. Ibid., 4.

12. Ibid., 5.

13. This quote and most of the other information in this paragraph is based on A. K. Mukherjee, *Librarianship: Its Philosophy and History* (London: Asia Publishing House, 1966), 83–84.

14. D. N. Marshall, "Libraries in Ancient India," in Sat Paul Goyal, ed., *Indian Librarianship: Essays in Honour of S. R. Bhatia* (Delhi: Scientific Book Store, 1972), 6.

15. Ibid.

16. G. L. Trehan, *Learning and Libraries in Ancient India—A Study* (Chandigarh: Library Literature House, 1975), 54.

17. Ibid., 54–55.

18. Ibid., 38.

19. Ibid., 56.

20. Ibid.

21. Marshall, "Libraries in Ancient India," 15.

22. Marshall, *History of Libraries: Ancient and Medieval*, 118.

23. Trehan, *Learning and Libraries in Ancient India*, 34–35.

24. Ibid., 14–15.

25. Marshall, "Libraries in Ancient India," 14.

26. Trehan, *Learning and Libraries in Ancient India*, 32.

27. Ibid.

28. Marshall, "Libraries in Ancient India," 15.

29. Sharma, "Forces behind the Indian Public Library Movement," 5.

30. Quoted in ibid., 6.

31. Quoted in Anis Khurshid, "Growth of Libraries in India," *International Library Review* 4 (1972), 22.

32. Quoted in ibid.

33. Ibid., 23.

34. Kalpana Das Gupta, "How Learned Were the Mughals: Reflections on Muslim Libraries in India," *Journal of Library History* 10 (1975), 243.

35. Ibid., 245.

36. Ibid., 247.

37. Ibid., 248.

38. Anirudh Prasad, "Libraries in Medieval India," *Library Herald* 20 (1982), 157.

39. B. K. Datta, *Libraries and Librarianship of Ancient and Medieval India* (Delhi: Atma Ram & Sons, 1970), 85.

40. Ibid.

41. Ibid.

42. S. N. Sadhu and B. N. Saraf, *Library Legislation in India: A Historical and Comparative Study* (New Delhi: Sagar, 1967), 3.

43. B. K. Datta, *Libraries and Librarianship*, 86.

44. Ibid.

45. Mohamed Taher, "India," in *Encyclopedia of Library History* (New York: Garland, 1994), 272.

46. D. N. Marshall, *History of Libraries*, 118.

47. B. K. Datta, *Libraries and Librarianship*, 172–173.

48. C. G. Viswanathan, "A Hundred Years of Indian University Libraries, 1857–1956: A Historical and Critical Survey," *Library Association Record* 49 (December 1957), 393.

49. Mumtaz A. Anwar, "The Roots of a Free Public Library Movement in South Asia," *Pakistan Library Bulletin* 21 (3–4) (September–December 1990), 15.

50. Ibid., 16.

51. Ibid.

52. Ibid.

53. Quoted in P. N. Kaula, "Libraries in India," *Herald of Library Science* 16 (2–3) (April–July 1977), 165.

54. Sadhu and Sarat, *Library Legislation in India*, 4.

55. Ibid.

56. Sharma, "Forces behind the Indian Public Library Movement," 254–255.

57. Quoted in M. L. Nagar, *Foundation of Library Movement in India* (Ludhiana: Indian Library Institute and Bibliographical Centre, 1983), 3.

58. Ibid.

59. Ibid.

60. P. N. Kaula, "Facets and Phases of Indian Library Development," in N. B. Sen, ed., *Development of Libraries in New India* (New Delhi: New Book Society of India, 1965), 159.

61. Nagar, *Foundation of Library Movement in India*, 3.

62. Khurshid, "Growth of Libraries in India," 44.

63. Ibid., 45.

64. D. C. Johnson, "Government Concern for the Development of Libraries: Sanskrit Manuscript Libraries in India, 1858–1937," unpublished Ph.D. dissertation, University of Wisconsin, Madison, 1980.

65. Quoted in A. K. Ohdedar, "The Library Profession in India: Its Status and Responsibilities," *IASLIC: Special Publication*, no. 12, pts. 1–2 (1969), 87.

66. N. B. Inamdar and M. R. Riswadker, "India," in M. Miles, ed., *International Handbook of Contemporary Developments in Librarianship* (Westport, Conn.: Greenwood Press, 1981), 194.

67. Ibid., 1981.

68. Taher, "India," 274.

69. Shera, "Of Peacocks, Elephants, and the Philosophy of Librarianship," 24.

70. Ibid., 21.

71. L. J. Kipp, "Four Libraries: Enough of Their Histories to Explain Their Problems," *Library Herald* 10 (2 and 3) (July and October 1968), 181.

SELECTED BIBLIOGRAPHY

Anwar, Mumtaz A. "The Roots of a Free Public Library Movement in South Asia." *Pakistan Library Bulletin* 21 (3–4) (September–December 1990), 12–17.

Basham, A. L. *The Wonder That Was India*. 3d rev. ed. London: Sidgwick & Jackson, 1967.

Butler, Pierce *An Introduction to Library Science*. Chicago: University of Chicago Press, 1933.

Chandler, George. *Libraries in the East: An International and Comparative Study*. London and New York: Seminar Press, 1971.

Chitale, T. B. "A Review of Library Profession in India." *Herald of Library Science* 10(1) (January 1971), 42–54.

Das Gupta, Kalpana. "How Learned Were the Mughals: Reflections on Muslim Libraries in India." *Journal of Library History* 10 (July 1975), 241–254.

Datta, Bimal Kumar. "Early Monastic Libraries and Other Institutional Libraries in India." *Library History Review* 1 (1974), 18–42.

———. *Libraries and Librarianship of Ancient and Medieval India*. Delhi: Atma Ram, 1970.

Datta, Rajeshwari. "The India Office Library: Its History, Resources and Functions." *Library Quarterly* 36(2) (April 1966), 99–148.

Davis, Donald G. "Indian Library History: A Bibliographic Essay on Major English Language Printed Works." *South Asia Library Notes and Queries* 26 (fall–winter 1989–1990), 17–23.
———. "Status of Library History in India: A Report of an Informal Survey and a Selective Bibliographic Essay." *Libraries and Culture* 25(4) (fall 1990), 575–589.
Harvey, John F. "Libraries in Bombay." *Indian Librarian* 28 (December 1973), 129–136.
Johnson, D. C. "German Influences on the Development of Research Libraries in Nineteenth Century Bombay." *Journal of Library History* 21 (1986), 215–277.
———. "Government Concern for the Development of Libraries: Sanskrit Manuscript Libraries in India, 1858–1937." Unpublished Ph.D. dissertation, University of Wisconsin, Madison, 1980.
Kaula, P. N. "Facets and Phases of Indian Library Development." In N. B. Sen, ed., *Development of Libraries in New India*. New Delhi: New Book Society of India, 1965, 158–167.
Khurshid, Anis. "Growth of Libraries in India." *International Library Review* 4 (1972), 21–65.
Kipp, L. J. "Four Libraries: Enough of Their Histories to Explain Their Problems." *Library Herald* 10(2 and 3) (July and October 1968), 175–181.
Kipp, Laurence J., and Cecilia R. Kipp. *Indian Libraries and the India Wheat Loan Educational Exchange Program: A Report* (August 1961).
Krzys, Richard. "Library Historiography." In *Encyclopedia of Library and Information Science*. Vol. 15. New York: Marcel Dekker, 1975, 294–330.
Kumar, P.S.G. *Indian Library Chronology*. New Delhi: Metropolitan, 1977.
Mangala, P. B. et al., eds. *Fifty Years of Librarianship in India: Past, Present and Future*. Delhi: Indian Library Association, 1983.
Marshall, D. N. *History of Libraries: Ancient and Medieval*. New Delhi: Oxford & IBH, 1983.
———. "Libraries in Ancient India." In Sat Paul Goyal, ed., *Indian Librarianship: Essays in Honour of S. R. Bhatia*. Delhi: Scientific Book Store, 1972.
Misra, Jogesh. *History of Libraries and Librarianship in Modern India since 1850*. Delhi: Atma Ram, 1979.
Mukherjee, A. K. *Librarianship: Its Philosophy and History*. Bombay: Asia Publishing House, 1966.
Nagar, M. L. *First American Library Pioneer in India*. 2d ed. Ludhiana: India Library Institute and Bibliographical Centre, 1983.
———. *Foundation of Library Movement in India*. Ludhiana: India Library Institute and Bibliographical Centre, 1983.
Ohdedar, A. K. *Growth of the Library in Modern India: 1498–1836*. Calcutta: World Press, 1966.
———. "Library Development in Calcutta, 1700–1900." *IASLIC Bulletin* 37 (1992), 1–14.
———. "The Library Profession in India: Its Status and Responsibilities" (IASLIC Special Publication, no. 12, pts. 1–2). Calcutta: IASLIC, 1969, 87–97.
Prasad, Anirudh. "Libraries in Medieval India." *Library Herald* 20 (1982), 155–59.
Rajagopalan, T. S. *Year's Work in Indian Librarianship, 1987*. Indian Library Association, 1988.
Rao, K. Ramakrishna. "Library Development in India." *Library Quarterly* 31(2) (April 1961), 135–153.

Sharma, Om Prakash. "Forces behind the Indian Public Library Movement, 1858–1892." Unpublished Ph.D. dissertation, Graduate Library School, University of Chicago, 1970.

Sharma, R. N., ed. *Indian Librarianship: Perspectives and Prospects*. New Delhi: Kalyani, 1981.

Shera, Jesse. "Of Peacocks, Elephants, and the Philosophy of Librarianship." In V. Venkatappaiah, ed., *March of Library Science: Kaula Festschrift*. New Delhi: Vikas, 1979.

———. "On the Value of Library History." *Library Quarterly* 22 (July 1952), 240–251.

Singh, Mohinder. "Progress in Librarianship in India, 1911–1978." *Libri* 29(2) (June 1977), 158–168.

Taher, Mohamed. "American Studies in India." In B. M. Gupta, ed., *Handbook of Libraries, Archives and Information Centers in India*. Vol. 8. Delhi: Aditya, 1990, 230–240.

———. "American Studies Research Center, Hyderabad." In B. M. Gupta, ed., *Handbook of Libraries, Archives and Information Centers in India*. Vol. 8. Delhi: Aditya, 1990, 165–174.

———. "India." In W. A. Weigand and D. G. Davis, eds., *Encyclopedia of Library History*. New York: Garland, 1994.

Taher, Mohamed, and Davis, Donald Gordon. *Librarianship and Library Science in India: An outline of Historical Perspectives*. New Delhi: Concept, 1994.

Trehan, G. L. "Dewey Conquers Library India." *Herald of Library Science* 15 (1976), 295–301.

———. *Learning and Libraries in Ancient India—A Study*. Chandigarh: Library Literature House, 1975.

Vashishthi, C. P. "Libraries in Delhi: A Scenario." In R. Saha, ed., *Souvenir*. Calcutta: Bengal Library Association, 1988, 48–56.

❧ 2 ❧

National Libraries

What is a national library? UNESCO provides the following definition, which was adopted by the UNESCO General Conference at its sixteenth session in 1970:

Libraries which irrespective of the title are responsible for acquiring and preserving copies of all significant publications published in the country and functioning as a deposit library, either by law or under other arrangement. They will also perform some of the following functions: produce a national bibliography; hold and keep up to date a large and representative collection of foreign literature including books, etc.; act as a national bibliographical center; compile union catalogs; and publish the retrospective national bibliographies.[1]

There are three national libraries in India: the National Library, Calcutta; the National Medical Library, new Delhi; and the National Science Library, New Delhi.

THE NATIONAL LIBRARY, CALCUTTA

History

The present National Library evolved out of the old Imperial Library, located in Calcutta, and established by the British government in India in 1891. Calcutta was then the capital of India. The Imperial Library was founded by Lord Curzon, then viceroy of India. It was "conceived as housing the best of European thought, with an emphasis on English."[2] The *Gazette of India* reported the objectives of the Imperial Library, which included:

The existing Imperial Library will form the nucleus of the new institution, which will be provided with Reading Rooms, public and private, as at the British Museum and Bodleian Libraries. It is intended that it should be a library of reference, a working place for students, and a repository of material for the future historians of India, in which, so far as possible, every work, written about India at any time can be seen and read."[3]

There were no changes in the foregoing objectives when the Imperial Library was renamed the National Library in 1948. After a careful study of the same objectives, P. N. Kaula suggested the following basic objectives of the National Library, Calcutta:

1. To preserve the national cultural heritage of India
2. To provide leadership and promote co-operation in library affairs in India
3. To act as a dynamic resource center dedicated to the development of nationwide library and information services of all types, at all levels, and for all people
4. To act as the national agency dedicated to the exchange of information in all fields with other nations of the world
5. To assist the government in promotion of the learning, use, and the advancement of the culture
6. To support research and inquiry on a national scale
7. To assist cooperation in bibliographical activities
8. To publish the National Bibliography[4]

Some of these objectives meet the needs of a modern national library. The Imperial Library moved to the present Belvedere Campus in Calcutta. The great Indian leader and internationally well known Jawahdrlal Nehru commented on the Belvedere, "I do not want Belvedere for the mere purpose of stacking books. We want to convert it into a fine central library where a large number of research students can work and where there will be all the other amenities which a modern library gets."[5] Another great leader, Mahatma Gandhi, also commented, "I do not want my house to be walled in on all sides and my windows to be stuffed. I want cultures of all lands to be blown about my house as freely as possible. But I refuse to be blown off my feet by any."[6]

Legal Base

The National Library is administered by the Ministry of Education and Culture. In 1954 the Delivery of Books Act was passed, which required every publisher to send a copy of every book to the National Library in Calcutta, the Connemara Public Library in Madras, and the Central Library in Bombay. Since December 16, 1991, Delhi Public Library has received one copy of each publication published in India free of cost. This is in addition to the three other libraries mentioned. In 1956 the act was amended to cover all periodical publications. As a result a comprehensive national bibliography of new published materials in all the fourteen languages of India became possible since 1954. The role of the National Library became apparent after the enactment of the Delivery of Books Act of 1954. It also lends out books received through legal deposit. Learning resources were not included in the legal deposit. There was a suggestion that

legal deposit in Free India should also cover all non-book materials such as gramaphone records and motion picture films, which come within the purview of the Copyright Act. Without non-book materials the efficacy of modern-day library service loses much of its weight. The scope of the Delivery of Books Act should therefore be extended to include non-book materials.[7]

The basic functions of the National Library are:

1. Acquisition and conservation of all significant national production of printed material to the exclusion only of ephemera
2. Collection of printed material concerning the country, no matter where this is published, and, as a corollary, the acquisition of a photographic record of such material that is not available within the country
3. Acquisition and conservation of manuscripts of national importance
4. Planned acquisition of foreign material required by the country
5. Rendering of bibliographical and documentation services of current and retrospective material, both general and specialized (implying the responsibility to produce a current national bibliography and retrospective bibliographies on various aspects of the country)
6. Acting as a referral center purveying full and accurate knowledge of all sources of bibliographical information and participation in international bibliographical activities
7. Provision of photocopying and reprographic services
8. Acting as the center for international book exchange and international loan[8]

The National Library in the past was not performing some of the basic functions. One library educator in the 1960s wrote, "Its reading rooms are used mostly by local day scholars with a sprinkling of outstation readers who can afford time and money. . . . Readers are often frustrated when they get indifferent response to their queries and do not get their required materials."[9] A critical study of the National Library of India was published by Kaula in 1970. In his opinion, it is "functioning no differently from a mere lending library though of a grand size. . . . The emphasis and concentration on the lending function alone is a negation of the functions of a National Library."[10] In the preface to Kaula's critical study of the National Library, a well-known library educator, S. Bashiruddin, commented:

Its functioning since it has been raised to the status of a National Institution has not been in the traditions of similar institutions in the advanced countries of the world. While it was expected that it should be organized as the repository of the literary and intellectual output of the country and function as an instrument of its expansion through research and higher learning, it has fallen short of these expectations to a marked degree.[11]

Organization and Tasks

Under the reorganized plan of the library, the director is the head of the library who is assisted by two professional librarians and a large staff, which in 1989 numbered 779, including 205 professionals. The work of the library is divided into three main divisions: professional, conservation, and administrative. As of 1986, professional divisions are responsible for technical and patron services. The Division of Conservation is in charge of reprography, preservation and laboratory. The Administrative Division is concerned with personnel and maintenance of buildings and facilities.[12] The detailed reorganized plan of the library is as follows:

Director
Librarian
Deputy Librarians
Assistant Librarians
Administrative Officers
(Each division is headed by an assistant librarian.)

Acquisition and Processing
Acquisition (Book Orders) Division
Acquisition (Book Selection) Division
Coordination Division
English Serials Division
Foreign Official Documents Division
Gift and Exchange Division
Indian Official Documents Division
Maps and Prints Division
Printed Catalogue Division
Processing Division
Stock Verification Division

Languages
Arabic and Persian Division
Assamese Division
Bengali Division
European Languages Division
Gujarati Division
Hindi Division
Kannada Division
Malayalam Division
Marathi Division
Oriya Division
Panjabi Division

Sanskrit, Pali and Prakrit Division

Tamil Division

Telugu Division

Urdu Division

Services

Asutosh Collection

Bibliography (General) Division

Bibliography (Indology) Division

Children's Library

Esplanade Reading Room

Lending Section

Reading Room (Reference) Division

Science and Technology Division

Stacks (Annexe) Division

Stacks (Main) Division

Conservation and Preservation

Conservation Division

Laboratory Division

Rare Books Division

Reprography Division

Administration and Allied Agencies

Administrative Division

Gardens Division

Other Sections

Source: Handbook of Libraries, Archives and Information Centers in India, Vol. 1 (New Delhi: Information Industry Publications, 1984–85), 9–10.

Resources

The collection of the National Library is the largest in the country, with a total of 1,476,752 volumes in 1974, 1,607,528 books in 1978, 1,730,530 in 1983, and almost 1,950,000 books in 1989. In the early 1990s its collection included 2,002,910 books, 112,158 bound periodicals, 78,158 maps, and 3,124 manuscripts.[13] The library receives annually about twenty thousand books and eighteen thousand periodicals in English and Indian languages published in the country through a legal deposit system.[14] in 1987–1988 it purchased sixty-seven hundred books and received about forty-six hundred as gifts and sixty-one hundred on exchange.[15]

Its collection included over sixty thousand Indian and foreign official documents, including the publications of the United Nations and other international bodies and almost 77,500 maps, 3,024 manuscripts. In the mid-1970s, "the United

Nations and League of Nations publications and the United States and foreign government publications together exceeded 2,051,845."[16] Among its rare items are the approximately twenty-five hundred books in European languages published between the fifteenth and eighteenth centuries and another thirty-five hundred rare titles published in India.

A total of 15,670 current periodical titles and 809 newspaper titles are being received by the library.[17]

Bengali literature is comprehensively represented in collections with old and rare items, as is Sanskrit literature. The official Indian documents of the central and state governments from the early British time to the present have proven to be useful for scholarly research in social science, and foreign scholars interested in linguistic, historical, and sociological research visit the library to consult its materials. There are about one thousand daily users of this library.

Technical Services

The library has made an effort to build an effective collection by its acquisitions of various materials, domestic as well as foreign, in various fields, such as humanities and social sciences, based on the information needs of users. Those materials have been collected through legal deposits, purchases, gifts, and exchanges.

According to the Delivery of Books Act of 1954, along with its amendment in 1956, publishers are required to deposit a copy of every book with the National Library within thirty days from the date of its publication. In 1956 the act was amended to cover all periodical publications. The legally deposited materials include not only books but also periodicals from all parts of India. All material published in India is to be preserved permanently as a cultural heritage through this legal system.

Apart from the legal deposits, the library has been acquiring materials by means of purchases, gifts, and exchanges, and it is a depository of UN, U.S., and international organizations' publications (and houses other documents as well). The library has been purchasing foreign books that are mostly related to India in any language, published anywhere in the world. It has also been acquiring books by Indian authors, published abroad. The foreign books, which have a considerable need in the nation, are acquired by this library either by purchase or by gift and exchanges. Unfortunately, the budget for materials of the library has never been enough to acquire foreign materials comprehensively. The books in foreign languages have been acquired as far as budgets allow. Biographies of famous world leaders have also been acquired.

As for exchanges, the library has been quite active in the international exchange of materials. Since 1904, the library has exchange agreements with foreign governments and institutions. In 1986–1987, it had 170 exchange institutions located in fifty-six countries around the world. The status of their depository library was given to this National Library by several international institutions and organizations, and under this agreement it has received all publications of the United

Nations, UNESCO, International Civil Aviation Organization, Food and Agricultural organization, and International Monetary Fund.[18] It also acts as a center for international loan.

Manuscripts of national importance have also been acquired by the library. It is rich in manuscripts in Sanskrit, Persian, Arabic, and Tamil languages and literature. More efforts are needed to acquire manuscripts. Fortunately, some valuable collections of books and manuscripts acquired by private collectors have been donated to the library. The first of these was the private collection of Sir Asutosh Mukhopadhyay in 1949. The seventy-six thousand volumes that make up this collection cover the whole range of the humanities and sciences. This private collection of Sir Mukhopadhyay (also known as Mukherji) is comparable with some of the private libraries of European national libraries. A number of donors followed the example set by Sir Mukhopadhyay: the Ramdas Sen collection of about 3,500 volumes (1951), the Tej Bahadur Sapru papers (1952), the Baird Baran Mukherji collection (1953), the Jadunath Sarkar collection of about 2,500 items (1959), the Surendranath Sen collection of 3,620 volumes (1960), and the Vaiyapuri Pillai collection comprising 2,943 books and manuscripts out of which 265 are palm leaf manuscripts (1960). These personal collections have been proved to be useful and precious resources for scholarly research.

In regard to the classification system used in this library, the first librarian, John Macfarlane, modeled a scheme for the classification of books into European languages which was used in the British Museum, now the British Library. Macfarlane came from the British Museum. There has been influence of British Museum methods on the classification and cataloging of the early history of the library. The system was then known as Relative Location. In 1930 his successor librarian, Khan Bahadur Asadullah, developed a new classification scheme for Arabic, Persian, and Urdu books. Since 1954 Dewey Decimal Classification has been adopted as the classification scheme.

In the case of cataloging rules, Anglo-American Cataloging Rules, North American Text 1967 and AACRII 1978, the Rules for Descriptive Cataloging in Library of Congress, 1949 and Notes used in catalog cards; a List of Examples, 1963, have been in use. The Subject Headings Used in the Dictionary Catalog of the Library of Congress, with supplements, have been used to achieve uniformity in subject headings. The development of Indian Machine Readable Cataloging (INMARC) at the National Library was suggested in the mid-1980s. However, "In computerized cataloging the Indian librarian would face some problems in inserting all diacritical marks (as presently used) for machine readable cataloguing. One of the reasons is that the machine does not accept all forms of diacritical marks used in the National Library."[19] There are fifteen official languages in India, and entries of all Indian Languages are Romanized and transliterated with diacritical marks. The library has made efforts to preserve its material as long as possible by controlling temperature, humidity, and insects. The rare books in the library have been separated and protected by temperature control. The library began work on computerizing its operations and services since the late 1980s. MINISIS is being used for bibliographic control of library operations and CDS/ISIS for creation of small databases for special areas or subjects.

Public Services

The library is freely available to all citizens over eighteen years of age. The library extends its services to scholars worldwide and scholars who come from outside the location of the library (Calcutta) are even provided with accommodation in the Readers' Hostel for a nominal charge a day. This Readers' Hostel is conveniently located within walking distance of the library. The library is open from 9 A.M. to 8 P.M. and 10 A.M. to 5 P.M. on Sundays and other holidays and is closed on the three national holidays.

The library has tried to provide several service points by operating such rooms as the Main Reading Room and Reference Division. During 1988 and 1989 this Reading Room and Reference Division served almost 184,000 users. Apart from this Main Reading Room, there are some other specialized reading rooms for the library collections. Some, among others, are: Asian and European languages other than English, United Nations Documents, Rare Books, Science and Technology, and Foreign Official Documents. These Reading Rooms and other divisions of the library, for example, Bibliography Division, also provide reference service by mail and telephone. The library on requests from scholars compiles lists for reading or selected bibliographies. The library also provides a lending service, which is appreciated by local students and scholars. The library also acts as the center for international loan.

As far as public catalogs are concerned, both in the form of book and card are available in the National Library. Most of the materials in the library are accessible through card catalogs. The card catalogs for documents in the European and Indian languages are available in the main building of the library. The Annexe reading room has catalogs of the Indian official documents, serials, and UN documents. Book form catalogs have been published in several volumes, covering different periods, collections and languages.

Publications

The National Library has been active in publishing retrospective European and Indian languages catalogs. It has published a few volumes in this series. The other volumes include the printed catalogs of the Calcutta Public Library, the Imperial Library and the National Library. There are eighteen volumes of bibliographies including *Index Translationum Indicarum*, *Bibliography of Dictionaries and Encyclopedias in Indian Languages*, and *Bibliography of Indology*. A series of general publications of thirteen volumes have been published, including *Author Table for Indian Names*, which was brought out as an alternative to Cutter's author table. Since 1984, it has published thirty-one brochures, including the *National Library of India, 1903–1978: A Pictorial History*.

Staff

A total of 784 people of various titles and status were employed at the National Library in 1985. The staff numbered one hundred in 1947. A scholar librarian with an academic status of a vice chancellor of a university becomes the director of the National Library. He is assisted by a librarian, four deputy librarians and other professional and non-professional staff.[20]

Budget

The annual budget of the library in the mid-1970s was 38,370,000 rupees. In 1984–1985 it was 152,550,000 rupees. The budget for books and periodicals was 25,820,000 rupees. The book budget has decreased from 1.493 million rupees in 1980–1981 to 1.425 in 1984–1985. With the increase in book prices, the budget increase of about 5,615,000 rupees is not enough to meet the developments of the library.[21] For 1992–1993, it had a budget of 44.7 million rupees (U.S.$1=Rs.42.00).[22]

Problems and Prospects

Growth of the library was witnessed in the 1950s and early 1960s, thanks to the 1954 Delivery of Books Act. The collection also grew through other ways such as gifts, donations, and exchanges. There was an increase in staff. However, "the period of expansion did not last long, as problems of growth—critics say unplanned growth—began to surface in the mid sixties. Prolonged staff unrest coupled with unimaginative management"[23] brought the government of India to appoint a commission to evaluate the staff problem and a review committee to examine the functioning of the library and suggest possible solutions.

The review committee made a number of recommendations, including an autonomous status of the library and the appointment of a scholar director for the library with the status and salary of a university vice chancellor. A university professor was appointed as the first director of the library. There were no significant changes in the library from 1977 to 1981, under the scholar director without library credentials. In the mid-1980s, the problems continued of staff, space and management.[24]

The first director of the National Library, Professor R. K. Das Gupta has commented on many problems. The library "has the problem of shelf-space, problem of preservation, the usual administrative problems in a country . . . for building up and maintaining public institutions. But we can take care of these problems only when we are in a position to function as a National Library and we can do so only when there is a National Library system."[25]

The director of the library has requested the government of India twice "to appoint a Union Library Advisory Commission as the first step towards the reorganization of our National Library which can function as such only when there is a network of well stored and well administered libraries in the country."[26]

In the late 1980s the plans for the development of the library were: "(1) modernization, i.e., computerization of major library operations and housekeeping functions; (2) national union catalog; (3) maintaining a library of microforms and compaction of reading materials; and (4) monitoring book production statistics."[27]

Conclusion

The services provided by the National Library are far below the ones expected from the national library of a large country like India. It has failed to play its role of leadership. It needs to be strengthened and to receive necessary support.[28] The literature of librarianship on the library revealed that the problems that face the library are historical and can be solved when the library is considered in a wider national context. P. B. Mangla, in the late 1970s, suggested that the government of India should appoint a National Libraries Commission "to go into the whole matter" of the national libraries of India. The United States and the United Kingdom have appointed such commissions and their recommendations have greatly helped the development of the national library systems in those countries.[29]

NATIONAL MEDICAL LIBRARY, NEW DELHI

History

The government of India in 1966 designated the former library of the director general of Indian Medical Services at New Delhi as the National Medical Library. It is one of the largest medical libraries in South Asia and the best medical library in India. In 1971 it moved to its present independent four-floor building on the campus of the All India Institute of Medical Sciences.

Functions

The National Medical Library functions as the focal point for collecting, processing, and disseminating knowledge with the medical community worldwide.

The library serves to meet the information needs of the biomedical community of researchers, teachers, practitioners, administrators, planners, journalists and others concerned with health science and its related disciplines. It has also conducted surveys and studies on medical libraries. Additionally, it has provided training to health science librarians in India and South Asia.[30] Since 1980 it has also organized several seminars and workshops with the assistance from the World Health Organization (WHO).

The organization plan of the professional manpower is as follows:

Deputy Director
Additional Deputy Assistant Director
  Periodical Services

Acquisitions Services

Technical Services

Assistant Director (Training)

Training Division

Senior Documentation Officer

Reference and Photocopying Services

Documentation and Indexing Services

Source: Handbook of Libraries, Archives and Information Centers in India, vol. 1 (New Delhi: Information Industry Publications, 1984–85), 25.

Resources

The collection of the National Medical Library has grown from twenty thousand volumes in 1946 to 1.2 million in 1980 and its subscription of periodicals from two hundred in 1946 to two thousand in 1980.[31] At the end of 1981 its collection contained 226,934 volumes, including 96,144 books and reports, 118,240 volumes of periodicals, 12,500 pamphlets and offprints. It has a rich collection of nineteenth-century medical literature.[32] This rich collection has been listed in the published library catalog of 1937. An important collection of medical journals since 1944 have been acquired. Examples of these journals are *Archives of Pediatrics, Indian Annals of Medical Sciences, Lancet, Indian Medical Gazette,* and *British Medical Journal.* The library receives indexes and abstracts through subscription, for example, *Index Medicus, Drug Literature Index, Nutrition Abstracts, Current Contents,* and *Hospital Abstracts.*[33]

Technical Services

The books are classified by the Dewey Decimal Classification (DDC). There are two parts of the library catalog: the first includes items up to 1976, and the second has materials from 1977. Medical Subject Headings (MESH) have been used for making subject entries. There is a separate catalog of government of India documents.[34]

Public Services

In the late 1980s the library had about 1,192 registered borrowers. About thirty thousand users visit the library and consult its materials annually. In 1986–1987, 4,725 items were issued out on loan and 442,800 items were consulted within the library. Additionally, 770 items were issued on interlibrary loan. About nine thousand reference inquiries were answered by the staff of the library in a year during the late 1980s.[35]

The library has conducted, through the courtesy of the WHO Regional Office for Southeast Asia, New Delhi MEDLINE Search Service (a computerized bibliographical search) since 1978. All MEDLINE search requests emerging from India were processed through the National Medical Library (NML). Occasionally, it has also been operating Cancer Literature Search Service through the courtesy of the British Library.[36] It has in the past compiled about 150 bibliographies. At present, NML provides literature search service using MEDLINE and POPLINE databases on CD-ROM.

Publications

The Documentation Section of the National Medical Library has been preparing indexes and abstracts of medical literature in Indian and English languages, union catalogs, manuals, and directories in the discipline of health-related sciences. Its publications include a bimonthly accessions list, *Library Bulletin*; a fortnightly service, *Selective Dissemination of Information*; and a quarterly *Index to Indian Medical Periodicals*. It has also compiled the *Union Catalogue of Medical Periodicals in Indian Libraries*. This catalog is revised every five years. In 1991 work began on its seventh edition. The library has also prepared a catalog of publications of the Ministry of Health and Family Welfare. In 1969 a printed catalog of books and reports in the collection was published. In 1980 a *Directory of Medical Libraries in India* was published. An attempt has been made to computerize the production of *Index to Indian Medical Periodicals* and to maintain a machine-readable database. In addition, the library brings out *Highlights from Current Health Literature* (monthly); *Chetna*, *1982–*(quarterly) and *ADISDOC*.

Staff

A total of eighty-seven people of various titles and status were employed at the National Medical Library in the late 1980s. The staff included about forty-seven professionals, paraprofessionals, and others.

Budget

The annual budget of the library in the mid-1980s was four million rupees for its resources.[37]

NATIONAL SCIENCE LIBRARY, NEW DELHI

History

The National Science Library was founded in 1964. It is a part of the Indian National Scientific Documentation Center (INSDOC) and is located in the INSDOC building. A sum of twenty million rupees was provided for developing the National Science Library in the early 1970s.

Functions

The functions of the National Science Library are

to build up a central collection of material and to offer documentation and information services on a national scale; to survey the holdings of scientific institutions in the country and to fill up the gaps by acquiring relevant documents; to introduce cooperative acquisition programs and integrate them through a national union catalogue to act as a center of exhaustive information on documentation, information and library techniques to make special efforts to acquire Indian literature—books and periodicals in Indian languages, including those written in English on science and technology and to act as a dormitory for housing every old periodical run.[38]

Resources

The collection of the National Science Library numbered about two hundred thousand volumes and received about five thousand periodicals in the late 1980s. The library has been acquiring periodicals by means of purchases, gifts, and exchanges. In 1986–1987 it received 1,624 periodicals by exchange and 1,524 periodicals by gift. It had about 380 exchange institutions located in some thirty-five countries.[39] In 1994 it had 136,000 bound volumes and received thirty-five hundred serial titles.[40] At present the library has a collection of 150,000 books, reference books, back volumes of periodicals, and Russian monographs; it receives over 3,320 periodicals (out of these 1,200 periodicals are on CD-ROMs); and it has acquired full text databases on CD-ROMs.[41] It acquires materials in all areas of science and technology. It has a good reference collection, conference proceedings, research and industrial reports, Indian university dissertations, and publications in library and information science.

The library has acquired the back volumes of periodicals in the fields of science and technology in microfilm and microfiche. It also has one of the finest collections in the field of information science and technology in the country.

Technical Services

The National Science Library was planning "to introduce automation / mechanization of serials control and cataloguing operations"[42] in 1987. At present, different activities have been computerized.

Public Services

In 1985–1986, the collection of the library was consulted by about thirty-six thousand outside users and about 26 items were checked out on interlibrary loan.[43]

Staff

In the late 1980s, it had a staff of forty-five, including thirty-two professionals, some paraprofessionals, and others.

Budget

The annual budget of the library in 1986–1987 was thirty-six million rupees.

CONCLUSION

The library aims to acquire all Indian science and technology monographs and periodicals. In addition, it gives emphasis to procurement of foreign periodicals in electronic form. The library has succeeded in computerizing its various activities. It serves as a major information resource center in the field of science and technology in the country.

NOTES

The statistics (both general and for libraries) in this chapter have been drawn from *Year's Work in Librarianship 1987* (Delhi: Indian Library Association, 1988); *ALA World Encyclopaedia of Library and Information Services* (Chicago: American Library Association, 1980, 1993); *International Handbook of Contemporary Developments in Librarianship*, ed. Miles M. Jackson (Westport, Conn.: Greenwood Press, 1981); and *Handbook of Libraries, Archives and Information Centres in India*, vol. 1 (New Delhi: Information Industry Publications, 1984–85).

1. P. N. Kaula, "National Library of India: Functions and Activities," *Herald of Library Science* 20(3–4) (July–October 1981), 191.

2. B. S. Kesavan, "India, Libraries and Information Centers in: the National Library," in *Encyclopedia of Library and Information Science*, vol. 11 (New York: Marcel Dekker, 1977), 417.

3. B. S. Kesavan, *India's National Library* (Calcutta: National Library, 1961), 14.

4. Kaula, "National Library of India," 193.

5. Kesavan, "India, Libraries and Information Centers," 418.

6. Legend at the entrance to the National Library of India.

7. A. K. Ohdedar, "Legal Deposit and Libraries in Free India," in N. B. Sen, ed., *Progress of Libraries in Free India* (New Delhi: New Book Society of India 1967), 131.

8. Kesavan, "India, Libraries and Information Centers," 418.

9. Amitabha Chatterjee, "National Libraries—Their Scope, Structure and Functions," in N. B. Sen, ed., *Progress of Libraries in Free India* (New Delhi: New Book Society of India, 1967), 246.

10. P. N. Kaula, *The National Library of India: A Critical Study* (Bombay: Somaiya Publications, 1970), 25.

11. Ibid., preface.

12. Uma Majumder, *India's National Library: Systematization and Modernization* (Calcutta: National Library, 1987), 33–34.

13. D. N. Banerjee, "India's National Library," *Herald of Library Science* 31 (3–4) (July–October 1994), 237.

14. R. K. Das Gupta, "India," in *ALA World Encyclopedia of Library and Information Services* (Chicago: American Library Association, 1980), 246.

15. P. B. Mangla, "India," in *ALA World Encyclopedia of Library and Information Services*, 3d ed. (Chicago: American Library Association 1993), 362.

16. Kesavan, "India, Libraries and Information Centers," 417.

17. Banerjee, "India's National Library," 238.

18. V. K. Jain, "'National Library of India," in B. M. Gupta et al., eds. *Handbook of Libraries, Archives and Information Centers in India*, vol. 1 (New Delhi: Information Industry Publications, 1984–85), 11.

19. Majumder, *India's National Library*, 131.

20. T. S. Rajagopalan, *Year's Work in Indian Librarianship 1987* (Delhi: Indian Library Association, 1988), 10.

21. Majumder, *India's National Library*, 61.

22. Banerjee, "India's National Library," 238.

23. K. M. Govi, "India's National Library," in P. S. Kawatra, ed., *Comparative and International Librarianship* (New Delhi: Sterling, 1987), 69.

24. Ibid.

25. The first director of the National Library of Calcutta quoted in Gupta et al., eds., *Handbook of Libraries, Archives and Information Centers in India*, 15.

26. Ibid.

27. Rajagopalan, *Year's Work in Librarianship*, p. 12. Rajagopalan wrote the chapter on "National Libraries" in this book on the basis of materials on the National Library of Calcutta supplied by Mrs. Kalpana Das, Gupta, Librarian, National Library.

28. Krishan Kumar, *Library Organization* (New Delhi: Vikas, 1989), 116–117.

29. P. B. Mangla, "The Concept of National Library," *Journal of Library and Information Science* 3(1) (1978), 14.

30. M. K. Bhatt, "National Medical Library (India)," in Gupta et al., eds., *Handbook of Libraries, Archives, and Information Centers in India*, 25.

31. S. A. Chitale and M. K. Bhatt, "Medical Libraries," in Allen Kent et al., eds., *Encyclopedia of Library and Information Science*, vol. 11 (New York: Marcel Dekker, 1977), 406–414.

32. Bhatt, "National Medical Library (India)," 25–26.

33. Ibid., 26.

34. Ibid.

35. Rajagopalan, *Year's Work in Indian Librarianship 1987*, 17.

36. Bhatt, "National Medical Library (India)," 27.

37. Ibid., 25.

38. N. B. Inamdar and M. R. Riswadkar, "India," in M. Miles, ed., *International Handbook of Contemporary Developments in Librarianship* (Westport, Conn.: Greenwood Press, 1981), 190.

39. Rajagopalan, *Year's Work in Indian Librarianship 1987*, 16.

40. *Annual Report, 1993–94* (New Delhi: INSDOC), 30.

41. INSDOC, *National Information Laboratory* (New Delhi: INSDOC, 1998), 14.

42. Rajagopalan, *Year's Work in Indian Librarianship 1987*, 17.

43. Ibid.

SELECTED BIBLIOGRAPHY

Chatterjee, Amitabha. "National Libraries—Their Scope, Structure and Functions." In
    N. B. Sen, ed., *Progress of Libraries in Free India*. New Delhi: New Book Society
    of India, 1967, 240–247.
Chaudhuri, Sibdas. "National Library for Developing Countries with Special Reference to
    India." In K. K. Bhattacharjee, ed., *Modern Trends in Librarianship in India*. Cal-
    cutta, World Press, 1979, 83–103.
Das Gupta, Kalpana. "New Role of Libraries in a Developing Society with Particular Ref-
    erence to India." *ILA Bulletin* 16(1–2) (January– June 1980), 37–42.
Downing, Joel C. "The Indian National Bibliography—Its Present State and Future Pros-
    pects." *Library Resources and Technical Services* (January– March 1984), 20–24.
Govi, K. M. "India's National Library." In P. S. Kawatra, ed., *Comparative and Interna-
    tional Librarianship*. New Delhi: Sterling, 1987, 65–74.
Gupta, B. M. et al., eds. *Handbook of Libraries, Archives and Information Centers in India*.
    Vol. 1. New Delhi: Information Industry Publications, 1986.
Inamdar, N. B., and M. R. Riswadkar. "India." In M. Miles, ed., *International Handbook of
    Contemporary Developments in Librarianship*. Westport, Conn.: Greenwood
    Press, 1981, 183–199.
Jain, V. K. "National Library of India." In B. M. Gupta et al., eds. *Handbook of Libraries,
    Archives and Information Centers in India*. Vol. 1: Libraries and Archives. New
    Delhi: Information Industry Publications, 1986, 3–23.
Kaula, P. N. *The National Library of India: A Critical Study*. Bombay: Somaiya Publica-
    tions, 1970.
———. "National Library of India: Functions and Activities." *Herald of Library Science*
    20(3–4) (July–October 1981), 190–200.
Kesavan, B. S. "The Concept of the National Library as a Network Institution and as a
    National Documentation Base." *Timeless Fellowship* 12 (1978–79), 1–15.
———. "The Indian National Library." *Library World* 63(741) (March 1962), 216–221.
———. *India's National Library*. Calcutta: National Library, 1961.
———. "The National Library." In *Encyclopedia of Library and Information Science*. Vol.
    11. New York: Marcel Dekker, 1977, 417–419.
Khanna, S. N. "National Library of India." In S. P. Goyal, ed. *Indian Librarianship: Essays
    in Honour of S. R. Bhatia*. Delhi: Scientific Book Store, 1972, 44–51.
Girja, Kumar. "National Library of Calcutta; A Critical Review." *IASLIC Bulletin* 19(2–3)
    (1974), 94–118.
Majumder, Uma. *India's National Library: Systematization and Modernization*. Calcutta: Na-
    tional Library, 1987.
Mangla, P. B. "The Concept of National Library." *Journal of Library and Information Sci-
    ence* 3(1) (June 1979), 1–15.
———. "India." In *ALA World Encyclopedia of Library and Information Services*. 3d ed.
    Chicago: American Library Association, 1993, 361–364.
Nagaraj, M. N. "The National Library of India—Brief Note." *Library Scene in Calcutta,
    Seminar Papers of 100th IASLIC Study Circle Calcutta*. February 26–27, 1977,
    9–12.
Nagaraj, M. N., and A. K. Ghosh. *National Library of India 1903–1978*. Calcutta: National
    Library, 1978.
National Library. *The National Library of India: 1903–1978: A Pictorial History*. Calcutta,
    1978.

Ohdedar, A. K. "Legal Deposit and Libraries in Free India." In N. B. Sen, ed., *Progress of Libraries in Free India.* New Delhi: New Book Society of India, 1967, 122–131.

Rajagopalan, T. S. "National Libraries." In T. S. Rajagopalan, ed., *Year's Work in Indian Librarianship 1987.* Delhi: Indian Library Association, 1988, 10–18.

❦ 3 ❦

Academic Libraries

PART 1: COLLEGE LIBRARIES

In general, a college is an institution of higher learning that offers a three-year degree course after secondary school. Most professional degrees are earned in four years. In medicine the duration is four and one-half years. Some colleges offer postgraduate courses, which generally take two years. Research is usually the prerogative of universities.

Colleges can be categorized into three categories: university, government, and private colleges. Private colleges consist of either aided colleges, which receive funding from the state or central government or both, or unaided colleges, which do not get any public funding. Another categorization consists of constituent colleges, affiliated colleges, and recognized colleges.

In 1947 the number of colleges rose to about 650. In 1990–1991, there were 7,121 colleges.[1] In 1993–1994, there were eighty-six thousand colleges. In 1994–1995, there were 5,099,436 students and 231,510 teachers.[2] These numbers continue to increase.

HISTORY

The educational system in India has its roots in the Vedic period. Oral communication was used for giving instruction and imparting knowledge. From Buddha's time onward, written word began to be used for instruction. Academic libraries were established during this period, but these passed into oblivion. During the medieval period, Muslim royalty and aristocracy set up libraries at their palaces and houses. Not much is known about these libraries. However, there is "a mention of an academic library in a college in Bidar. This was built by Mehmud Gawan who was a minister at the Court of Mohammad Shah Bahmani III (1463–1482). Having conquered this region, Aurangzeb took away the collection of about 3,000 volumes to Delhi where it was amalgamated in the palace library."[3]

With "the rise of British paramountcy, the college libraries preceded the university libraries. Governor Warren Hastings felt that in order to rule judiciously the areas occupied by the East India Company, the officers as well as the employees of the Company should familiarise themselves with Arabic and Persian. For this purpose, he commissioned a Madarsa at Calcutta in the year 1781. Jonathan Duncan emphasized the need to collect books of the most ancient and valuable general learning and tradition so that the officers could benefit from these in the course of their studies."[4]

In 1811 Viceroy Lord Minto proposed that a "library be attached to each of the colleges under the charge of a native with a small establishment of servants for the care of the manuscripts."[5] This was an important statement about the significance of libraries in academic institutions like colleges.

According to Mathew, during the British period, "the British East India Company and Christian missionaries took the initiative to start colleges with well-stocked libraries in their early settlements like Bombay, Madras, Calcutta and Agra."[6] Agra College, Agra and St. Johns College, Agra, were established in 1823 and 1850, respectively.

In 1857 three universities were established in Calcutta, Bombay, and Madras. This gave impetus to the setting up of colleges, leading to establishment of libraries.

The Hunter Commission (1882) reported about the progress made by the college libraries. The commission observed:

As regards the extent to which libraries are used, the information obtained seems to show that among the students of some colleges, a perceptible taste for general reading has sprung up. Yet, the Bombay, the Bengal and North Western Provinces reports agree in saying that the general reading of students is confined to a very narrow range, being almost entirely limited to books which have some bearing on the subjects of examination; though an exception to a limited extent is made in Bombay in the case of the Elphinstone College.[7]

The commission also reported that there were a number of colleges in existence with small collections such as SPG College, Trichinapally, (1,120 books); Presidency College, Madras (3,289 books); the Government College, Lahore (1,400 books); the government College, Jabalpur (1,000 books).

Colleges in India have been the forerunners of the universities. The same can be said about the libraries. For instance, University of Delhi was established in 1922. However, five of its well-known colleges—Zakir Hussain (formerly Delhi College), the St. Stephens College, the Hindu College, Lady Hardinge Medical College, and Ramjas College—were founded in 1710, 1881, 1899, 1916, and 1917, respectively. These colleges came into being before the founding of the university.

However, libraries attached to Lady Hardinge Medical College and Zakir Hussain College (Day) were established in 1932 and 1792, respectively.

COLLECTION

Collection is usually limited to books and periodicals. Very few of them acquire nonbook materials. The only nonbook material may be in the form of maps. In Delhi University College Libraries, the collection ranged from 2,158 volumes to 151,508, the average size being 39,668 volumes.[8] On average about eighteen hundred books are added every year. The number of periodicals subscribed ranged from 5 to 350, the average being about 83 periodicals.[9] It may be kept in mind that in Delhi, college libraries are much better than in many other states.

In Tripura[10] the size of collection ranges from 1,500 volumes to 65,000 volumes (books), the average being 17,300 volumes. This shows the disparity between collections in Delhi colleges and elsewhere.

In Haryana[11] the size of collection varies from 2,750 volumes to 80,741 volumes (books), the average being 27,500 volumes. The average number of volumes is fairly high.

ACCESS

Most of the college libraries do not have provision of open access to books. In Haryana "books on open shelves with free access to them by the readers is a rarity."[12]

CLASSIFICATION AND CATALOGING

A majority of college libraries follow Dewey Decimal classification. Some libraries follow Colon classification. About one-third of the colleges in Delhi used Colon classification.[13] Generally, these libraries use Anglo-American Cataloging Rules (2d ed.) for cataloging reading materials. Some libraries used Classified Catalog Code, by S. R. Ranganathan, to catalog reading materials.

SERVICES

College libraries provide a variety of services. They all render lending service, although publications like periodicals and newspapers are generally lent to teachers only.

On demand users are given help in the location of reading materials and use of the library catalog. Often they render an orientation program for the new members. Only a small percentage of them provide services such as interlibrary loan (only for teachers), bibliographic services and current awareness services.[14]

As regards bibliographical services, "some of the college libraries are providing reading lists to different categories of users based on their courses/trades in the colleges. Teachers are also provided such lists from time to time. During the academic seminars, the college libraries provide such services to the organisers/teachers/participants of the seminars."[15] Thus bibliographical services are rendered to a limited extent in college libraries in Delhi.

In some colleges in Delhi, "in order to make the users aware of the current literature on various subjects/courses, the photocopies of brief contents of books and related periodicals, literature and book jackets are displayed on the library notice board and also kept in the staff room for consultation."[16] These kinds of bibliographical services are being provided to serve the needs of the users.

The UGC provided grants for the purpose of a photocopier in college libraries, but no provision was made for a machine operator. Library attendants are given an honorarium to operate the copy machines, but sometimes this results in their neglecting their basic responsibility of stocking books. When told to carry out their basic responsibility fully, then they tend to neglect the operation of the machine.

No provision has been made for consumables and maintenance of the machine in the library fund. The machines are maintained through the College General Maintenance Grant, generally operated by the office in charge of the college. As a result, a library has to depend on grants from the college funds, which are often delayed unnecessarily by the administrative officer/section officer, who may not get along well with the librarian and may not accept the librarian's higher status as bestowed by the authorities. Sometimes this leads to the shutting down of the copier for a few days. Considerable tension arises between the library staff and office staff when copies cannot be made as quickly as they are needed.

In college libraries, there is a trend to ask a private vendor to provide photocopying services under the conditions laid out by the authorities. The vendor may set up his machine within the library or anywhere on the college campus. The librarian then does not have to worry about tending to the machine.

The reprographic services have become very popular, and fortunately, due to competition, the prices have come down.

FINANCE

The sources of finance may be broken down in the following manner:

1. Library fee
2. Reading room fee
3. Grants from the state
4. Grants from UGC
   a. Recurring grants
   b. Nonrecurring grants (grants for new subjects, grants for construction of library buildings, grants for developing special collections, special grants for specific occasions, etc.)
5. Grants from the parent body/management (for colleges run by a nongovernment agency)

6. Donations

7. Library fines and deposits

8. Sale of library publications

9. Sale of newspapers, magazines, discarded books, and so on as scrap

10. Charges on services provided to users, such as reprographic service, translation service, bibliographic service, database search service, and so on

With regard to colleges affiliated with the University of Delhi, "the UGC from its inception to 1968 was contributing at the rate of Rs. 10/-per student subject to a maximum of Rs. 10,000. Thereafter in 1969 the rate was charged to Rs. 15/- and the limit was also raised to Rs. 15,000/- in day colleges and Rs. 22,500/- in extended colleges. But the rate of UGC book grant continues at the old rate in evening colleges even now. Besides UGC also gives grants in the form of Book Bank Scheme, Student Aid Fund Scheme, and ad hoc library grants for new subjects from time to time. Since the amount received from the UGC is not much, the colleges collect Library and Reading Room fee at the time of admission each year from each student."[17]

The fee being charged at present varies from Rs. 15 to Rs. 300, per annum. Library and reading room fees are considered as important sources of funds. In addition to fees collected from the students, the UGC provides its share at the rate of Rs. 55 per student, to a maximum of Rs. 55,000 per college as recurring grants for books and periodicals. At present, a basic grant for strengthening the library collection (during a five-year plan period) is available for a college, amounting to Rs. 2 lakh, for a college having more than twelve hundred students on its rolls.

A study carried out by Bavakutty indicates that the expenditure on college libraries in Kerala is less than 2 percent of the total expenditure on colleges in the state.[18] This figure is much less than the 6.5 to 10.0 percent as recommended by the Kothari Commission on Education (1964–1966). However, in the case of Delhi University Colleges, "it has been found that 95% of the colleges spend between 3–6% of the total budget of the college on library."[19] Thus the situation in Delhi is much better as compared with Kerala. The situation in other states is comparable with Kerala.

The college libraries earlier often did not have a regular source of income. After the UGC was established in 1953, college libraries started getting a regular flow of funds.

NORMS

The UGC Workshop on Standards for College Libraries was held at Khandala March 5–7, 1979. The recommendations made by the workshop were approved by a UGC subcommittee at its meeting held on August 30, 1979. However, the recommendations were never accepted by the UGC itself.

The Committee on University and College Libraries[20] was appointed by the UGC in 1957, under the chairmanship of Dr. S. R. Ranganathan, to examine the conditions of academic libraries and suggest the standards for libraries, pay scales of library staff, and training and status of the staff. Many of the recommendations of this committee were accepted and implemented. The report gave a big push to the development of college libraries and status of college librarians.

The government of Kerala appointed an expert committee "to examine the functioning of College Libraries and suggest suitable measures for their improved functioning.[21] V. P. Joy was the convener of the committee. The committee wrote an excellent report that touches every aspect of the functioning of a college library, keeping in mind the recent developments in higher education. Some of the significant recommendations are given below.

1. Every college library should offer Ready and Long-Range Reference Services, Selective Dissemination of Information, Current Awareness Service, and so on and should provide facility for borrowing materials from outside sources.
2. The committee recommends that the college librarian should be given status and rank as recommended by the UGC subject to satisfying the qualifications and other conditions prescribed by the UGC.
3. The committee recommends that library services in all colleges should be centralized to bring them under supervision of a qualified professional. Departmental libraries should be abolished and their collections and staff should be transferred to the central library.
4. The committee considers it desirable to computerize the college libraries to enable the college to utilize the possibilities in information services offered by current information technology and also INFLIBNET and other systems sponsored by the UGC.
5. The committee recommends that opportunities like those available to teachers should be provided to librarians also to improve their professional qualifications and to keep them in touch with experts in their subject and related fields.

LIBRARY COMMITTEE

Usually a college constitutes a library committee for the management of a library. The principal or a senior teacher may serve as a chairman and the college librarian as member–secretary, with teachers and student representatives as members. There are instances where a teacher instead of a librarian is made a member-secretary or convener. A library committee may be advisory or administrative in nature. Most often it is advisory in nature. The size of the committee varies. Out of sixty-six[22] colleges affiliated to the University of Delhi, sixty-five colleges had a library committee. Out of fifty-one[23] colleges surveyed in Andhra Pradesh, thirty-nine colleges had a library committee. The main functions performed by it cover planning and formulation of library policy including formulation of rules and regulations for use of library, book selection, budget approval, distribution of funds, and so on.

Now the library committee for Delhi University colleges is a statutory body. The composition of the library committee consists of (1) principal (chairman), (2) librarian (convener), and (3) teacher in charge of all subjects (members).

Statutory provision is a positive step. However, there is no provision for a student representative. In some colleges, where the number of subjects is large, the library committee becomes unwieldy.

STAFFING PATTERN

The Committee on University and College Libraries[24] of the UGC (1957) laid down the strength of the staff on the basis of the criteria formed for the purpose. This became the basis of the UGC staff formula.

The following staff was sanctioned by the UGC (vide letter no. F.1-1-18/63 [CUP] of 25.9.1964 and letter no. F.1-35/47 [CU] of 18.2.1968):

1 Librarian

1 Professional Assistant

1 Semiprofessional Assistant

1 Library Assistant

1 Typist

2 Attendants (up to a collection of fifteen thousand volumes)

If the collection contains thirty thousand volumes, then four attendants are provided. For an extended college (having more than fifteen hundred students), two additional attendants are given. If a library is open for twelve hours, then two additional attendants are provided. Fifty percent of the attendants are placed in the senior scale, but the staff provided for an extended college is inadequate.

In evening colleges, the following staff was sanctioned:

1 Librarian

1 Semiprofessional Assistant

1 Typist

2 Attendants (up to a collection of fifteen thousand volumes)

If the collection contains thirty thousand volumes, then four attendants are provided. Fifty percent of the attendants are placed in the senior scale. Logically speaking, an evening college library should have the same number and level of staff as in day colleges. However, the UGC has given stepmotherly treatment to evening college libraries. It should also be noted that the UGC has discriminated against evening college libraries in the matter of provision of staff. They have not been provided positions of professional assistant and library assistant, which is difficult to justify.

Staff provision for colleges offering undergraduate courses and those offering undergraduate and postgraduate courses is the same. It also does not take into consideration the amount of budget allocated to a library. A library having a budget of Rs. 2.5 lakhs and another one having a budget of Rs. 30,000 would have the same number of staff provided the size of the collection is the same. This is certainly unrealistic.

The norms given above are inadequate as the formula is attendant oriented. As the collection increases or the opening hours are extended, then more attendants are provided. In a service library, the stress should be on increasing the number of professional staff so that the services can be improved.

The UGC Workshop [25] on formulating standards for college libraries was held at Khandala March 5–7, 1979. The recommendations made by the workshop were considered and approved by the UGC subcommittee at its meeting held on August 30, 1979.

The subcommittee recommended that basic staff for the college having the strength of five hundred students and five thousand volumes in the library should be as follows:

1 Librarian

1 Assistant Librarian

2 Library Assistants

1 Library Clerk-cum-Typist

3 Library Attendants

Besides the above staff, the following provisions were made based on library size:

1. For an increase of every five hundred students' enrollment, one library assistant and two library attendants should be added.
2. Similarly, a college will be required to appoint one library assistant and two library attendants for every addition of twenty-five thousand volumes up to the limit of eighty thousand volumes.
3. When the strength of students exceeds two thousand, one more assistant librarian and one library clerk should be appointed.
4. The figures mentioned above are based on the following tentative framework of the main functions that are expected to be carried out in the college library: (a) Acquisition of new books, (b) periodicals, (c) technical processing service, (d) reference service, (e) circulation of books, (f) maintenance, (g) administration, (h) supervisory work, and (i) documentation.

The recommendations of the subcommittee were sound but the UGC did not accept these. The UGC Standing Committee (1980) instead recommended the following staff pattern:[26] Core staff for a college having an enrollment of five hundred students and ten thousand volumes in the library:

1 Librarian

1 Assistant Librarian

1 Library Assistant

3 Attendants

For every additional enrollment of five hundred students, one library assistant and one attendant is added. For every addition of ten thousand volumes, one attendant is added. The staff formula for Delhi University Colleges was adopted by the university. It provides for:[27]

1 Librarian

1 Professional Assistant

3 Semiprofessional Assistants, one each for: Circulation Department, Accessioning work, and Periodical Department and Library correspondence

3 Attendants (up to fifteen thousand books)

One extra attendant is allowed for each ten thousand books. An extended college, operating twelve hours a day, is further allowed:

1 Attendant extra (up to twenty thousand books)

2 Attendants extra (beyond twenty thousand books)

Although this formula is a step forward, it is still attendant oriented, which is a weakness. Attendants often refuse to perform tasks (e.g., the dusting of the books in college libraries) because they claim that they are in a higher salary scale.

The college libraries in metropolitan towns may have a staff ranging from five to ten persons. However in small towns, the librarian may be the only professional assisted by one or two attendants. In some cases, the librarian may be the only person manning the library with some part-time assistance from the college. The position in professional colleges (agriculture, medicine, engineering, etc.) on the whole is much better. The size of the staff may vary from ten to fifteen persons. There may be two to three professionals. These are not very often governed by UGC staff formula. The staff may be sanctioned in such institutions by the state government or state agency or nongovernment organization, which may be the major source of income.

Norms for the strength of the college library staff were decided sometime in 1964 (the post of a professional assistant was sanctioned in 1968) and again marginally revised in 1980. During the past thirty years or so, tremendous changes have taken place. Many libraries have shifted from a single room to multistoried buildings. The number of users has increased. Some of them have changed over from close access to open access. Certain additional services have been introduced. Many of them have either initiated computerization or intend to do so in the near future. Under the changing environment, the existing UGC staff formula needs to be revised so that college libraries can meet the challenges of the twenty-first century.

QUALIFICATIONS

The minimum qualifications for appointment to the post of a college librarian, vide UGC letter of February 20, 1990, are given below:

(i) Qualifying the national level test conducted for the purpose by the UGC or any other agency approved by the UGC; (ii) Master's degree in Library Science/Information Science/documentation or an equivalent professional degree with at least fifty-five percent marks or its equivalent grade plus a consistently good academic record; or master's degree in Arts/Science/Commerce or equivalent degree with at least fifty-five percent marks or its equivalent grade with bachelor's degree in Library Science/Information Science/Documentation or an equivalent professional degree with at least fifty-five percent marks or its equivalent grade plus a consistently good academic record.

SALARY SCALES

The UGC recommended the following salary scales vide letter no. F.1-9/89 (CPP-1) dated February 20, 1990:

College Librarian	Rs. 2,200 (beginning level); Rs. 75 (annual increment up to Rs. 2,800); Rs. 100 (annual increment up to Rs. 4,000)
College Librarian	Rs. 3,000 (Senior Scale); Rs. 100 (annual increment up to Rs. 3,500); Rs. 125 (annual increment up to Rs. 5,000)
College Librarian	Rs. 3,700 (Selection Grade); Rs. 125 (annual increment up to Rs. 4,850); Rs. 150 (annual increment up to Rs. 5,700)

A merit promotion scheme has been extended to professional librarians. The UGC has laid down evaluation criteria similar to college teachers. These criteria cover qualifications, attendance of at least two refresher courses, evaluation by a committee, and so on.

The UGC recommended the following salary scales vide letter no. D.O. F.3-1/94 (PS) dated July 30, 1998, effective from January 1, 1996:

College Librarian	Rs. 8,000–13,500
College Librarian (Senior Scale)	Rs. 10,000–15,200
College Librarian (Senior Grade)	Rs. 12,000–18,300

A merit promotion scheme has been extended to college librarians. The UGC has laid down evaluation criteria. The implementation of revised salary scales and a personal promotion scheme are in process.

BUILDINGS

At one time college libraries were located in a single room, originally meant for a classroom. Now many college libraries are located in multistory buildings, constructed specifically for the purpose. However, the situation varies from region to region. According to a survey of college libraries in Jammu and Kashmir, it was found that "of the thirty degree colleges just four had separate library buildings. All other libraries are housed in inadequate, shabby apartments in one of the college buildings lacking all the facilities of a functional library building. All these libraries had acute shortage of space which had forced them to virtually dump their collections in every nook and corner of the library, leaving them to the care of insects, rodents, dust and dampness. Most of these libraries wore the look of a godown."[28] The situation as described above is an extreme one. It cannot be generalized as such. There are colleges having excellent library buildings. These are mostly located in metropolitan towns or attached to professional colleges (e.g., Hans Raj College Library, Delhi and Regional Engineering College Library, Nagpur, etc.).

PHYSICAL FACILITIES

In a survey of college libraries in Haryana, the author concluded that "in short, by and large norms and specifications laid down by the Indian Standards Institution have not been adhered to in designing these physical facilities."[29]

In a survey of college libraries in Jammu and Kashmir, the researcher found that "so far as the other physical facilities like furniture, fixture, etc. are concerned, the condition in all the libraries was found most unsatisfactory."[30]

INFORMATION TECHNOLOGY

To modernize college libraries, the UGC provides funding, out of nonrecurring plan grants. A college is supposed to send a proposal to the UGC through its principal. Already, a number of colleges have received grants for computerization of their libraries.

Indian college libraries are trying to automate their libraries at a time when financial resources are dwindling, the costs of automated systems are quite high and the telecommunication infrastructure is still unreliable.

There are many college libraries that have initiated computerization of their libraries. College of Business Studies (University of Delhi), Delhi, has computerized all operations of the library. It has developed LIBTEK inhouse, an online library information software. The library has computerized acquisition, circulation, catalog, bibliographies, serial control, masters, stock verification, reports/registers, and maintenance.[31]

The Library of the College of Vocational Studies has two PCs and one dot-matrix printer. The library has created databases for budget expenditure and allocation, borrowers file, and so on. Further work is going on.

Sri Ram College of Commerce, Delhi, has initiated computerization of its library and has created a number of databases.

CONTINUING EDUCATION

Continuing education programs are organized by various organizations in the country to serve the needs of library professionals. Such programs have been organized by INSDOC, DRTC, DESIDOC, Indian Library Association, IASLIC, and so on with the support of NISSAT. These are short-term programs for a duration varying from four to six weeks.

UGC-sponsored refresher courses, offered for a duration of four weeks each, are organized by Academic Staff Colleges attached to universities with the assistance of the faculty of the Department of Library and Information Science of the concerned university. College librarians with a minimum of five years' experience are eligible to attend such courses. Each participant is paid a traveling allowance (TA) and a daily allowance (DA) for attending the course. Eighty-five to 90 percent of the seats are reserved by the catchment areas (as specified by the UGC) and the remaining 10 to 15 percent of the seats are filled on an all-India basis.

The attendance of at least two refresher courses has been made compulsory for college librarians at the time of promotion into senior scale. This is a good step but the number of refresher courses conducted by the Academic Staff Colleges is insufficient to cover total college librarians. Such courses are also needed for other staff members.

AUTONOMOUS COLLEGES

In recent years the UGC has recognized some leading colleges all over the country as autonomous colleges. As of March 31, 1996,[32] there were 113 autonomous colleges. They are free to frame their own curriculum and conduct examinations. They are provided with special assistance from the UGC, and their libraries also get higher financial support.

PROFILES OF TYPICAL COLLEGE LIBRARIES

There is a whole range of college libraries, from a first-rate library to a poor one. The college libraries in metropolitan towns like Delhi, Bombay, Calcutta, Madras, Bangalore, and Hyderabad are well developed. However, college libraries in small towns located in economically poor states such as Bihar, Orissa, Madhya Pradesh, and Uttar Pradesh are in a poor state. They may be unattractive, poorly lit and ventilated, and may have rickety furniture.

A typical library from a metropolitan town (Delhi) is equipped with the following:

Staff: 2 professionals, 3 semiprofessionals, 1 clerk, 8–10 attendants

Collection: 50,000 volumes; 100 periodicals, including newspapers and magazines

Access: Open access
Services: Lending, limited reference services, reprographic services, library orientation
Space: 5,000 square feet
Seats: 50–100
Furniture: Decent
Lighting and ventilation: Good
Members: 1,000

A typical library from a small town (Madhya Pradesh) is equipped with the following:

Staff: 1 professional
Collection: 10,000–20,000 volumes; 40–50 periodicals, including newspapers and magazines
Access: Close access
Services: Lending, limited reference service
Space: 1,000–2,000 square feet
Seats: 40–50
Furniture: Unattractive
Lighting and ventilation: Poor
Readers: 600

PROBLEMS

Some of the major problems experienced by college librarians include:

Staff. Usually a college library has only one professional to look after the library. There is no support staff.

Collection. Due to rising prices and budget cuts, libraries are finding it difficult to acquire reading materials to serve the needs of the users adequately. A library may have few reference books, but these are likely to be out of date. Usually college libraries do not have a well thought out book selection policy. This can adversely affect collection building process.

Access. In many libraries, librarians prefer to adopt close access because often librarians have to pay from their pocket for loss of books, and lack of supporting staff makes it difficult to keep strict vigilance on deviant users.

Space for books and readers. Often there is lack of adequate space for books and readers.

Services. Usually, these libraries provide only lending service. This may be due to lack of professionalization on the part of the librarian. User education, often given halfheartedly, if undertaken seriously would lead to greater and better utilization of the resources. In recent years, many college libraries have started reprographic service using photocopy machines. Some libraries have started computerization of their libraries. This is a healthy sign.

Authorities. There is usually lack of adequate support from the authorities. Authorities at different levels need to be educated about the significance of a library and its services.

Funding. Lack of funding is a major problem. Colleges attached to central universities are economically better off than states; professional colleges and autonomous colleges get higher financial support. Most of the other colleges get stepmotherly treatment. The cost of books and periodicals has risen to a high level, and increasing staff salaries have cut heavily into budgets. Thus there is an urgent need for the UGC to review its system of funding. The authorities and the college librarians should approach the public for donations and also make an effort to generate funds through provision of library and information services to the public or industry.

CONCLUSION

Various studies indicate that the development of college libraries has not been satisfactory, mainly due to lack of funds, staff, and support from the authorities.

In a survey of college libraries in Haryana, Janak Raj remarks that "it is not difficult to conclude that the college libraries in Haryana, as they are with their collection, staff, building, equipment and services cannot achieve the objectives.... The services rendered by majority of these libraries fall terribly short of the standards as envisaged in the model list of college library services proposed by the Standing Committee of the University and College Libraries of the UGC."[33]

There are "tremendous disparities between college libraries in different parts of the country. Libraries in UP, MP, Bihar and Orissa are really in bad shape. The condition in Delhi is certainly better thanks to the financial support provided by the UGC directly to the Delhi University, being a central university, and to its constituent colleges."[34]

College libraries need to take a new direction so that they are prepared to meet the challenges of the twenty-first century. Higher financial support and support from the authorities can go a long way to respond to the challenges.

PART II: UNIVERSITY LIBRARIES

IMPORTANCE

University Education Commissions were appointed by the government of India from time to time. All of these have given high importance to the role of university libraries in higher education, expressed their concern about lack of proper library facilities and gave recommendations to improve the situation. Some of the comments and recommendations are quoted in the next few paragraphs.

The University Commission appointed in 1902 by the then government of India observed the following:

Of the present university libraries there is not much to be said. The library at Madras appears to be entirely neglected; Bombay has a good collection of oriental and other books—but the library is little used by graduates and hardly at all by students. Calcutta has a library and moneys have been granted for the purpose of making it supplementary to other libraries in

Calcutta. It is open to fellows and to persons permitted by the syndicate to use it for the purpose of literary research. The Allahabad University has no library.[35]

The Report of the Radhakrishnan Commission on University Education (1948–1949) emphasized the importance of libraries:

The library is the heart of all the University's work; directly so, as regards its research work, and indirectly as regards its educational work which derives its life from research work. Scientific research needs a library as well as its laboratories, while for humanistic research the library is both library and laboratory in one. Training in higher branches of learning and research is mainly a question of learning how to use the tools, and if the library tools are not there, how can the student learn to use them? . . . Both for humanistic and scientific studies, a first class library is essential in a university.[36]

The Radhakrishnan Commission (1948–1949) felt concerned about the unsatisfactory position of university libraries. The report notes:

While at a few universities the libraries are fairly well-stocked, grants for their upkeep are more or less reasonable, arrangements for lending books to teachers and students are efficient and the reading room space is reasonably adequate; it was distressing to find that in most colleges and universities the library facilities were very poor indeed.[37]

The Kothari Commission on Education (1966) gives a high priority to libraries in higher education, as described below:

No University, College or Department should be set up without taking into account its library needs in terms of staff, books, journals, space, etc. Nothing could be more damaging to a growing department than to neglect its library or to give it a low priority. On the contrary, the library should be an important centre of attraction on the college or university campus.[38]

The UGC was set up in 1953 by the central government and was given the statutory status in 1956. From its inception, the UGC has recognized the role of libraries in higher education. From time to time, review committees have been appointed by the UGC to advise the UGC in library matters. The UGC panel on Library and Information is a regular body, which examines library problems and gives recommendations. The UGC has set up information centers to cater to the needs of the academic community. It has given financial support to university and college libraries in a big way. Thus we find that it has given a high priority to the development of university libraries.

Dr. C. D. Deshmukh was the first full-time chairman of the UGC. According to Deshpande, "his contribution to the development of the Universities in general and Libraries in particular was singularly great. But for him, the University Libraries, instead of becoming the very hearts of the Institutions, would have continued to be mere appendages. He was a man of great vision and firm convictions and largely because of his efforts, the status of the University Library and its profes-

sional staff was elevated." He was responsible for implementing "the recommendations of the Sadler and the Radhakrishnan Commissions regarding the upgrading
of the entire University Library System, including the status of the professional
staff ".[39] He was also responsible for upgrading college libraries during his tenure at
the UGC. Thus he gave the big push to the university and college library movement in India.

HISTORY

During the early period of education in India, a number of centers of learning
came into existence. These were called parishads or associations of Brahmins
(Brahmins were learned in Vedas and Dharam Sutras), which attracted a large
number of students. During the later period, great centers of learning got established in different parts of the country, such as Nalanda and Taxila (North India);
Kanchi (South India); Vallabhi (Kathiawad); and Ujjain (Central India). Other
centers included Odentapuri and Jagaddale (famous for Buddistic learning).

Some of the "centres of learning in the East and South continued their work
throughout the middle ages, the Muslim rulers encouraged the establishment of
colleges (madrasas) at places such as Lahore, Ajmer, Delhi, Lucknow, Rampur,
and Allahabad. These institutions specialized in the teaching of subjects such as
logic, astronomy, theology and natural philosophy. While most of those institutions have disappeared some still carry on the traditions of old Madrasas."[40]

During the British period before 1857, a number of colleges and other institutions of higher learning were established by the East India Company and the
Christian missions. Some of these still exist.

Sir Charles Wood's Education Despatch of 1854 is regarded as an important
document. One of its recommendations was to establish universities in the presidency towns of Bombay, Calcutta, and Madras. As a result of this recommendation, in 1857, the first three universities were established, namely, the University
of Bombay, the University of Calcutta, and the University of Madras. These are
the first Indian universities in the modern sense. These were set up in the year
1957, but their libraries were established in 1864, 1873, and 1907, respectively.[41]
Two more universities—Panjab University and University of Allahabad—were
subsequently established in 1882 and 1887, respectively.

According to Isaac, "in the case of the early universities, libraries were started
long after the starting of the universities themselves. This is because they had no
teaching and research functions that needed library support. But after the enactment of the Indian University Act of 1904 which wanted the universities to assume direct teaching and research functions, it became necessary for libraries to be
established in the universities. . . . This is indicative of a general lack of appreciation of the importance of the library in university education."[42]

In 1947 (the year of independence), there were nineteen universities and 636
colleges with a student enrollment of about 106,000. In 1950–1951 there were 28
universities and 695 colleges. The enrollment was about 174,000 and the total

number of teachers was 21,264. In 1993–1994, there were 190 universities, 7,600 colleges, 4.6 million students and 249,000 teachers.[43]

During 1994–1995,[44] there were 229 university-level institutions, enrollment of students being 1,014,393 and the 69,283 faculty members in these. It may be noted that between 1857 and 1947, the rate of increase was extremely slow due to the neglect of higher education by the British, who ruled India until August 14, 1947.

From 1947 onward there has been a tremendous growth in higher education due to the high priority given to higher education by the government of India. The first five-year plan commenced in 1951 and the ninth five-year plan is in progress. Two education commissions for higher education were set up in 1948 and 1964, respectively. The UGC was established in 1953 and has brought important changes and played a crucial role in the sphere of higher education.

Early in 1985 the central government reviewed the educational situation. On the basis of the review, the new education policy was adopted by the Parliament in 1986. The government of India announced its national Policy on Education (NPE)[45] in 1986. This has been a landmark in the educational development of the country. The NPE was reviewed by a committee (chaired by A. Ramamurthi) in 1990. A revised Programme of Action (POA) was placed in the Parliament on August 9, 1992, and approved by it. The eighth five-year plan (1992–1997) was formulated, keeping in view the 1986 NPE and 1992 POA. These developments in higher education have given tremendous impetus to higher education in the country.

India is a vast multilingual and multicultural country, which poses a great challenge to planners and administrators in providing access to its citizens to higher education. In spite of the proliferation of institutions of higher education in the 1960s and 1970s, these institutions were found to be inadequate to meet the ever-growing demand. Thus a committee was constituted by the then Ministry of Education, under the chairmanship of Professor D. S. Kothari to examine the feasibility of establishing correspondence courses in India. On the basis of the recommendations of the committee, the University of Delhi started correspondence courses in 1962. Today there are more than thirty-eight universities offering correspondence courses at the graduate and postgraduate levels.

There has been a growing demand for higher education from the masses. The Indian state has been unable to meet the demand adequately due to the lack of resources including qualified personnel. Formal education is considered quite costly and the country does not have the necessary resources to fulfill in a satisfactory manner the objectives. Thus it was decided to conduct higher education through distance education (open universities). Today, there are eight open universities.[46] Indira Gandhi National Open University (IGNOU) and such other institutions have done a commendable job. At present, the open university system is heavily dependent on printed material. Modern technologies are beginning to be used. TV and radio broadcasts have been in use for quite some time, though these have not proved to be adequate.

Today India has a large infrastructure of higher education consisting of 229[47] university level institutions and 8,600 colleges, with an enrollment of 6,113,929 students and having 300,793[48] teachers. These university-level institutions include conventional universities, institutions deemed universities, institutions of national importance and universities specializing in subjects like agriculture, medical science, science, engineering and technology, and so on. There are four women-only universities and eight open universities (providing distance education).

NORMS

The Committee on University and College Libraries was appointed in 1957 to advise the UGC regarding the proper functioning and management of libraries. Dr. S. R. Ranganathan was made its chairman. In 1959 the UGC organized a seminar titled "From Publisher to Reader: Work-flow in University and College Libraries."

The report of the Ranganathan Library Committee (1957) and proceedings of the seminar (1959) were published together in 1965.[49] The report is indeed a landmark document. It contained recommendations regarding finance, collection, services, buildings, furniture and equipment, staff, and so on. The UGC adopted these recommendations as norms for the working of college and university libraries.

One major recommendation which had a far reaching effect was this: "The high academic and professional qualifications, the combination of academic and administrative responsibilities and the practice in the universities all over the world indicate that the status and salary scale of library staff should be the same as of teaching and research staff."[50] This is a clear and precise statement about academic status and salaries of library staff. This recommendation regarding parity of pay scales was accepted by the UGC and implemented by central universities. However, other universities were rather slow in this regard.

The Pay Commission (government of India) (1974) did not recommend equal status and salaries to the librarians. This was a retrograde step. After a long a struggle, the government of India finally decided to give parity with teachers regarding salary scale effective from April 1, 1980. However, the UGC revised the set of laid-down qualifications and made it obligatory for authorities to follow revised qualifications for recruitment of library staff in the future.

The UGC has formulated standards for college and university libraries, but it has been slow in the matter of accepting for implementation and revising these standards. The Library Committee (1957) of the UGC laid down a staff formula, which forms the basis of allocating staff to university and college libraries. These standards are outdated and need to be revised in light of the changing environment.

SALARY SCALES

The UGC recommended the following salary scales vide letter no. F.1-9/89 (CPP-1) dated February 20, 1990:

Assistant Librarian/Documentation Officer	Rs. 2,200 (entry level); Rs. 75 (annual increment up to Rs. 2,800); Rs. 100 (annual increment up to Rs. 4,000).
Assistant Librarian/Documentation Officer	Rs. 3,000 (Senior Scale); Rs. 100 (annual increment up to Rs. 3,500); Rs. 125 (annual increment up to Rs. 5,000).
Assistant Librarian/Documentation Officer	Rs. 3,700 (Selection grade); Rs. 125 (annual increment up to Rs. 4,950); Rs. 150 (annual increment up to Rs. 5,700).
Deputy Librarian	Rs. 3,700; Rs. 125 (annual increment up to Rs. 4,950); Rs. 150 (annual increment up to Rs. 5,700).
Librarian	Rs. 4,500; Rs. 125 (annual increment up to Rs. 5,700); Rs. 200 (annual increment up to Rs. 7,300).

The parity of salary scales with teachers was maintained. The merit promotion scheme has been extended to professional librarians. The UGC has laid down evaluation criteria similar to university teachers. The criteria cover qualifications, attendance of at least two refresher courses, evaluation by a committee, and maintaining parity with teachers. Recently salary scales have been again revised vide letter no. F-3-1/94 (PS) dated July 30, 1998/August 10, 1998 from the UGC:

Assistant Librarian/Documentation Officer	Rs. 8,000-13,500
Assistant Librarian/Documentation Officer (Senior Scale)	Rs. 10,000-15,200
Deputy Librarian	Rs. 12,000-18,300
Librarian	Rs. 16,400-22,400

It may be noted that parity of scales with those of teachers has been maintained. This is a positive step. The Merit Promotion Scheme has been extended to library professionals. The UGC has laid down evaluation criteria. The implementation of revised scales and personal promotion schemes is in progress.

PATTERN OF ORGANIZATIONAL SYSTEM

Functional arrangement as a basis of pattern of organizational system has been adopted by and large by Indian university libraries. Usually, there is a provision for the following sections or departments: (1) Acquisition section, (2) Technical section, (3) Reference section, (4) Circulation section, (5) Periodical section, (6) Maintenance section, and (7) Administrative section.[51] In addition, some libraries have a Documentation section. This pattern more or less conforms to the pattern recommended by the UGC Committee on University and College Libraries. The committee recommended the following departments and sections: (1) Book section, (2) Periodical section, (3) Documentation section, (4) Technical section, (5) Reference section, (6) Circulation section, (7) Maintenance section, (8) Administrative section, and (9) Supervisory section.

CENTRALIZATION VERSUS DECENTRALIZATION

Whether a university library should be centralized or not continues to be a controversial topic. This issue has four aspects: physical location, administrative control, processing, and services. On one extreme we have a highly dispersed library system, and a completely centralized library system having no departmental libraries belongs to another extreme. The history of departmental libraries is very old. The departmental libraries are as old as university libraries themselves. These have existed all along.

By and large librarians have advocated one strong central university library. They have tried to get the departmental libraries merged into the central library. Sometimes they have succeeded and other times they have failed. The reverse has also happened sometimes, where departmental libraries get created out of a central library.

The organizational system varies from complete centralization (with regard to central control) to complete decentralization. Delhi University Library System is a large system consisting of Central Reference Library, Ratan Tata Library (for social sciences), Arts Library, Science Library, South Campus Library and Faculty/departmental libraries. Administratively, each unit is responsible to the dean of the concerned faculty or Head of the concerned academic department or the director. However, the university librarian has complete control over the Central Reference Library and coordinates certain functions.

The year 1966 is a landmark in the history of Delhi University Library because structural and organizational changes were made in the governance of the library. The statutes and ordinances of the University of Delhi were revised so that all university maintained libraries were organized into a "system of libraries" under the charge of the university librarian. The university librarian was made directly responsible to the vice chancellor. The Library Committee became an advisory body. Earlier it was an administrative body responsible for managing the library. However, "the 'System' with its highly centralised administration could not stand the strains and pressures of the sprawling components and thus the 'System' was decentralised rather disintegrated in 1983. The ordinances were again changed and the structural changes in the governance of the library were brought about. Under the new ordinances, the Library Committee under the chairmanship of the Vice Chancellor is an administrative committee charged with the responsibility to manage and administer the library. Each component of the erstwhile 'System' is for purposes of administration and management under their respective Head of the Department, Deans, Directors, etc as the case may be."[52]

In most of the university libraries, there exists partial centralization. This means that central library (or main library) and many of the departmental libraries are under the control of chief librarian, but certain professional school libraries, departmental libraries, and special collections have autonomous position.

Jawaharlal Nehru University, New Delhi, has a university library, which is a good example of complete centralization (in all respects including administrative control). On the issue, the Education Commission (1964–1966) recommended that "in addition to having departmental and seminar libraries stocked with a working collection of books and journals, the central library should facilitate inter-disciplinary communication as also the work of research scholars in border-line disciplines."[53] The UGC Committee on University and College Libraries recommended that departmental libraries should be given a permanent loan of two thousand volumes to a post-graduate department. This is a good suggestion.

LIBRARY COMMITTEE

For the purpose of the governance, most of the university libraries have a library committee. The first library committee was constituted in 1873 by the Calcutta University. They are either formed on a statutory basis or constituted through an executive order. These are usually concerned with policy and developmental matters. They may be either advisory or executive in nature. The vice chancellor or a senior professor of the university is the chairman and the university librarian is usually the member-secretary of the library committee.

USERS

User population[54] among 129 university libraries consists of 64,411 teachers, 55,135 researchers, 352,286 students and 78,347 others. The average number of members is 4,256. Thus, the number of members to be served by a university library is fairly large. Over the year, the number of users to be served has been increasing. Not only the number is increasing but the range of fields of interest is also increasing. Newer specializations are appearing from time to time. Thus, not only the numbers of users is large but their information needs are highly varied, which can be considered a big challenge.

COLLECTION

In the early 1960s an average university library of the country had a stock of one lakh volumes. It received 750 periodicals. The combined grant for purchase of books received from the university and the UGC enabled a university library to procure about seventy-five hundred books a year.[55]

By 1971 an average Indian university library had a stock of about 150,000 volumes subscribed to about 1,000 current periodicals, its average annual acquisition being about ten thousand volumes.[56] However, a large portion of this material especially of book resources (i.e., excluding the back sets of periodicals) consisted of multiple copies of textbooks and reading material not of significant importance to research and development.

In 1972 data were collected from fifty-eight university libraries concerning the number of periodicals each library subscribed to. These figures appear as follows:[57]

Number of Periodicals Subscribed To	Number of Universities
2,000 or above	6
1,000–2,000	14
500–1,000	19
100–500	14
Less than 100	5

These data show that about 66 percent (two-thirds) of university libraries subscribed to 1,000 or fewer periodicals.

In 1970 Gidwani remarked that "by international standards, our library collections are so inadequate as to hardly support any worthwhile research in topics other than indigenous. Even in this field, the American Book Procurement Centre has ensured that more university libraries in the United States of America will have better library resources on India than a similar number within our own country. It is now imperative for a scholar doing quality research on India to knock at the doors of libraries in UK or USA."[58] This is indeed a pathetic situation. Today the situation has gone from bad to worse.

Sethi and Moorthy analyzed data from ninety-seven university libraries collected in the early 1980s.[59] They concluded that nearly 45 percent of the university libraries in the country possess moderate collections of 100,000 volumes or less; about 70 percent of the libraries have collections not exceeding 2 lakh volumes; only 3 percent of libraries have collections exceeding 5 lakhs and not a single one has hit the figure of one million.

The INFLIBNET report appeared in 1988. The data given in the report are based on 177 responding libraries, which included besides the university libraries, department/campus libraries, having a collection exceeding 10,000 volumes. According to the report, 29.4 percent university libraries have a collection less than 25,000 volumes, 28.8 percent of libraries between 25,000 to 100,000 volumes and 27.1 percent of libraries between 100,000 to 300,000 volumes and 11.8 percent of libraries over 300,000 volumes. Thus 85.3 percent of libraries have a collection of less than 300,000 volumes. The report further adds that "Between 120,000 and 200,000 volumes are added every year by all the libraries in a region totally [North, South, East and West regions]. If all the university libraries in the country are taken together, about 700,000 volumes are added every year totally. On an average, between 4,000 and 6,000 volumes are added annually by a medium/large size library."[60]

According to *Universities Handbook* (published 1992), the size of the collection ranges from 12,000 volumes to 1,149,000 volumes. Delhi University Library had 1,149,000 volumes.[61] The number of volumes added per year ranges from 200 to

13,969. According to Sethi and Moorthy, 72 percent of university libraries subscribe to fewer than 1,000 current periodicals; 15 percent of those libraries subscribe between 1,000 and 1,500 periodicals; only 2 percent of them acquire between 1,501 and 3,000.[62] Thus, 99 percent of university libraries subscribe to fewer than 3,000 periodicals annually.

The periodical collections in the 129 university libraries[63] together comprise 1,940,547 items. Out of these 944,875 items (48 percent) are located in university libraries belonging to the north region. This implies that university libraries in the north region as a whole is stronger in terms of periodical collections. This indicates disparity in the periodical collections in the country as a whole.

The 129 university libraries are subscribing to 2,352 abstracting and indexing periodicals, involving an expenditure of Rs. 2 crores. *Chemical Abstracts*, *Biological Abstracts*, and *Physics Abstracts* are being subscribed to by 58, 56, and 41 university libraries, respectively.

The number of periodicals subscribed to[64] varies from forty-eight to four hundred. According to Krishan Kumar,

During the recent years, the number of periodicals subscribed to has come down drastically due to severe budget cuts. The solution lies in resource sharing. A university library should establish linkages for resource sharing with other university libraries in the region and other libraries also especially with libraries attached to institutions of higher education and research organizations. They should become active members of networks. INFLIBNET has mentioned about large duplication in subscription to indexing and abstracting periodicals. Can we avoid this duplication? Provision of effective current awareness services and SDI can help in this direction. Establishing of national information centers by UGC and networks (such as DELNET, CALIBNET etc.) are steps towards sharing of resources, offering opportunities for avoiding duplication.[65]

The suggestions mentioned are relevant even today.

FUNDING

The UGC assists universities and colleges by giving grants for different purposes:

1. Grants for books and journals
2. Grants for buildings
3. Grants for furniture
4. Grants for purchase of equipment such as photocopy machines, computers, and so on.

The UGC meets total expenses of central universities. This is true today. However, in the case of state universities and institutions deemed to be universities, it adds to their funds for various development activities under the five-year plans.

Higher education is highly subsidized. For instance, "Tuition fees in Delhi University colleges have not been changed for the last 30 years, thanks to UGC subsidies. The monthly tuition fees are still only Rs. 15. Apart from tuition fees, Delhi colleges collect funds under various other heads like sports, library, development etc."[66] A paper on government subsidies in India was prepared by India's Ministry of Finance. It classifies higher education in the list of 'non-merit goods/services' and excludes it from "subsidies on the basis that the benefits in this case, accrue principally to the recipient." Further it recommends that "the subsidies for high education should be reduced from 90 to 50 percent in the next three years with a further goal of reducing the subsidies to 25 percent in another two years."[67] The UGC as well as teachers and students have opposed such a move. Subsidies are in the process of being reduced. Therefore, university libraries should prepare themselves for marketing their services to earn so that the income this obtained can be used for improving the services. It can be said that they are not ready for the change.

State university libraries all over the country are starving for funds. This is because

the existing system of funding of state university libraries in the country is based on the old Victorian pattern of maintenance grant-in-aid. In this system, the state government puts upper ceiling on the expenditure of a university. It gives grant-in-aid to the extent the university's resources fall short of the upper ceiling amount. University's resources include income from examination fee, tuition fee and endowment grants. The state government hardly shows any dynamism and commitment in considering the development proposals of the university. The state government policy has been to give just enough to pay for salary of the staff and other sundry expenses including some amount for libraries and laboratories. In respect of libraries this system does not take into account its developmental and research needs, increase in prices of books, purnals, microform literature and increase in foreign exchange rates."[68]

In the seventh five-year plan there was an outlay of 15.7 percent on higher education out of a total education budget, but in the eighth five-year plan (1992–1997), the percentage was reduced to 8 percent only. Thus the percentage of expenditure on higher education has come down drastically. This has severely affected funding to university libraries.

The figures for nonplan allocation to the UGC in 1993–1994, 1994–1995 and 1995–1996 budgets are Rs. 336.95 crores, 343.18 crores, and 341.82 crores, respectively. Thus, nonplan allocation to the UGC is almost stationary. As a consequence many universities and colleges are reluctant to fill up vacancies and some of the facilities are being withdrawn.

In recent years, there has been severe resource crunch. There was a 19.5 percent cut in the maintenance grant as imposed by the UGC for the financial year 1997–1998. This was in addition to a 3.25 percent cut announced by the union government earlier. This has led to lopsided growth of library collections, resulting in lots of gaps.

RESOURCE CRUNCH

Upendra Baxi, the then vice chancellor of the University of Delhi, wrote in 1993 that

At no time since the independence have Indian universities been subjected to such sustained ideological offensive as in the last two years. The technique adopted is twofold. On the one hand, declining allocations to Central and State universities, in an era of deregulation, devaluation and inflation and on the other by the thoughtless insistence that universities should meet additional dearness allowance payments out of their already impoverished grants. Both these techniques have been severely invoked, more recently by the recent Union Budget without any sustained national debate on how, if at all, should the four decade old policy, mandated by the Indian Constitution, of state support for university education should be fundamentally modified.[69]

Thus it is being insisted that universities somehow manage with their vastly limited means. They are being told to raise resources on their own. There has been a keen concern to enhance quality of university education. Toward this end education has been placed into the concurrent list with state and central government by the Forty-Second Amendment. Besides, the New Education Policy has sought to expand state support by dedicating progressively 6 percent of the GNP to education as a whole. Although privatization of university education is not mentioned in the policy document, there is now a nationwide movement to deprivatize college education. This is getting wide political support as many politicians have benefited from such an arrangement in the past.

During recent years, there has been a serious resource crunch in terms of support to university libraries. Owing to shortage of funds, the Delhi University Library System has virtually reached a serious situation of decline as can be seen in Table 3.1.

Table 3.1
Number of Journals Subscribed and Renewed in Delhi University Library System

Library	Journals Subscribed in 1990	Renewed in 1991	Renewed in 1992	Likely to be Renewed in 1993
Arts	582	285	219	168
Science	795	350	275	uncertain
Ratan Tata	920	600	200	247
Law Faculty	280	248	177	163
South Campus	350	250	200	175

Source: The Gathering Storm: Resource Crisis for Universities (Delhi: University of Delhi, 1993), 49.

It may be noted that although there has been a proportionate increase in the library budget, this becomes nullified due to fiscal measures and increased subscription costs.

According to the chair of the UGC, "instead of the usual increments in our budget, it has been reduced by 3.22 percent which is reflected in the budget for all UGC centrally supported institutions. . . . Our budget estimates of 1997–98 are less than the budget estimates of 1996–97 and no increase was given at the revised estimates stage in 1996–97."[70] As a consequence, central universities and colleges, supported by the UGC, are facing a resource crunch crippling the growth and development of university and college libraries attached to these institutions. The only way out for these libraries is to market their services and charge the users. This profit can then be used to improve the services.

BUDGET

Laurence J. Kipp and Cecilia R. Kipp compiled in 1961, on behalf of the U.S. Wheat Loan Office in India, certain data on thirty university libraries.[71] They found that six libraries had a book budget (annual) less than Rs. 100,000, eleven between Rs. 100,000 and 149,000, five between 150,000 and 199,000, and eight more than Rs. 200,000.

Book budget is based on data provided by eighty-one university libraries. Nearly half the number of university libraries have book budgets of less than Rs. 10 lakhs; only seven libraries have budgets ranging between 25 lakhs and 50 lakhs and just one library has crossed the figure of Rs. 50 lakhs.[72] Sources of budget for university libraries are included in Table 3.2.

Table 3.2 shows that the total budget of 129 university libraries was Rs. 16.01, 18.94 and 23.14 crores for the years 1985–1986, 1986–1987, and 1987–1988, respectively. If we use 1985–1986 as a base, then we find that the budget has increased by 18 percent and 44 percent during 1986–1987 and 1987–1988, respectively. The budget for books has increased by 1.48 crores from 1986 to 1987–1988. But in the case of periodicals, the increase is of the order of Rs. 2.66 crores. This is due to the fact that price rise in the case of periodicals is higher than that of books. The budgeted amount for nonbook items, preservation and maintenance and staff training is certainly inadequate. According to *Universities Handbook*, the budget ranges from Rs. 56,000 to Rs. 11,500,000.[73] The budgets vary widely. There is no pattern. Older universities have better support.

The data provided by Sethi and Moorthy indicate that "nearly half the number of university libraries have book budget of less than Rs. 10 lakhs." This amount is too small. In fact, three libraries had a book budget less than rupees one lakh. There were only five libraries having a book budget more than thirty lakhs. *Universities Handbook* shows that the budget ranges from a low of Rs. 56,000 to Rs. 1,150,000. This shows a great disparity. The budget varies widely depending on various factors like age, number of members, subject(s) covered, and so on. Libraries attached to central universities, Indian Institutes of Technology are in a far

Table 3.2
Budget of University Libraries

Source of Budget	1985–1986	1986–1987	1987–1988
Books	67,146,060	80,032,389	94,859,295
Periodicals	83,759,179	98,423,938	125,045,740
Serials	1,278,842	2,297,674	2,006,402
Nonbook items	734,665	1,035,368	1,026,939
Preservation and maintenance	2,657,756	3,280,956	3,345,488
Staff training	56,400	56,400	81,350
Database search	538,000	528,029	112,860
Other	3,947,591	3,834,421	4,954,518
Total	160,118,493	189,489,175	231,432,582

Source: University Grants Commission (India), *Development of an Information and Library Network*, 403.

better position than state universities. State universities in Madhya Pradesh, Uttar Pradesh, Bihar, Orissa, Rajasthan, and so forth are starved for funds. The reasonable norm for a university library should be 6.5 to 10 percent of the university budget, as suggested by the Kothari Commission report. Most of the university libraries fall below this norm. Newer university libraries should have higher support. In practice, however, the reverse is the case.

SERVICES

According to Sewa Singh, "During 1960s interaction of the university librarians with their counterparts in the USA (maybe through PL 480) and other western countries increased, and they brought home the new techniques, new library services, and procedures; and when applied back home a new environment was generated in university libraries in which users started getting better service."[74] This is a significant statement.

More than 95 percent of the libraries provide reference, circulation and interlibrary loan services. These provide reprographic service (80 percent), microfilming facility (15 percent), bibliography compiling work (65 percent), indexing/abstracting work (11 percent), current awareness services (51 percent), selective dissemination of information (20 percent), press clippings service (2 percent), translation service (2 percent), and user education (1 percent).[75]

Libraries were asked to rate by priority the various services.[76] The order of priority listed by librarians was reference services, lending to internal users, reprographic service, current awareness, referral service, lending to external users, SDI, and computerized database access. Thus SDI and computerized database access are given low priority.

The provision of services is indeed a matter of concern because university libraries have neglected provision of certain services such as microfilming and user education. Reference and interlibrary loan services are provided by most of the libraries. But these are neither effective nor efficient. The INFLIBNET report indicates that librarians give top priority to reference service and computerized database access gets the least priority. The low priority to computerized database access is understandable in the context of priorities but this is rather unfortunate.

Computerization in university libraries started in early 1990s and picked up in late 1990s. Databases are being created, but it will take a year or two before there will be an impact on library services.

INFLIBNET CENTER (UGC)

The Information and Library Network (INFLIBNET) program was initiated by the UGC in April 1991. The INFLIBNET center was set up in 1991 at Ahmedabad, with the objective "to make optimum use of the treasure of information available in all the academic and research libraries in the country by modernizing library operations, creating union databases and providing speedy access to information through the network(s)."[77] The center has given funding to sixty-nine universities for "creating required computing facilities, creating databases and automating library operations." Another eighteen university libraries were funded under the same program recently.[78] It has trained more than three hundred staff members in computer application from different libraries. Five union databases have been created by the center. It has encouraged the development of Integrated Library Management software.

An INFLILBNET report was submitted in 1988. It is a landmark document. INFLIBNET has initiated a number of activities such as training, standardization of formats, development of software application interfaces, development of software for library management (Integrated Library Management software) developed in collaboration with DESIDOC, creation of databases (books, serial holdings, theses/dissertations), services (COPSAT Service, e-mail access to INFLIBNET databases), ADINET, and Technical Support to Libraries.

UGC INFORMATION CENTERS

The UGC realized that in addition to providing resources for purchase of books and reading materials, it was also necessary to provide bibliographic help and support to the academic community. Thus three information centers were established at Bangalore, Bombay, and Baroda, with the aim to improve information access and also to provide bibliographic support.

The National Science Information Centre (NSIC) was established in 1983 at the Indian Institute of Science (Bangalore) to provide services in the fields of mathematics, physics, chemistry, biology, and earth sciences. In 1988 engineering was also added. This was the first center to be set up.

The NSIC offers the following services:

Current Awareness services. The center acquires a number of databases and matches them against the interest profiles of the research scholars and sends abstracts of relevant references to them. Initially this service was free of charge to the users from colleges and universities. In 1991 a decision was taken to extend this service to the nonacademic sector and also to charge a fee for the service.

Document delivery service. Indian Institute of Science, Bangalore, National Library of Australia, Sydney and the French National S&T Information Centre serve as supporting agencies.

Retrospective search service. This service was started in late 1989. This service is provided through accessing DIALOG using online access facility, and CD-ROM databases are used for retrospective searches.

Referral service. The center uses CODATA referral database and numeric databases on floppy disks, for provision of numeric information. It has designed a database of Biotechnology Scientists of Indian origin.

Training. Courses of a year's duration in information technology application are conducted, enrolling six to eight students for a course.[79]

The UGC established in 1986 a second center named National Information Centre at SNDT Women's University Library, Mumbai. Its coverage includes sociology, women's studies, home science, special education and library science. The center has designed a computerized database covering books, journal articles, theses, newspaper reports and other materials published in 1987. Older material is being added on a selective basis. The database consists of ninety thousand records.

The center provides the following services:

1. Literature search
2. Quarterly alerting bulletins that are tailored to individual interest profiles
3. Photocopying
4. Interlibrary loans
5. Compilation of bibliographies
6. Referral service
7. Remote online access to Centre's databases through telephone.[80]

A third center, called the Social Science Information Centre, was established in 1992 at M.S. University (Baroda). Its coverage includes Economics, Political Science, Education, and Psychology.

ACADEMIC STATUS

University and college librarians have been fighting for academic status for a long time. At a meeting of the Academic Council of the University of Delhi held on December 24, 1983, the then vice chancellor stated that "the question of recognition of Librarians as teachers had been pending for a long time." He suggested that "Librarians, Deputy Librarians, Assistant Librarians and Documentation Officers in the University/College Libraries be recognized as teachers of the University subject to the condition that they would not be entitled to any summer and other vacations available to other teachers in the University but would continue to be governed by the various types of leave available to their case as at present" (Resolution 245, passed at the Meeting of the Academic Council).

The executive council of the University of Delhi at its meeting, held on November 19, 1988, passed the following ordinance:

Staff working in the Delhi University and its colleges of the rank of professional junior or equivalent and above will be termed as 'non-vacation academic staff'. The Executive Council/Governing Body of the college may on the recommending of the Vice-Chancellor/Chairman Governing Body, as the case may be, *re-employ* any distinguished incumbent working against the post of professional junior/college librarian or equivalent and above after he has attained the age of 60 years.

In view of the above ordinance, university and college librarians have been given the same salary scales as recommended for teachers. Further, they are given reemployment for five years after attaining the age of sixty years. Library professionals at the University of Delhi have been recognized as academic staff. Professionals elsewhere have not been granted this status.

STAFFING PATTERN

Ranganathan's General Staff Formula

A mathematical formula for calculating staff can be extremely helpful. Once such a formula is accepted by authorities, then the increase of staff based on an increase in quantum of work would become somewhat mechanical. General staff formula formulated by S. R. Ranganathan[81] has proved to be extremely useful. This formula is applicable to different types of libraries. Ranganathan has recommended the following staff formula.

(a) Professional staff

$$SB + SC + SL + SM + SP + SR + ST$$

(b) Non-professional staff

$$B/30,000 + S/100$$

(c) Unskilled staff

SB/4 + SC/2 + SL + SM/4 + SP/2 + SR/8 + A/20,000 + D/500 + B/60,000 + (S/100)/4 + V/30,000

Explanation

SB = Number of persons in book section
   = A/6,000 = (Number of books accessioned in a year/6,000)

SC = Number of persons in circulation section
   = G/1,500 = (Number of gate hours for a year/1,500); One gate hour = one counter gate kept open for one hour)

SL = Number of persons as librarian and his deputies
   = HW/1,500 = (Number of hours library is kept open × Number of working days in a year/1,500)

SM = Number of persons in maintenance section
   = A/3,000 = (Number of volumes accessioned in a year/3,000)

SP = Number of persons in a periodicals section
   = P/500 = (Number of periodicals currently taken/500)

SR = Number of persons in a reference section
   = (R/50) (W/250) = (Number of readers per day/50 × Number of working days/250)

ST = Number of persons in technical section (that is, classification and cataloging section)
   = (A+40D)/2,000 = (Number of volumes accessioned in a year + 40 × Number of periodicals abstracted and indexed in a year/2,000)

 B = Annual budget allotment in rupees
 S = Number of seats for readers
 A = Number of volumes accessioned in a year
 D = Number of periodicals abstracted and indexed in a year
 V = Number of volumes in the library

It may be noted that the requirement of staff for each section has been calculated on the basis of assumptions based on experience. For instance, the number of professionals required for a periodical section has been worked out based on the assumption that one professional is sufficient for procuring and recording five hundred periodicals per year. The above formula needs to be revised in the context of information technology.

UGC Library Committee (1957)

The Library Committee of the UGC (1957) laid down the strength of the different sections in university and college libraries to be determined roughly on the following basis:

Book section. One person for every six thousand volumes added in a year

Periodical publications section. One person for every five hundred current periodicals taken

Documentation section. One person for every one thousand entries prepared in a year

Technical section. One person for every two thousand volumes added in a year

Maintenance section. One person for every six thousand volumes added in a year, one person for every five hundred volumes to be replaced in a day, and one person for every one hundred thousand volumes in the library

Publicity section. No staff provided for this section

Administrative section. Minimum of one library accountant, one stenotypist, and one correspondence clerk

Reference section. One person for every fifty readers (other than the users of the textbook collection) in a day

Circulation section. One person for every fifteen hundred hours for which one wicket gate of the library has to be kept open in a year

Supervisory section. One librarian and one assistant or deputy librarian

Unskilled staff. One cleaner for every thirty thousand volumes in the library, one attendant each for every six thousand volumes added in a year, for every five hundred current periodicals taken, and for each of the shifts in the circulation section, besides unskilled and the semi-skilled workers normal to any institution.[82]

Later on, Ranganathan suggested certain changes in the above mentioned norms, as noted below:

Periodical publications section. Fifteen hundred periodicals subscribed.

Documentation section (to supplement the work done by the INSDOC and the international abstracting services: Thirty research workers (in the university).

Maintenance section. Fifteen hundred volumes newly added, fifty thousand volumes to be looked after (one person).[83]

QUALIFICATIONS

The minimum qualifications for appointment to the posts of librarian, deputy librarian and assistant librarian/Documentation Office (vide UGC letter No. F-1/89 [CPP-1] of February 20, 1990) are as follows.

Librarian (University)

(1) Master's degree in Library Science/Information Science/Documentation with at least 55 percent marks or its equivalent grade and a consistently good academic record; (2) one-year specialization in an area of Information Technology/Archives and Manuscript Keeping, master's degree in an area of specialization of the institution; (3) at least ten years' experience as a deputy librarian in a university library or fifteen years' experience as a college librarian; (4) evidence of innovative library service and organization, published work. *Desirable*: M.Phil./Ph.D.

degree in Library Science/Information Science/Documentation/Archives and Manuscript Keeping.

Deputy Librarian

(1) Master's degree in Library Science/Information Science/Documentation with at least 55 percent marks or its equivalent grade and a consistently good academic record; (2) one year's specialization in an area of Information Technology/Archives and Manuscript Keeping or master's degree in an area of specialization of the institution; (3) eight years' experience as assistant university librarian/college librarian; (4) evidence of innovative library services, published work and professional commitment. *Desirable*: M.Phil./Ph.D. degree in Library Science/Information Science/Documentation/Archives and Manuscript Keeping.

Assistant Librarian/Documentation Officer

(1) Qualifying the national level test conducted for the purpose by the UGC or any other agency approved by the UGC; (2) master's degree in Library Science/Information Science/Documentation or an equivalent professional degree with at least 55 percent marks or its equivalent grade plus a consistently good academic record; or master's degree in Arts/Science/Commerce or equivalent degree with at least 55 percent marks or its equivalent grade with bachelor's degree in Library Science/Information Science/Documentation or an equivalent professional degree with at least 55 percent marks or its equivalent grade plus a consistently good academic record.

Since the very beginning, there has been heavy reliance on nonprofessionals and semiprofessionals. During the first quarter of the twentieth century, the highest qualification was matriculation. The post of the person was designated assistant librarian. The second in command had studied up to the lower secondary examination. The third and the last had not reached beyond the primary school class.[84]

Kipp and Kipp wrote that during 1961, out of the thirty university libraries, eight university libraries had six to nineteen members, fifteen between twenty to thirty-nine and the remaining seven fell within the range of forty to sixty-three staff members.[85] Out of these more than 50 percent belonged to unskilled or Class IV staff and 25 percent belonged to ministerial and nonprofessional categories.

The table that follows sums up the situation in the 1968–1969 period.[86]

Staff Range	Number of University Libraries
3–20	20
21–40	26
41–60	13
61–80	7
81–100	2
Over 101	3

About 50 percent of the staff belonged to unskilled or Class IV category. Barely 20 to 25 percent of the total staff is professionally equipped to provide efficient library services.[87]

POSITIONS OF UNIVERSITY LIBRARIANS

Data were collected by Professor P. B. Mangla, who found that as of March 1992, 51 percent of the top positions in the libraries of university institutions were vacant.[88] This is a sad reflection on the attitude of authorities, who have not cared to fill up the top and crucial positions. The present position may be slightly better, as many posts have been filled up in recent years.

BUILDINGS

"Till the 1930s, the university library buildings were ornamental, designed for decorative purposes."[89] Among university libraries, the Bombay University Library building was the first to be constructed. It was constructed during 1864–1878. This became possible due to donations amounting to Rs. 4 lakhs, made by Premchand Roychand for the same. The Calcutta University Library was initially housed in the Senate House. In 1912 it was shifted from the Senate House to its own building. Madras University Library was initially housed in the Connemara Library building. In 1928, the library was shifted to the Senate House, remaining there up to 1936. The library shifted to its building in 1936, located opposite to the Marina Beach. Andhra University Library got its new library building in 1936. The foundation stone of Banaras Hindu University library was laid in 1926. It is a two-story building consisting of a big hall with a rotunda, in the tradition of the British Museum.

The University Grants Commission was established in 1953. It gave impetus to the construction of university library buildings. "During the First, Second and Third plan periods and up to the year 1972–1973 of the Fourth Plan period, UGC had sanctioned a sum of Rs. 38,375,289/- for the construction or expansion of university library buildings. Up to March 1973, UGC had sanctioned over 10 lakh rupees for the purpose to seven university libraries, between 5 lakh to 10 lakh to 23 university libraries, between 1 to 5 lakh to 16 university libraries, and less than 1 lakh to 6 university libraries."[90]

INFORMATION TECHNOLOGY

University libraries have been rather slow in the matter of application of information technology. Up to the 1980s university libraries were hardly affected by information technology except in the field of reprography. Under the INFLIBNET program the UGC started funding university libraries in 1991 to promote automation activities. Since 1991[91] seventy universities have been funded for creating core facilities for information access. Thus, in the 1990s, university libraries have been affected by the rapid changes taking place in information technology.

According to the latest position, "till now, 87 universities have been funded by the UGC under this programme for automation and networking. Remaining universities have been given funding for creating core facilities to enable them to access information. By the end of the current plan period, most of the remaining universities will be covered under the program."[92]

Out of fifty-four[93] university libraries for which data were available, twenty-five university libraries have procured and implemented the computer system. Fifty-one university libraries have been covered under a manpower training program. Twenty have a networking facility. Some of the university libraries that have done quite well in introducing computerized services include Panjap University Library, Jawaharlal Nehru University Library, North-Eastern Hill Library, Nagpur University Library, Pune University Library, Indian Institute of Science, Bangalore, and so on.

Panjab University Library has a computer network, CD-ROM server, Internet, Fax, e-mail facilities, and so on. Similar facilities are also available at other libraries. Nagpur University Library has already acquired a CD-recording (scribe) system to transfer its manuscript collection onto CDs. Nagpur University Library has made good progress in computer application. It has computerized most of its inhouse operations, and acquired a CD-NET facility with ten drives and Internet connection. They have created a number of databases. A campuswide network has become operational. The users can search the library catalog of the university library from their respective departments and also from CD-ROM databases.

JNU Library opted for HP 3000 X E mini-computer system, as MINISIS software was available free of cost by IDRC, Canada to the nonprofit institutions in developing countries. HP 3000 X E, on which MINISIS software was running, has become out of date. It is too costly to add more terminals, cartridges required for backup of data are not available and maintenance charges are too high. The library plans to transfer data on a 486/Pentium system and run it on another software. The library has acquired one 486, three 386 and two 286 PC ATs purchased with the UGC grants. The library has created bibliographic records of documents and articles from periodicals of social sciences, building large databases in social sciences, the humanities, and science and technology. Work is going on retrospective conversion of bibliographic records for the 1972–1989 period. The library shall soon start giving information retrieval services to users through computer terminals. The future plan includes computerization of circulation, acquisition, searching of press-clippings files, documentation and cataloging work, serial control. The library is a member of DELNET and INFLIBNET. They are connected to other libraries of India, through e-mail.

The Indian Institute of Science, Bangalore, a deemed university "has set up a digital library, the first of its kind in the country. The new cyber library uses the IBM's Digital Library software running on fast computers. This software has already been installed at the Vatican and in many large universities in other countries. With communication links, the IISc's digital library will be accessible from anywhere in the country and the world."[94] The papers produced at the institute, doctoral theses submitted to it and the journals published by the Institute will be available from the digital library. This new digital library will be accessible over the Internet through the Institute's web site.

NETWORKING

The UGC has taken an active role in promoting library and information network of university and college libraries. INFLIBNET is a major program initiated in 1991 to automate and network libraries both in academia and research-and-development systems for the purpose of resource sharing. INFLIBNET became an Inter-University Centre in May 1996. INFLIBNET Centre is an autonomous body. It is trying to achieve networking of databases created by university libraries. The UGC gave special funds to some of the university libraries in the year 1993/94 and 1994/95 for computerization and automation.

INFLIBNET has released a list of software and hardware recommended by it. It has also recommended standards for inputting resources and communication, such as *Common Communication Format*, 1988, and *Anglo-American Cataloguing Rules* (2d ed., 1988 revision).

INFLIBNET supports CDS/ISIS software on a DOS environment on stand-alone 286/386/PC ATs. It also supports 486/586 PC ATs with multiuser network on a UNIX environment.

The UGC has allocated grants to eighty-seven university libraries to equip them for computerization. INFLIBNET plans to link resources of all academic institutions of India through a network, a process that is already under way. A number of university libraries have started the work of converting their catalogs into machine-readable form. These include JNU, IGNOU, Poona University, Nagpur University, and Panjab University. There are a number of colleges in Delhi and elsewhere that have also taken steps toward this. Some libraries have started sending their records to INFLIBNET for merging in its OPAC, which in due course of time shall be made available online through satellite. At present, one can send request to INFLIBNET Centre at Ahmedabad, for searching the catalog via e-mail.

Delhi University Library System received a special grant of Rs 1 crores from the UGC outside the plan allocation during 1996–1997. It has taken steps to implement a scheme of computerization and networking of the system with facilities like e-mail.

CONCLUSION

Although the university libraries have developed steadily they have not yet realized their expectations. They have not succeeded in building sound library collections as they have not been able to evolve sound principles for acquisition of documents. This has sometimes resulted in a lopsided and haphazard collection of documents not satisfactory for study and research.[95] However, there are some bright spots. The collection on economics of Ratan Tata Library (University of Delhi) is an excellent one and the collection on international relations at Jawaharlal Nehru University Library is extremely good. Bombay University Library has a strong collection in economics and psychology and has built a substantial collection of nonbook materials. Panjab University has a rich collection of rare and out-of-print books on modern Indian history, travel, and geography. Rajasthan has a strong collection on South Asia. Delhi University Library has a rich collection in the field of chemistry. Indian Institute of Science, Bangalore, has built up an excellent collection in the field of sciences. Panjab University Library has a good collection in geology. These are but a few examples.

University libraries have failed to provide satisfactory services. They need to give a high priority to the improvement of services. Provision of satisfactory services will go a long way in improving the sagging image of university libraries.

Indian higher educational system is under great strain. A paucity of resources is wreaking havoc. At times universities do not have enough funds to pay the salary of teachers and other staff in time. This is true even for some of the prestigious universities.

Higher education in India is highly subsidized. However, subsidies are in the process of being reduced. University libraries must prepare themselves to market their services and earn money so that the income can be used for improving collections and services.

University libraries in India also must cope with the increasing number of users and users from newer fields of study, teaching, and research. The interdisciplinary approach in many of these fields has added an additional dimension to the situation.

University libraries in the United Kingdom and the United States have been in the forefront of library automation. However, university libraries in India have been lagging behind with a few exceptions. The situation is likely to improve during the next few years due to the grants given by the UGC under INFLIBNET program for computerization. Already eighty-six university libraries have been given grants for the purpose. The major problem remains the lack of trained manpower with expertise in computer application. By the year 2003, most of the university libraries would have created "core facilities" for automation and networking. Thus we may conclude that the process of library automation is quite slow.

NOTES

1. Gita Mathew, "College Libraries in India: Present Condition and Future Prospects," *Lucknow Librarian*, 26(1–4) (1994), 33.

2. University Grants Commission (India), *Annual Report, 1994–95* (New Delhi: University Grants Commission, 1995).

3. N. Datta, *Academic Status for University and College Librarians in India*, 3d ed. (Delhi: Indian Bibliographies Bureau, 1989), 35–36.

4. Ibid., 36.

5. India, Bureau of Education, *Selections from Educational Records*, Part 1, 1781–1839 (Calcutta: Superintendent Government Printing, 1920), 21.

6. Mathew, "College Libraries in India," 33.

7. Hunter Commission (1882), *Report*, para. 317.

8. J. K. Anand, "College Libraries in Delhi," in Krishan Kumar and J. K. Anand, ed., *College Libraries in India* (Delhi: Indian Library Association, 1988), 6–7.

9. Ibid., 7.

10. G. P. Chakraborty, "College and Academic Institutional Libraries in Tripura: A Survey," in Krishan Kumar and J. K. Anand, ed., *College Libraries in India* (Delhi: Indian Library Association, 1988), 126.

11. Janak Raj, "Problems of College Libraries in Haryana," in Sewa Singh, ed., *Librarianship and Library Science Education* (New Delhi: Ess Ess Publications, 1988), 110–120.

12. Ibid., 115.

13. Krishan Kumar and S. D. Vyas, "Classification Practice in Delhi University College Libraries," *Journal of Library and Information Science* 4(1) (June 1979), 41–76.

14. P. K. Walia and Shalini Gautam, "Library Services in Colleges of Delhi: A Survey," in Krishan Kumar and J. K. Anand, ed., *College Libraries in India* (Delhi: Indian Library Association, 1988), 17–19.

15. S. K. Bajpai, "Evaluation of College Library Services in Delhi," *Library Herald*, 32 (3–4) (October 1994–March 1995), 141.

16. Ibid.

17. C. P. Vashishth, "College Libraries in Delhi: A Scenario" in IASLIC Conference (1983) (New Delhi), *Souvenir* (New Delhi: INSDOC, 1983), 10.

18. M. Bavakutty, "Development of Book Collection in College Libraries in Kerala," in P. B. Mangla, ed., *Building Library Collections and National Policy for Library and Information Service* (Delhi: Indian Library Association, 1985), 83.

19. Madan Lal, and S. Jyothirmayi, "Library Finance in Delhi University Colleges," in Krishan Kumar and J. K. Anand, ed., *College Libraries in India* (Delhi: Indian Library Association, 1988), 27.

20. University Grants Commission (India), Committee on University and College Libraries, *University and College Libraries containing the Report of the Library Committee of the University Grants Commission and the Proceedings of the Seminar on "Publisher to Reader,"* 1959 (New Delhi: University Grants Commission, 1965).

21. "College Libraries in Kerala," *University News* 33 (January 23, 1995), 1–8, 13.

22. Vashishth, "College Libraries in Delhi," 12.

23. B. Sreepathy Naidu, "College Libraries in Andhra Pradesh with Special Reference to Andhra University," *Library Herald*, 19 (3–4) (October 1980–March 1981), 138.

24. University Grants Commission (India), Committee on University and College Libraries, Report, 72–73, 199.

25. P.S.G. Kumar, "Manpower Planning for College Libraries," in Sewa Singh, ed., *Librarianship and Library Science Education* (New Delhi: Ess Ess, 1988), 136–137.

26. Ibid., 137.

27. University of Delhi, *Governance of Colleges* (Delhi: University of Delhi, 1996).

28. W. A. Alvi, "Resource Sharing among University and College Libraries in Jammu and Kashmir with a Proposed Model." Unpublished Ph.D. thesis, University of Kashmir, 1994, 78, 81.

29. Raj, "Problems of College Libraries in Haryana," 119.

30. W. A. Alvi, *Resource Sharing among University and College Libraries in Jammu and Kashmir*, 81.

31. Narendra Kumar and Jaiversh Anand, "Computerising a College Library," *University News* (August 5, 1996), 7–8.

32. *Universities Handbook* (New Delhi: Association of Indian Universities, 1997), xi.

33. Raj, "Problems of College Libraries in Haryana," 125–126.

34. Mathew, "College Libraries in India," 36.

35. Quoted in S. N. Srivastava and S. C. Verma, *University Libraries in India: Their Organisation and Administration* (New Delhi: Sterling, 1980), 11.

36. India, University Education Commission (1948–49) (Chairman: S. Radhakrishnan), *Report*, 2 vols. (Delhi: Manager of Publications, Government of India, 1949).

37. Ibid., 111.

38. India, Education Commission (1964–66) (Chairman: D. S. Kothari), *Report* (New Delhi: NCERT, 1971).

39. K. S. Deshpande, "My Encounters with Dr. C. D. Deshmukh," *ILA Magazine*, 2 (4–2) (April–Sept. 1995), 9.

40. P. B. Mangla, "University Libraries and Libraries in India: An Overview," *University News* 30 (35) (August 31, 1992), 3.

41. Datta, *Academic Status for University and College Librarians in India*, 38.

42. K. A. Isaac, "University Libraries in India," paper read at IFLA General Conference (New Delhi) (1992), 3–4 (mimeograph).

43. G. Ram Reddy, "Quality of Higher Education," *University News* 32 (49) (December 5, 1994), 12.

44. University Grants Commission (India), *Annual Report, 1994–95* (New Delhi: University Grants Commission, 1995).

45. *National Policy on Education* (New Delhi: Government of India, Ministry of Human Resource Development, 1986).

46. *Universities Handbook*, x–xi.

47. Ibid., x.

48. University Grants Commission (India), *Annual Report, 1994–95*.

49. University Grants Commission (India), Committee on University and College Libraries, *University and College Libraries, Containing the Report of the Library Committee of the University Grants Commission and the Proceedings of the Seminar on "Publisher to Reader,"* 1959 (New Delhi: UGC, 1965).

50. Ibid., 66–67.

51. Ibid., 72–73.

52. A. L. Kapoor and H. C. Jain, "University Libraries in Delhi," in IASLIC Conference (1983) (New Delhi), *Souvenir* (New Delhi: INSDOC, 1983), 5.

53. India, Education Commission (1964–66) (Chairman: D. S. Kothari), *Report*, 520.

54. University Grants Commission (India), *Development of an Information and Library Network: Report of the Inter Agency Working Group* (Delhi: University Grants Commission, 1988), 359.

55. N. N. Gidwani, "Indian University Library: Problems and Prospects," in Seminar of University Librarians (Jaipur) (1966), *Proceedings*, Vol. 2 (Jaipur: University of Rajasthan, 1967), 3.

56. Krishan Kumar, *Research Libraries in Developing Countries* (Delhi: Vikas, 1973), 139.

57. S. N. Srivastava and S. C. Verma, *University Libraries in India*, 86–87.

58. N. N. Gidwani, "The Universities," *Seminar*, 126 (1970), 25.

59. A. R. Sethi and Shyamala Moorthy, "University Libraries in India: Some Facts, Some Figures," *ILA Bulletin*, 20 (1–2) (April–September 1985), 73.

60. University Grants Commission (India), *Development of an Information and Library Network: Report of the Inter Agency Working Group*, 359.

61. Association of Indian Universities, *Universities Handbook*, 1992.

62. Sethi and Moorthy, "University Libraries in India: Some Facts, Some Figures," 73.

63. University Grants Commission (India), *Development of an Information and Library Network*, 360.

64. Association of Indian Universities, *Universities Handbook*, 1992.

65. Krishan Kumar, "Development of University Libraries during 1980s," *University News* 30 (35) (August 31, 1992), 55.

66. Sonal Manchanda, "UGC Opposes Move to Reduce Subsidies," *Indian Express* (Delhi), July 30, 1997, 1.

67. Ibid.

68. M. S. Rana, "Funding of University Libraries," *University News* 30 (35) (August 31, 1992), 101–102.

69. Upendra Baxi, "On Pain of Death," *The Hindustan Times* (Delhi), April 14, 1993, 11.

70. A. S. Desai, "The Letter of the UGC Chairperson." *University Today* 17 (22) (November 15, 1977), 1, 3.

71. Laurence J. Kipp and Cecilia R. Kipp, *Indian Libraries and the Indian Wheat Loan Educational Exchange Programme* (1961), 6.

72. Sethi and Moorthy, "University Libraries in India," 72–73.

73. Association of Indian Universities, *University Handbook*, 1992.

74. Sewa Singh, "From Librarianship to Information Science," *University News* 30 (35) (August 31, 1992), 75.

75. Sethi and Moorthy, "University Libraries in India," 74–75.

76. University Grants Commission (India), *Development of an Information and Library Network*, 360–361.

77. Pramod Kumar, "Address of Director, INFLIBNET" in *Souvenir* (Caliber, 1998), 6.

78. "New Varsities under INFLIBNET," *University News* 36 (38) (September 21, 1998), 20.

79. Harsha Parekh, "UGC's Information Centres," *University News* 30 (35) (August 1992), 87–88.

80. National Information Centre, *Suchak Services* (Mumbai: SNDT Women's University Library), 3. (a pamphlet).

81. S. R. Ranganathan, *Library Administration*, 2d ed. (Bombay: Asia Publishing House, 1959), 27–30.

82. University Grants Commission (India), *University and College Libraries*, 72–73, 199.

83. S. R. Ranganathan, "Academic Library System: Fourth Plan Period," *Library Science* 2 (4) (December 1965), 227–228.

84. S. R. Ranganathan, "University Libraries Then and Now," *Library Herald* 6 (1963), 63.

85. Kipp and Kipp, *Indian Libraries and the Indian Wheat Loan Exchange Programme*, iii.

86. Srivastava and Verma, *University Libraries in India*, 23.

87. Ibid., 24.

88. P. B. Mangla, "University Libraries and Librarians in India: An Overview," *University News* 30 (35) (August 31, 1992), 8.

89. Srivastava and Verma, *University Libraries in India*, 25.

90. Ibid., 26.

91. I. K. Ravichandra Rao, "Automation of Academic Libraries in India: Status, Problems and Future," *CALIBER-97* (1997) 1.

92. *CALIBER-99* (a brochure for the convention issued by Nagpur University) (1998), 2.

93. V. S. Cholin and K. Prakash, "Status of computerisation and networking of university libraries in India," *CALIBER-97* (1997), 6–7.

94. "IISC's Digital Library," *University News* 36 (14) (April 6, 1998), 15.

95. Kumar, *Research Libraries in Developing Countries*, 141–42.

SELECTED BIBLIOGRAPHY

Alvi, W. A. "Resource Sharing among University and College Libraries in Jammu and Kashmir with a Proposed Model." Unpublished Ph.D. thesis, University of Kashmir, 1994.

Bavakutty, M. "Development of Book Collection in College Libraries in Kerala." In P. B. Mangla, ed., *Building Library Collection and National Policy for Library and Information Service*. Delhi: Indian Library Association, 1985.

"College Libraries in Kerala." *University News* 33 (January 23, 1995), 1–8, 13.

Committee on University and College Libraries. *Report of the Committee on University and College Libraries, 1959*. New Delhi: University Grants Commission, 1965.

Datta, N. *Academic Status for University and College Librarians in India*. 3d ed. Delhi: Indian Bibliographies Bureau, 1989.

Janak Raj. "Problems of College Libraries in Harayana" in Sewa Singh, ed., *Librarianship and Library Science Education*. New Delhi: Ess Ess Publications 1988, 107–127.

Kapoor, A. L., and H. C. Jain. "University Libraries in Delhi" in IASLIC Conference. *Souvenir*. New Delhi: INSDOC 1983, 4–8.

Krishan Kumar, "Development of University Libraries during 1980's." *University News* 30 (35) (August 31, 1992), 53–56.

———. *Research Libraries in Developing Countries*. Delhi: Vikas, 1973.

Krishan Kumar, and J. K. Anand, ed. *College Libraries in India*. Delhi: Indian Library Association 1988.

Kumar, P.S.G. "Manpower Planning for College Libraries." In Sewa Singh, ed., *Librarianship and Library Science Education* (New Delhi: Ess Ess, 1988), 129–138.

Mathew, Gita. "College Libraries in India: present condition and future prospects," *Lucknow Librarian* 26 (1–4) (1994), 33–45.

Moorthy, A. L., and P. B. Mangla, ed. *Information Technology Applications in Academic Libraries in India with Emphasis on Network Services and Information Sharing*. Ahmedabad: Information and Library Network Center, 1997.

Naidu, B. Sreepathy. "College Libraries in Andhra Pradesh with Special Reference to Andhra University." *Library Herald* 19 (3–4) (October 1980–March 1981), 134–147.

Seminar of University Libraries. *Proceedings*. 4 vols. Jaipur: University of Rajasthan, 1967.

Sethi, A. R., and Shyamala Moorthy. "University Libraries in India: Some Facts, Some Figures." *ILA Bulletin* 20 (1–2) (April–September 1985), 72–78.

Srivastava, S. N., and S. C. Verma, *University Libraries in India, their Organisation and Administration* (New Delhi: Sterling 1980).

University Grants Commission (India), *Development of an Information and Library Network: Report of the Inter Agency Working Group.* Delhi: University Grants Commission 1988.

University of Delhi. *Governance of Colleges.* Delhi: University of Delhi, 1996.

Vashishth, C. P. "College Libraries in Delhi: A scenario" in IASLIC Conference (1983) (New Delhi) *Souvenir.* New Delhi: INSDOC, 1983, 9–14.

❧ 4 ❧

Public Libraries

In India, as elsewhere, the spread of knowledge through recorded communication and the development of libraries are interrelated. The growth of education spreads knowledge which stimulates the practice of building collections and preservation of reading materials, thus leading to formation of libraries.

EARLY PERIOD

Archaeological as well as literary evidence indicates that the writing and reading of manuscripts were regularly practiced in ancient India since the fourth century B.C. This must have led to the growth and development of collections of manuscripts at important centers of learning. Many of these centers received royal grants. Scholars from all over India and also from abroad came to these centers to receive education. Obviously, these institutions maintained their own manuscript collections. Many original works and commentaries were written here. Important centers of learning, such as Nalanda, Vikramsila, Odantapuri, Somapuri, Jaggadal, Mithila, Vallabhi, and Kanheri, had famous libraries attached to them.[1]

The Buddhists of India laid special emphasis on the writing of manuscripts and maintaining of their collections. The Jains and Hindus also made immense contributions to the field of learning. They patronized education and literary activities and established innumerable institutions called upasrayas and temple colleges. These institutions established and maintained their respective libraries.

From the seventh century kings and nobles patronized education and encouraged the writing of manuscripts and their preservation. The emperors of the

Timuride dynasty were patrons of learning. With the exception of Aurangzeb, all the early Mughal rulers extended their support to art, music, literature.[2] The libraries also made remarkable progress during this period.

In the seventeenth and eighteenth centuries, the development of libraries received an impetus due to the rise of European settlements in India. The Christian missionaries with a view to propagate religion, promoted learning, introduced printing, and also established libraries.

The early libraries did not serve as an instrument of mass education. These were almost an exclusive possession of royal and feudal courts and scholarly individuals of the priestly classes and the various religious and monastic organizations. These libraries were more like storage warehouses. The modern concept of a library being a service institution was missing.

THE NINETEENTH CENTURY

Certain important developments took place during the nineteenth century, which gave impetus to the library movement. The year 1808[3] is considered an important date because the then government of Bombay initiated a proposal to register libraries, which were to be given copies of books published from "Funds for the Encouragement of Literature."

The Calcutta Public Library was established in August 1835 from private sources. It was meant to serve the needs of all the people.

By the middle of the nineteenth century, the towns of Bombay, Calcutta, and Madras had subscription libraries, established with the active support and initiative from Europeans. These cannot be regarded as free public libraries as they loaned books for home reading only to their members, who paid subscription fees and also deposited money as security against loss of books. In fact, the membership was confined to the upper classes of the society.

In 1867 the government of India enacted the Press and Registration of Books Act XXV, under which the printer of a book was supposed to deliver free to the provincial government concerned one copy of the book and one or two more copies, if the provincial government so desired. The additional copies were to be sent to the central government.

Khuda Baksh Oriental Public Library (Patna) was established in 1875. In 1891 it was opened to the public. It has an excellent collection of Arabic and Persian manuscripts. In 1969 it was declared under the act an Institution of National Importance.

In 1860 a small library was set up by Jean Mitchel in Madras as a part of the museum. The library was opened to the public in 1896. It was renamed Connemara Public Library. It was a free public library; only a nominal deposit was required, which was refundable. In 1948 the library became the state central library.

Toward the end of the nineteenth century, social, economic and political preconditions necessary for the origin of public libraries were coming into being. This was the time when national awakening was taking place. National awakening was encouraged by the formation of the Indian National Congress (1885), the speech of Swami Vivekananda at the Parliament of World Religions (1895) held in Chicago and his subsequent work in awakening national cultural pride, and the crucial role played by national leaders like Bipinchandra Pal and Lala Lajpat Rai in leading the Swadeshi movement.[4]

Therefore, as the necessary conditions for the establishment of public libraries became available, before the nineteenth century ended all the provincial capitals and many district towns had so-called public libraries. In addition many princely states had public libraries in their capitals (e.g., Indore, Travancore-Cochin, Patiala). However, in general the masses did not take full advantage of these institutions.

THE TWENTIETH CENTURY

Beginnings of the public library movement in India can be traced to 1885, when the Indian National Congress was founded. This was the time when national awakening was taking place, leading to cultural renaissance. The Swadeshi movement was taking root.

The contributions made by Maharaja Sayajirao III, Gaekwar of Baroda, to the modern public library movement in India is really remarkable During the course of his visit to the United States in 1906 he felt greatly impressed by the role played by public libraries in the advancement of education. Therefore he decided to establish public libraries throughout his state. To organize libraries along modern lines, he invited W. A. Borden, librarian of the Young Men's Institute, in New Haven, Connecticut, to lead the proposed system of free public libraries in Baroda. During his tenure of office, 1910–13, he established the Central Library and initiated a public library system. He also conducted library training classes to train staff in 1910. The modern public library movement in India is said to have begun in Baroda during the first decade of the century.

By the time Borden left the state, on May 15, 1913, "Baroda city had its Central Library, comprising Reference and Lending Departments with a book stock of 40,000 volumes. Twenty-five thousand more books were awaiting addition as soon as more space was provided. . . . Two of the three *prant* libraries had been established and thirty-six of the thirty-eight towns had provided their own libraries. Two hundred sixteen of the four hundred twenty-six large villages had founded their libraries. Even the small villages had come forward and had initiated their own libraries. There were 140 travelling libraries as well."[5] By the time Borden left Baroda, he had achieved a great deal, in the form of planning and establishing a network of public library systems in Baroda. Due to the far-sightedness of Sayajirao III, Baroda State was able to provide free library facilities to citizens of the state. The maharaja passed away in 1936. It is a pity that an excellent library system developed as early as 1910 could not be sustained, due to lack of support on the part of the state government. The library system had deteriorated to a large extent by 1947.

"It was at the time when the nationalist spirit was surging forth with an over-spill of enthusiasm, when Dr. Annie Besant's Home Rule Movement met with repression by the foreign British Government, that the Indian Public Library Movement was conceived. The movement took a concrete shape in 1919 and set itself on the path of enlightening the people throughout the length and breadth of our vast sub-continent. The Gandhian Movement later made the Library Movement an indispensable necessity to the people and the spring board for the successful organization of the Independence Movement."[6] This indicates the environment prevailing at the time when the concept was conceived.

The Public Libraries Acts

The public library movement has received impetus due to enactment of library legislation in different states of India. These acts have provided for funding, structure of library systems, powers and functions of authorities and such other matters relating to public libraries. So far library legislation has been enacted in ten states.

1. Madras (Tamil Nadu) Public Libraries Act (1948)
2. Andhra Pradesh Public Libraries Act (1960)
3. Mysore (Karnataka) Public Libraries Act (1965)
4. Maharashtra Public Libraries Act (1967)
5. West-Bengal Public Libraries Act (1979)
6. Manipur Public Libraries Act (1988)
7. Kerala Public Libraries Act (1989)
8. Haryana Public Libraries Act (1989)
9. Mizoram Public Libraries Act (1993)
10. Goa Public Libraries Act (1993)

In the history of library legislation in India, the Kolhapur Public Libraries Act, 1945, is the first one in the preindependent India. According to Venkatappaiah, "Karveer Wachan Mandir, which was known as Central Library of the State later, was catering to the needs of the Kolhapur City. This Act was made mainly to maintain and organize the Karveer Wachan Mandir, Karveer (Kolhapur)."[7] The act is defunct now.

Due to the efforts of Dr. S. R. Ranganathan, the Madras (Tamil Nadu) Public Libraries Act was passed in 1948. It was put on the statute book on January 29, 1949. It was a landmark. This was the first library act to be passed in independent India. Thus Madras became the first state to provide a public library system through library legislation after independence. Next, the Hyderabad Public Libraries Act was passed in 1955. This was the second library act to be passed in independent India. Thus, Hyderabad state was the second state to pass library legislation. On November 1, 1956, Andhra Pradesh was formed as a linguistic state, with Andhra region of Madras state and Telangana region of Hyderabad state. The Andhra Pradesh Public Libraries Act was enacted in 1960. As a consequence, Hyderabad Public Libraries Act was repealed by the Andhra Pradesh Public Libraries Act of 1960.

Andhra Pradesh was formed in 1956.[8] Eleven districts from Andhra region and nine districts from Telangana region were merged in the state. Before the formation of the Andhra Pradesh, the Madras Public Libraries Act was in force in Andhra region and the Hyderabad Public Libraries Act was in operation in Telangana region. Lot of administrative difficulties were faced in the operation of two different acts in the same state. Thus a new act was passed, namely Andhra Pradesh Public Libraries Act (1960), applicable to the whole of Andhra Pradesh. It was amended in 1964, 1969, 1987, and 1989.

The Mysore (Karnataka) Public Libraries Act, 1986, was passed in the year 1965 and came into force on April 1, 1966.

The Maharashtra Public Libraries Act was passed in 1967. Under the act, no library tax is levied. However, there is a provision for state contribution for not less than Rs. twenty-five lakhs to the library fund every year as grant-in-aid. The subscription libraries are considered as public libraries for the purpose of grants. The act allows charging of fees or subscription. The act provides for a separate Department of Libraries with the director of libraries as its head.

The West Bengal Public Libraries Act was enacted and enforced in 1979. It does not levy tax, but under the act it is the responsibility of the state government to establish and maintain public libraries just as the state maintains other forms of educational institutions. The West Bengal government has established a separate Directorate of Library Services under a director. A considerable amount of money is being spent on the growth and development of public libraries in the state. The budget allocation has increased from year to year. In 1979–1980, the budget allocation was Rs. 22,646,000 and in 1991–1992, it increased to Rs. 200,000,000, almost ten times. The expenditure on public library services in West Bengal is the highest among all states of India.[9]

The Manipur Public Libraries Act was passed in 1988 and came into force on October 1, 1988. It provides for the State Library Committee which is chaired by the minister-in-charge of education. Each district has a District Library Authority. A separate Department of Public Libraries under a director was also provided. No library tax has been imposed, but the act says that "the State Government shall contribute annually to the Library Fund maintained by every District Library Authority" (section 21 [3]).

The Kerala Public Libraries (Kerala Granthashala Sanghom) Act, 1989, was enacted in February 1989. The act provides for three tiers of library authorities at state, district, and taluk levels. The Kerala State Library Council is the highest authority vested with advisory, supervisory, coordinating, and promotional functions. It administers the State Library Fund. Secretary functions as the chief executive authority. Each district has a District Library Council. Each taluk has a Taluk Library Union. The act "has not only ensured majority of non-official and elected members in the Library Councils and Unions but also provided for election of office-bearers of the library authorities at different levels."[10] There is no provision for library directorate. The Act has authorized the State Library Council to levy a library tax in the form of surcharge on the building tax or the property tax at the rate of 5 paise per rupee. In addition, the state government may give an annual grant to the state council consisting of a sum which "will not be more than one percent of the amount allotted for education."[11]

The Manipur Public Libraries Act, Kerala Public Libraries Act, and Haryana Public Libraries Act were passed in 1988, 1989, and 1989, respectively. The Mizoram Public Libraries Act and Goa Public Libraries Act were enacted in 1993. The Goa State Assembly passed the Goa Public Libraries Act on November 26, 1993. Thus Goa is the tenth state to have enacted library legislation. So far, ten states (Tamil Nadu, Andhra Pradesh, Maharashtra, Karnataka, West Bengal, Manipur, Kerala, Haryana, Mizoram and Goa) have enacted library legislation for establishment and maintenance of public libraries.

Public libraries acts have been enacted in the states of Manipur, Haryana and Mizoram, but unfortunately the implementation of the provisions of acts in these states has been inadequate and tardy. The library associations need to put pressure on the authorities to achieve their proper implementation.

The Role of Individuals

Philanthropists have not given much attention to the development of public libraries in India. However, there have been many individuals who have contributed immensely to the growth and development of the public library movement. In the former state of Baroda, "The library movement originated as the people's movement under the leadership of a public leader, Motibhai Amin, in the form of Mitra Mandal (Society of Friends) Libraries as early as 1906, and was accorded a substantial state patronage only in 1910."[12] He strove hard to make libraries popular in Gujarati-speaking areas. Maharaja Sayajirao III, Gaekwar of Baroda (1862–1939) was an enlightened person who succeeded in setting up a chain of public libraries. Newton Mohun Dutt became the curator of libraries in 1921. He "provided an effective leadership for the library movement in Baroda during the 1920's."[13]

The library movement in Andhra Pradesh[14] has been quite successful due to the efforts of a number of pioneers. One of them, Sir Iyyanki Venkata Ramanayya, holds a place of pride. From Bengal, we have the name of Manindra Dev Rai Mahashaya of Bengal, who was closely associated with the library movement in Bengal. He made great effort to get the Bengal Libraries Act enacted. In 1920 Master Motilal (1876–1949) established the Shri Shanmati Pustakalaya in Jaipur (a public library) by his own efforts and meager resources. He made pioneering efforts toward the promotion of free public library services at a time when the concept of a free public library was hardly known. From Punjab, we had Sant Ram Bhatia. He actively promoted the cause of public libraries in Punjab. Dr. S. R. Ranganathan is regarded as the father of the Indian library movement. He was instrumental in getting public libraries acts enacted in Tamil Nadu, Andhra Pradesh, and Karnataka. These acts have led to strengthening of the public library movement in South India. Ranganathan made pioneering efforts in the promotion of free public libraries.

The Role of Organizations

Various organizations have played a prominent role in building the public library movement in the country. These include Raja Rammohun Roy Library Foundation, Rajiv Gandhi Foundation, Indian Library Association, Indian Public Library Association, Andhra Pradesh Library Association, Bengal Library Association, etc.

The Raja Rammohun Roy Library Foundation

The Raja Rammohun Roy Library Foundation (RRRLF) was established in May 1972[15] on the occasion of the bicentennial birth anniversary of Raja Rammohun Roy. The foundation is an autonomous organization, established and sponsored by India's Department of Culture. With its headquarters located in Calcutta, its major aim is to promote and support the public library movement in the country through provision of adequate library services and popularization of reading habits among neoliterates and rural population.

The foundation promotes and develops public libraries under schemes of matching and nonmatching assistance. Its main program is to provide book assistance to the public libraries. Under this program, it operates two schemes, namely, (1) assistance with the building up of adequate stock of books and reading and other visual materials and (2) assistance with the development of rural book deposit centers and mobile library services. Under the program of financial assistance to libraries, it operates the following seven schemes:[16]

1. Assistance with organization of seminars, workshops, training courses (orientation/refresher), and book exhibitions
2. Assistance with the storage and display of books
3. Assistance to voluntary organizations providing public library services
4. Assistance to public libraries below district level for increasing accommodation
5. Assistance to state central libraries and district libraries to acquire TV-cum-VCR sets for educational purposes
6. Assistance to children's libraries or the children's section of general public libraries (nonmatching)
7. Assistance to public libraries with centenary celebrations

There are a number of schemes offered by the foundation to assist in the development of public libraries. Public libraries are taking full advantage of the scheme for purchase of books and other schemes are not being used fully. There is a need to simplify the rules and regulations governing the schemes and also greater publicity to various schemes should be given.

The RRRLF, under its scheme of central selection of books, provides books to selected public libraries in India. Selection of books is primarily done from current publications brought out by Indian publishers. Databases have been created for titles selected during various years.

The RRRLF has played a significant role in the growth and development of public libraries in India by providing grants for purchase of reading materials and for construction and extension of library buildings and various library-related activities.

The Rajiv Gandhi Foundation

The Rajiv Gandhi Foundation has undertaken a new program to establish in every village a rural library.[17] It has been reported that "The Foundation would put up about Rs. 25,000 towards setting it up. Each library would have 400 books, 2 daily newspapers, maps etc., suitable furniture, fixture and fittings. Young boys and girls are being trained as librarians. An operation manual and a set of rules have been designed. A nominal membership would be charged from members. Support would be provided for a library for the first 2 years and it would be expected to be self reliant from the very beginning.[18]

The Rajiv Gandhi Foundation has opened 256 rural libraries in the villages of Rajasthan, Uttar Pradesh, West Bangal, Madhya Pradesh, and Tamil Nadu.

The Indian Library Association

The Indian Library Association (ILA) is a premier professional organization in the field of library and information science. The ILA has given a high priority to the development of public libraries. "Promotion of the library movement" and "appropriate library legislation" are the main objectives laid down in its constitution.[19] The ILA has been on the forefront in actively pursuing enactment of library legislation. There is a separate Sectional Committee on Public Libraries, which looks after matters related to public libraries.

The All India Public Library Association

The All India Public Library Association was formed in 1920. In 1926 the All India Public Library Conference was organized in association with the National Congress. It has taken some interest in the development of public libraries.

The Andhra Pradesh Library Association

Under the auspices of the Ram Mohan Library, a conference of the representatives of libraries of Andhra Desa was convened in 1914. As a consequence, in 1914 the Andhra Desa Library Association was formed. This was perhaps the first library association to come into being in India.[20] Later, its name was changed to the Andhra Pradesh Library Association. Its headquarters are located at Vijayawada.

The association has published forty-two books in library science and eighteen books on audit education. It has been bringing out its house journal titled *Granthalaya Sarvaswamu*, published in Telugu since 1915. This is the first vernacular library journal to be published from India.[21]

In the early period, the association conducted two library training courses: the Granthalaya Pravesika and the Granthalaya Visarada. The Granthalaya Pravesika course was first conducted at Bezawada in 1920 with twenty students. Thus it became the first library association in India to conduct library training classes.[22] It has been conducting a certificate course since 1966, which is recognized by the government of Andhra Pradesh.

Boat libraries (floating library services) were organized by the late Dr. Paturi Nagabhushanam between 1935 and 1942 to serve the passengers. Library pilgrimages to popularize the library movement were organized by Iyyanki Venkata Ramanayya. A batch of library workers would tour a group of villages to create library consciousness among people.

The Andhra Pradesh Library Association has a rich history of contribution to the library movement in the state. Great personalities like Iyyanki Venkata Ramanayya, Godicherla Hari Sarvottama Rao, Chilakamarthi Lakshmi Narasimham, Suri Venkata Narasimha Sastry, Paturi Nagabhushanam, and Kodati Narayana Rao[23] successfully led the library movement as a parallel movement to the independence movement and contributed largely to the establishment of a large number of libraries in the state.

The Bengal Library Association

The first All Bengal Library Conference was held in Calcutta on December 20, 1925. The All Bengal Library Association was formed at the conference with a provisional committee under the Presidentship of Rabindranath Tagore.[24] With the establishment of the association, the library movement started gaining ground. The association was renamed the Bangiya Granthalaya Parishad and in 1933 the name was later changed to the Bengal Library Association. The Association is housed in a four-story building, consisting of office, library, classrooms, and so on. It holds seminars, conferences, lectures, and training programs. A large number of publications have been issued by it. The association brings out a monthly journal in Bengali, *Granthagar*. Due to the efforts of the association, the Public Library Bill was passed in 1979. It plays an important role in organizing the West Bengal Book Fair and district book fairs.

The Five-Year Plans

The central government took keen interest in the promotion of public library service as early as the First Five-Year Plan (1951–1956). The objective was to set up a national central library, a state central library in each state, and a network of circulating libraries consisting of deposit stations and mobile vans in villages. The plan included a scheme for the improvement of library services. Under the scheme, state central libraries and district libraries were established. The concept of social education with rural and mobile library service was also put into practice. By the end of the plan period, there were nine state central libraries and about one hundred district libraries.

During the Second Five-Year Plan (1956–1961), an amount of Rs. 140 lakhs was provided to the states for library development. The objective was to establish district libraries.

During the Third Five-Year Plan, the goal was to cover the entire country by means of a network of central, state, district, branch, village, and mobile libraries. The Working Group, set up by the Planning Commission, proposed a target of setting up a network of libraries reaching up to village level having a population of two thousand.

The Planning Commission Working Group was constituted to give a report on modernization of library services and informatics for the Seventh Five-Year Plan, 1985–1990. The report was submitted in July 1984. The Planning Commission set up a Working Group on Libraries and Informatics for the Eighth Five-Year Plan (1990–1995). The Working Group recommended that "the subject 'libraries' should be transferred from the State List to the Concurrent List to achieve integrated and coordinated development of library and information services. It has further recommended that a National Policy on Library and Information System (NAPLIS) as recommended by the Chattopadhyaya Committee be adopted by the Government of India with the approval of the Parliament and that for the implementation of the program suggested in the NAPLIS Report, a National Commission on Library and Information Services should be set up. The Commission should be an autonomous organization under the Department of Culture, Government of India. The Working Group recommended setting up of a Bureau of Library and Information Services in the Department of Culture headed by a Joint Secretary. Similarly in each state and union territory, there should be a separate Directorate of Libraries."[25] The Working Group also made useful recommendations regarding library finance. However, not much progress took place during the Eighth Five-Year Plan regarding the implementation of the recommendations.

SINHA COMMITTEE REPORT

The central government appointed in 1957 an Advisory Committee for Libraries under the chairmanship of K. P. Sinha. The Sinha Committee submitted its report in 1958. It recommended a twenty-five-year library plan, the main recommendations of which are:[26]

- Library service should be free to every citizen of India;
- The library pattern in the country should consist of National Library, State-Central Libraries, District Libraries, Block Libraries and Panchayat Libraries;
- State governments should enact a comprehensive state library law;

- Public libraries in the country should cooperate with one another as well as subscription libraries, school libraries, college libraries, departmental and research libraries, university libraries etc.;
- State governments should accept the responsibility of public library service in their areas.

The Central Government took the following steps to implement the recommendations of the Sinha Committee report:

1. A Model Library bill was drafted in 1963 and circulated to the state governments for adoption.
2. Instead of All-India Library Council, the Central Government set up the Raja Rammohun Roy Library Foundation in 1972, to serve as the central agency for supporting and promoting public library services all over the country.
3. Over the years, volume of central assistance given to the states through the Foundation, under various schemes for improvement of library services, has gradually arisen. The annual assistance being Rs. 140 lakhs by the end of the 7th Five Year Plan.

NATIONAL POLICY ON LIBRARY AND INFORMATION SYSTEM

In October 1985, the government of India constituted a committee under the chairmanship of Professor D. P. Chattopadhyaya to formulate the National Policy on Library and Information System (NAPLIS). The final report of the Committee was submitted to the minister of human resource development, government of India, vide letter of May 30, 1986, for its final approval. NAPLIS (1986) has recommended a policy on public library system, including these extracts:[27]

1. The most important task before the government is to establish, maintain and strengthen free public libraries in the country and enable them to work as a system.
2. The main thrust in this area should go to the rural public library.
10. All libraries within a state should form part of a network extending from the community library of the village through intermediate levels to the district and to the State Central Library. The state network should eventually connect with the national level.
12. To bring about this development of the public libraries in a State it is vital that each state enacts its own library legislation.

On November 1, 1986, the government of India set up the Empowered Committee to consider the recommendations of NAPLIS (1986). Professor D. P. Chattopadhyaya was the chairman of the Empowered Committee. The committee drew up an action plan for implementation and submitted the report on November 4, 1988, which include:[28]

1. The Committee recognises that the most important task is to establish, maintain and strengthen public libraries in the country and to enable them to work as a system. But instead

of free public library service it has recommended charging nominal fee ranging from Re. 1 to Rs. 10 to be fixed keeping in view the economic condition of the target group of users.

2. NAPLIS has recommended that the main thrust should go to the rural public library which should be developed like a community library and information centre.

3. The Empowered Committee has accepted the NAPLIS recommendation that a District Library should serve as an apex library of the public library network.

7. All public libraries within a state should form part of a network.

9. The Empowered Committee has also accepted the NAPLIS recommendation, that proposals for maintenance and development of public libraries should preferably be through State Legislative enactments.

NAPLIS (1986) is an excellent report. One wishes that the National Policy on Library and Information System should be passed by the Parliament. Even the action plan for its implementation is ready. This would give great impetus to the growth and development of public libraries. Perhaps the bureaucrats in the Department of Culture do not want the national policy to be implemented because this would result in the shifting of decision making from bureaucrats to library and information professionals. Once the national policy is accepted by the Parliament, then the action plan can be implemented, which would hopefully lead to faster growth and development of public libraries in India.

EXAMPLES OF LEADING PUBLIC LIBRARIES

The major public libraries are located mostly in large towns. These include Connemara (State Central) Public Library, Delhi Public Library, Khuda Bakhsh Oriental Public Library (Patna), State Central Library (Andhra Pradesh), State Central Library (Chandigarh), Trivandrum Public Library, and so forth.

In 1860 a small library was established by Jean Mitchel in Madras as a part of the museum. It was opened to the public in 1896 and was named Connemara Public Library. It was a free public library, with only a nominal refundable deposit required. In 1948 it was designated the State Central Library of Madras State (now called Tamil Nadu).

Connemara (State Central) Public Library (Tamil Nadu) has 457,521 books and subscribes to 3,809 periodicals. Under the Delivery of Books and Newspapers (Public Libraries) Act, every publisher is obliged to send at his own cost a copy of each book or newspaper published by him to this library.[29]

The State Central Library (Chandigarh) has about 1.6 lakh books and 19 newspapers, and subscribes to 175 journals. There are 13,011 members. The GISTNIC Informatics Centre was established in the library by the National Informatics Centre (NIC). Thus the library has access to NICNET. A number of databases including MEDLARS are available on NICNET. The library has computerized acquisition, membership record and catalog.[30]

The Delhi Public Library (DPL) was established in 1951 by India's Ministry of Education, with financial and technical assistance from UNESCO as a pilot project. It is administered by the Delhi Library Board and provides free library service to the public of National Capital Territory (NCT) of Delhi.

The DPL is a large system consisting of the following units:[31]

Central Library	1
Zonal Libraries	1
Branches	3
Subbranch Libraries	24
Community Libraries	7
Resettlement Colonies Lending Libraries (for weaker sections of the society)	22
Resettlement Colonies Reading Rooms	9
Braille Department for the Blind (6 depository libraries of Braille books)	1
Hospital library services	2
Prison Library	1
Sports Libraries	3
Deposit stations	28

As of March 31, 1997, it had a sanctioned staff strength consisting of 451 (298 professionals, 103 nonprofessionals, and 50 vacant positions).[32] It had 63,996 members (as of January 1, 1998) including 21,920 children. The collection consists of 1,401,536 books including 14,256 Braille books; 7,907 gramophone records and cassettes (as of September 30, 1997). It subscribed to 223 periodical publications. Since December 16, 1981, the DPL has received one copy of each of the publications published in India free of cost under the Delivery of Books and Newspapers (Public Libraries) Act, 1954.

Special services provided by the DPL include cultural activities through group activities and audiovisual programs and services to prisoners, sportsmen, and the visually handicapped. Five mobile vans served 5,188 members at forty points.

The DPL spent Rs. 34,130,425 during 1996–1997 and 413 lakh in 1997–1998. The budget estimate for 1998–1999 was Rs. 469 lakh (Rs. 389 lakh under nonplan and Rs. 80 lakh under plan). It receives grant-in-aid from India's Department of Culture, Ministry of Human Resource Development.

The library has taken steps to modernize. Computers have been recently installed at the Central Library and its Zonal Library at Sarojini Nagar. There are plans to acquire computers for the other three zonal libraries at Shahdara, Patel Nagar, and Karol Bagh.

At one time the Delhi Library Board undertook the job of producing books for neoliterates. It brought out thirty-five titles in Hindi and two in Urdu.

The Khuda Baksh Oriental Public Library (Patna) was established in 1876. Maulvi Muhammad Baksh Khan, on his death, left a collection of fifteen hundred manuscripts, which formed the nucleus of the library. In 1891 the library was opened to the public. This library is very rich in Urdu, Persian, and Arabic manuscripts (18,000)[33] and also in Chinese, Indian, Asian, and Persian paintings. The manuscripts cover subjects such as sciences, mathematics, medicine, religion, history, literature, biography, philosophy, and so on. It has over ninety-five thousand old and rare books. The library also acquires books in French, German, and Latin languages, and it serves the needs of scholars in the humanities.

The National Library Calcutta is a depository library. Under the Delivery of Books and Newspaper (Public Libraries) Act, it receives a copy of all published books in India. Central Reference Library housed in the National Library is compiling the Indian National Bibliography on the basis of the books received under the act.

The State Central Library (Mumbai) had 540,773 volumes, as of March 31, 1988. The new library building is under construction. It is a library having a rich collection of early books.

PRESENT SCENE IN THE STATES

In India the state governments are primarily responsible for the development of libraries, particularly public libraries. Under the constitution of India, library services come under the jurisdiction of state governments. The public libraries constitute the largest segment of the library sector. Thus it is the responsibility of the state government to establish, maintain, and develop comprehensive public library services in both urban and rural areas. However, the central government can render assistance to the states for the improvement of library services. The state governments are the implementing authorities. Assistance from the central government ultimately depends on active cooperation and efficiency of the implementing agencies.

We may identify four groups of public libraries in India. These are (1) state central and regional/divisional libraries, (2) city library systems, (3) district library systems, and (4) other libraries.[34]

Group 1. Twenty-four state central libraries (all states except Sikkim), five central libraries in union territories, and thirty divisional libraries at the headquarters of each revenue division, acting as branches of State central libraries.

Group 2. Fourteen city library systems (each city with a population of over one lakh has a city central library with branches in the city). Such a system exists in the cities of Madras, Delhi, and Hyderabad and also in eleven cities of Karnataka.

Group 3.

1. 392 district central libraries (Eighty-seven percent have district libraries. There were 451 districts as of March 31, 1989.)
2. 540 subdivisional/taluka/tehsil libraries as part of the district library system
3. 3,500 approximately block or town libraries as branches of subdivisional or district libraries
4. 51,000 village libraries, as of March 31, 1989, as branches of block libraries

Group 4.

1. 100 (approximately) city corporation and municipality libraries
2. 3,000 Zilla parishad/samiti/panchayat libraries
3. 20,000 subscription libraries at the time of independence (1947), out of which 5,000 were absorbed into state library systems
4. 37 information centers public relations centers/soochana bhawans
5. Adult education department libraries
6. Tribal welfare libraries
7. 100 children's libraries known as bal bhawans
8. 398 Nehru Yuvak Kendras

It should be noted that some of these data are approximate only. No correct and up-to-date figures are available. The data indicate that there are about fifty-nine thousand public libraries, excluding subscription libraries.

The present scene in different states and union territories is described in the subsequent paragraphs.

Andhra Pradesh

The number of public libraries is as follows:[35]

Government Libraries

State Central Library	1
Regional Libraries	6
Mobile Library	1
Total	8

Zilla Granthalaya Samstha Libraries

District Central Libraries	22
City Central Library (Hyderabad)	1
Branch Libraries	1,426
Mobile Libraries	98
Village Libraries	344
Book Deposit Centers	546
Total	2,437

Aided Libraries

Panchayats	1,197
Cooperative Societies	34
Private Management	653
Total	1,884
Grand Total	**4,329**

It has been estimated that 28.31 percent of villages have been covered by branch libraries. The budget for 1995–1996 was Rs. 953 lakhs. The public library system is well developed as compared with other states.

Arunachal Pradesh

Arunachal Pradesh has one state central library (in addition there are two branch libraries), ten district libraries, two subdivisional libraries and twenty-three block libraries, and forty-four circle libraries, for a total number of eighty-two public libraries. There is a state library committee at the apex to advise government on all matters relating to libraries. The budget of the Library Department during 1995–1996 was Rs. 95.20 lakhs. The financial support is quite high compared with other Indian states.

Assam

The history of public libraries in Assam goes back to 1904 when a small library was established at the British Capital of Assam (i.e., Shillong) by the government of Assam. It was a public library, but it mainly served the needs of high-ranked government officials. Public library services in the modern sense were introduced during the First Five-Year Plan.

The state central library (SCL) was established in 1954 in Shillong (then part of Assam). In 1956, the government library created in 1904 was merged with SCL. Meghalaya was created out of Assam in 1972. The SCL was bifurcated and Assam's share was transferred to Guwahati. From 1972 the SCL of Assam started operation from the first floor of the district library at Guwahati. In 1984 the Department of Public Library was upgraded to directorate. Following the creation of a directorate, the SCL ceased. The documents held by it were transferred to the district library at Guwahati and a branch library was started at Dispur with part of the collection held at the SCL.

At present the structure of the public libraries consists of[36] the directorate of public services at the top (which controls library services in the state); reference and research library (1), science and technology library (1) and branch library (1), children's library (1); district libraries (18); subdivisional libraries (14) (according to a recent decision, subdivisions have been declared as districts), and rural libraries (204) (out of these only 182 are functioning). In addition, libraries have been set up by the Community Development Department, private institutions, trusts, and municipal corporations.

It is a sad commentary on the state of affairs that there is no state central library. The rural libraries are in bad shape. The per capita expenditure on library service is Rs. 43,[37] which is extremely low.

Bihar

Bihar[38] has 1 state central library, 7 divisional libraries, 25 district libraries, 25 subdivisional libraries, 440 block libraries and 4,000 village libraries. Figures are not available about town and panchayat libraries. Total budget on libraries for 1988–1989 was Rs. 3,533,500. The amount is too small. The library scene is discouraging. The situation is going from bad to worse.

Delhi

The Delhi Public Library serves the Union Territory of Delhi. It is a large system. It has three branches, twenty-four subbranches and a large number of service points served by five book mobiles. It has a collection of 1,401,536 volumes of books and subscribes to 223 periodicals. The Hardayal Municipal Library (established in 1884) has a rich collection of rare and old books from 1634 onward. The Marwari Public Library (established in 1915) is a small library having a collection of 27,500 volumes. Parshottamadas Tandon Library has a collection of 53,541 volumes. For a large city like Delhi, the public library system has proved to be inadequate.

Goa

Goa is a small state, having a population of 1,168,622 (1991 census). Public libraries consist of the one state central library, five taluka libraries, one hundred village libraries, six municipal libraries, and twenty government-aided libraries. The budget allocation for 1995–1996 was Rs. 39.85 lakhs. The Goa State Assembly passed the Goa Public Libraries Act on November 26, 1993,[39] which will hopefully pave the way for fast progress of public libraries in the state.

Gujarat

The director of libraries serves as the head of the directorate [Department] of libraries. Administration of state central library, Gandhinagar and central library, Vedodara are under his direct supervision. Government and nongovernment libraries in districts are grouped under seven divisions and each division is placed under an Assistant Director.

Public libraries in the state may be broadly grouped[40] into government libraries and grant-in-aid libraries. Gujarat has 78 government run libraries (1 central state library, 1 central library, 18 district libraries, 49 Taluka libraries, 3 women's libraries and 6 other government libraries) and 7,517 public libraries (41 city libraries, 78 city branch libraries, 416 town libraries, 115 women's libraries, 101 children's libraries, 6 Braille libraries and 6,760 village libraries). Thus there are a total of 7,595 public libraries. More than one third of the rural area is served by public libraries.

The grant-in-aid libraries are eligible for maximum maintenance grant as follows:

Type of Libraries	Maximum Maintenance Grant per Year
City Libraries	Rs. 40,000
City Branch Libraries	Rs. 15,000
Town Libraries Category I	Rs. 12,000
Town Libraries Category II	Rs. 8,000
Women's Libraries	Rs. 3,000
Children's Libraries	Rs. 2,000
Village Libraries	Rs. 1,500

A library must mobilize 25 percent popular contribution to match the maintenance grant received each year.

In case of libraries located in tribal and backward areas, the popular contribution is exempted. In addition to maintenance grant, special grant is provided for specific purposes like construction and/or repairs of buildings and purchase of furniture, equipment, books, and so on to grant-in-aid libraries. During 1983–1984,[41] the government spent Rs. 34 lakhs on government-run libraries and grant-in-aid libraries received Rs. 38 lakhs, which is a meager sum.

Himachal Pradesh

The state has a central state library at Solan, eleven district libraries, two rural public libraries, three tehsil libraries, five community center libraries, thirty paragana village libraries, twelve paragana (integrated) village libraries, and nine block libraries under the education department of the state. In addition, there are 5 municipal committee/corporation libraries, 138 small panchayat libraries. The school libraries are being used as public libraries during extended hours.

Jammu and Kashmir

There are eighty-five public libraries in the state.[42] The public library system consists of two central libraries, one each at Jammu and Srinagar, fourteen district libraries, fifty-one tehsil libraries, and eighteen block libraries/lending depots. The collection of each central library is about fifty thousand volumes and those of district libraries range from fifteen thousand to twenty thousand volumes. Tehsil libraries have collections ranging from one thousand to seventeen hundred volumes. There is one book per ten literates in the state. The budget for libraries was 53.82 lakhs, 57.26 lakhs and 62.19 lakhs during 1987–1988, 1988–1989 and 1989–1990 respectively. The budget of libraries is about .5 percent of the total budget for education. Total staff strength is 237, out of which 101 are professionals or semiprofessionals. The membership of central libraries is about sixteen hundred and for district and tehsil libraries, it does not exceed one hundred. The physical condition of library buildings is deplorable. The only service provided by these libraries is lending service. There is no provision for services to special groups, such as blinds, neoliterates, and so forth. The collections are inadequate. Financial support is far below the standards laid down for the purpose.

Karnataka

The following is the picture of libraries in operation:[43]

State Central Library (Serves as a central reference library of the state)	1
City Central Libraries	15
Branch Libraries	125
District Libraries	20
Branch Libraries	324
Service Stations for District and City Central Libraries	295
Rural Libraries	1,051
Book Delivery Centers	300
Mobile Libraries	11
Grant-in-aid Libraries	42
Hospital and Prison Libraries	24
Reading Rooms	52

A separate public technical library at Peenya has been provided. The Karnataka Public Libraries Act (1965) provides a good source of income in the form of library taxes. The budget of the Department of Public Libraries for the year 1995–1996 was Rs. 1149.72 lakhs. Karnataka has a well-developed system of public libraries.

Kerala

Kerala has a fairly large number of public libraries. There are 5,239 public libraries including 1 state central library and 11 district libraries. The Kerala Public Libraries Act was enacted in 1989. There is a three-tier administrative system consisting of (1) the State Library Council, (2) the District Library Council, and (3) the Taluka Library Union. The system is decentralized. The Trivandrum Public Library (state library) has 187,980 book and subscribes to 287 periodicals. It is one of the oldest libraries in India. At present the state gives a grant of Rs. 138 lakhs and in addition Rs. 700 lakhs works out as library tax.[44] The state has a fairly well developed public library system.

Lakshadweep

The Union Territory of Lakshadweep consists of thirty-six islands, only ten of which are inhabited. There is a central library at Kevaratti and each of the constituent islands is provided with one public library. The budget allocation for 1995–1996 was Rs. 28.50 lakhs.[45]

Madhya Pradesh

The public library setup is:

Central Library	None
Regional Libraries	5
District Libraries	44
Libraries under the Directorate of School Education	50

The public libraries in Madhya Pradesh are totally inadequate. These are in a bad shape due to the paucity of funds. Because of lack of funds for maintenance of buildings three libraries have been closed down recently. No new books have been purchased for the last five years.

Maharashtra

Before the enactment of the 1967 Maharashtra Public Libraries Act, the number of public libraries in Maharashtra was 474. On March 1982 the number increased to 3,120. By the end of March 1988, the state had 4,241 public libraries as follows:[46]

Aided Libraries

Central Library at Bombay Managed by Asiatic Society of Bombay	1
District Libraries	28
Taluka Libraries	236
Other Libraries	3,963

Government Libraries

Government Divisional Libraries	4
Subcenter of the Bombay Division at Ratngiri	1
Government District Libraries in Vidarbha Region	8

The present structural setup of the state public library system consists of:

State Central Library	1
Government Divisional Libraries	5
Government District Libraries	8
Recognized Public Libraries	5,597

Recognized Libraries of Research a.ıd Literary   32
   Institutions

In 1968 there were 474 recognized public libraries. The number went up to 5,597 in 1995. Rs. 365.69 lakhs were spent by the state on development of libraries during 1994–1995. The library situation has improved over the years, but the library facilities are not satisfactory.

Meghalaya

The development of public libraries in the state can be traced to 1904, when the erstwhile government of Assam started a government public library in Shillong. In 1954 the state central library was established. The government public library was amalgamated into the state central library.[47] In Meghalaya[48] there are one state central library and four district libraries. Mobile library service is available in the district library, Jowai. The state central library has 115,615 books and subscribes to 106 periodicals. During 1989–1990, it spent Rs. 12,121,000, out of which only Rs. 80,000 was spent on the purchase of books and periodicals. In 1994–1995 it had a budget of Rs. 2,475,000 and collection was 162,000 volumes. District libraries more or less serve district headquarters. As a consequence, a large chunk of population has no access to libraries. There is a long way to go before the public library system can be considered well established.

Mizoram

In Mizoram, there are one State Library, two district libraries, three subdivisional libraries, and two hundred recognized village libraries (managed by voluntary organizations). The total budget for libraries in 1995–1996 was Rs. 29.91 lakhs. The 1993 Mizoram Public Libraries Act has not been implemented so far due to financial constraints. The library services are under the control of the Art and Culture Department of the state. The expenditure on aided libraries in 1987–1988 amounted to Rs. 27,798,832. The per capita expenditure (based on that of aided libraries only) is forty-four paise, which is far below the minimum expected.

Nagaland

Nagaland[49] has 1 state central library, 7 district libraries, and 110 rural libraries. The state central library has thirty-five thousand volumes, including books, periodicals and so on. The collection of district libraries varies between 500 and 3,206 volumes. Rural libraries have around five hundred volumes each.

Orissa

The following is the picture of public libraries in Orissa:

Central State Library	1
Block Libraries	314
Rural Libraries	1,600

The state of public libraries is poor. Due to paucity of funds, no books were purchased during 1993–1994.

Punjab

Fifteen public libraries are run by the Punjab Education Department. There are one central state library, thirteen district libraries, and one town library.

The central state library is located at Patiala. It has a rich collection, consisting of more than one hundred thousand volumes including rare books and manuscripts. All districts except Ludhiana have district libraries. However, Ludhiana has a municipal corporation library, a public library and Panjab University Extension Library. The municipal libraries have been established by all municipal committees. There are twelve hundred rural libraries and three thousand reading rooms. Some voluntary organizations have opened libraries in rural areas.

The services of most of these libraries consist of lending of books for home reading. Punjab is a prosperous state but library services are inadequate by and large. Except for libraries in major towns, the rest of the libraries more or less serve as reading rooms, which are kept open for few hours each day. The rural areas have been greatly neglected. Many of the block and panchayat/village libraries are mere store houses of books. It is unfortunate that a progressive state like Punjab has lagged behind in the matter of public libraries.

Rajasthan

Rajasthan has one state central library, five divisional libraries, twenty-seven district libraries, nine tehsil libraries, and sixteen reading rooms (providing newspapers and magazines). Library development is totally inadequate.

Tamil Nadu

The number of public libraries is:[50]

State Central Library	1
District Central Libraries	18
Branch Libraries	1,538
Mobile Libraries	7
Part-Time Libraries	1,099
Total	2,663

There are eighteen local library authorities, which run 18 district central libraries and 1,538 branch libraries. An outlay of Rs. 5.55 crores was made for the Public Libraries Department in the budget estimates for 1986–1987. During 1994–1995, the collection of library cess was Rs. 1,783 lakhs and Rs. 11 lakhs was provided as a special grant. The state central library has 457,521 books and subscribes to 3,809 periodicals. Tamil Nadu has been a pioneer in a number of ways. In 1948, Tamil Nadu was the first state after the independence of India in 1947 to pass the Public Libraries Act. This act has been a model for similar legislation in other states. In 1937, Madras University (Tamil Nadu) began post-graduate training for the first training for librarianship, with a one-year graduate diploma program. This was the first training program in the country and graduates served in public libraries in Tamil Nadu and other states. In addition, the state has been very successful in setting up a network of public libraries.

Tripura

In Tripura,[51] there is one state central library, three district libraries, seven subdivisional libraries, ten block level libraries, two rural libraries, one children's library and twenty-three book deposit centers. The state central library has a collection of 126,106 volumes. The budget for 1995–1996 was Rs. 5,885,000.

West Bengal

The number of public libraries is:[52]

Century Library	1
District Central Libraries	21
City Central Libraries	3
Town/subdivisional libraries	120
Rural Area/Primary Unit Libraries	2,276
Total	2,421

In recent years the West Bengal government has been spending about ten crores a year on public libraries. This is the highest amount of expenditure on public libraries in any state. This is in spite of the fact that the act does not provide for any library tax. The state has made good progress in developing a network of public libraries.

AWARDS/INCENTIVES

To provide incentive for the growth and development of public libraries in Maharashtra, the Dr. Babasaheb Ambedkar Granthalaya Puraskar award for the best public libraries has been instituted by the government of Maharashtra. Each year, eight libraries from four categories (based on the admissible expenditures incurred by the libraries in the previous year) are selected, four each from rural and city areas.

SCHOOL-CUM-PUBLIC LIBRARIES

According to the policy laid down under the National Literacy Mission,[53] libraries and reading rooms in educational institutions are to be opened to the public in the evening after the school hours. This approach has been introduced in Himachal Pradesh and a few other states. However, this arrangement is not working in a satisfactory manner due to lack of commitment on the part of states and also due to lack of sufficient funds.

PANCHAYATI RAJ AND PUBLIC LIBRARIES

In India autonomous library authorities for each district and city had been created, thus bypassing individual self-government for each library. A hierarchical structure was established in each state consisting of the directorate of public libraries, the state central library, divisional libraries, district central libraries, and branches of district central libraries in towns and villages. The idea of this hierarchical setup was that it would be possible to achieve resource sharing among libraries in the hierarchy, with larger units assisting the smaller units at each level. The idea was to create a network of libraries. However, this has not been achieved in practice.

In 1992 two amendments to the Constitution of India were enacted by the government of India. The Seventy-Third Amendment is related to panchayats for rural areas. The Seventy-Fourth Amendment pertains to municipalities for the urban areas. Panchayats and municipalities have been given constitutional status and some of the subjects from the state list have been transferred to these. Both amendments came into force on April 24, 1993. According to the editor of the *CLIS Observer,*

The panchayat system will have three tiers, namely the village panchayat for each village or a group of villages, intermediate panchayat at the Block level called Samiti and District Panchayat called Parishad. The state governments have been empowered to decide whether public libraries will be placed under the village panchayat, samiti panchayat or the parishad panchayat or under all the three in their respective areas. It is apprehended that in the absence of a common policy, each state may end up with a different system and there may not be any linkage between the parishad, samiti and village libraries. . . . As in the case of village panchayats, the state governments are empowered to decide whether to vest public library services in the Municipalities or some other authority. But the municipalities in the towns and the metropolitan areas may stake their claim for public libraries by taking them as part of cultural and educational activity.[54]

The amendments to the Constitution have led to uncertainties with regard to the future of library authorities and their manpower. It would be desirable that the Department of Culture should appoint a committee of experts to lay down guidelines for state governments so that an effective and efficient public library system could be developed.

INFORMATION TECHNOLOGY

Public libraries have lagged behind in the application of information technology. They are using photocopy machines. Some public libraries (e.g., the Delhi Public Library, Central State Library, Chandigarh, etc.) are using computers. The government of India and also some state governments are encouraging computer application, thereby encouraging a computer environment. Recently, the National Association of Software and Service Companies (NASSCOM) inaugurated video e-mail facility. For Rs. 15, one can transmit video images and the voices for a three-minute duration through public booths. Such facilities are being made available even in rural areas.[55] Thus rural public libraries can take advantage of such facilities.

PROBLEMS AND PROSPECTS

India became independent in 1947.

Lack of financial support has been the main problem faced by public libraries. After independence, there has been hard struggle for funds for different purposes. Libraries had to compete with basic services such as health, food, communication, etc. India has been faced with unfavourable circumstances due to rising unemployment, galloping inflation, growing population and the increasing threat of serious energy crisis. It is but logical, that any government under these circumstances would give high priority to the solution of these problems over library development. Obviously, in such a situation a government would be unwilling to increase financial support to a desirable level.[56]

India lacks a national policy on the development of public libraries. A report on the National Policy on Library and Information System (NAPLIS) formulated under the chairmanship of Prof. D. P. Chattopadhyaya was submitted (vide letter of May 30, 1986). An empowered committee appointed for the purpose drew up an action plan for implementation. The concerned report was submitted on April 11, 1988. Unfortunately, the NAPLIS has not been approved by the parliament and thus remains on paper without being implemented. National policy on development of public libraries can go a long way in giving direction to the public library movement.

Experience in India indicates that in order to set up a network of public libraries, an enactment of public libraries legislation is necessary. Those Indian states that have enacted a library law have, comparatively speaking, been more successful. At present ten states have enacted public libraries legislation. Mass movement needs to be built up to pressure the decision makers to take necessary steps in this direction. The Indian Library Association has given high priority to this aspect.

With the Indian economy getting strengthened and the literacy rate showing signs of improvement (though at the same time, the number of illiterates have been on the rise), there is every possibility that the public libraries shall get more attention as well as financial support. In the schemes of things, Raja Rammohun Roy Library Foundation, Rajiv Gandhi Foundation, and such other organizations are beginning to play a significant role in the development of public libraries. In view of the above, there is every possibility that in the twenty-first century the public library movement shall get a thrust and new direction.

CONCLUSION

Public libraries at different levels have multiplied in terms of quantity. According to the estimate there are about 59,000 public libraries excluding subscription libraries. A large majority of them are so-called libraries, being mere reading rooms that provide a few newspapers and magazines, with a small collection of outdated books, and are open for only a few hours. The quality of services leaves much to be desired. The book supplies are largely inadequate and there is a severe lack of qualified personnel. Some of the libraries providing good services include Connemara Public Library, Chennai; Delhi Public Library; Khuda Baksh Oriental Public Library, Patna; National Library, Calcutta; and the State Central Libraries in Bangalore, Calcutta, and Mumbai.

In India there has been uneven growth of public libraries between different states or regions and even within a local library system. A large majority of the population does not have access to free public libraries. Those regions that are economically backward are badly served in public libraries. Rural areas have been neglected compared with urban areas. In addition, the needs of special groups like children, the blind, the elderly, prisoners, and so on have been largely neglected.

NOTES

1. Krishan Kumar, Library Organization (New Delhi: Vikas, 1987), 140.

2. Ibid., 141.

3. Ibid.

4. Kodati Narayana Rao et al., Rise and Growth of the Public Library Movement in India (Eluru: Iyyanki Library Awards Committee, 1981), 4.

5. Murari Lal Nagar, Foundation of Library Movement in India (Ludhiana): Indian Library Institute and Bibliographical Centre, 1983), 79.

6. Rao et al., Rise and Growth of the Public Library Movement in India, 4.

7. V. V. Venkatappaiah, Indian Library Legislation, vol. 2 (Delhi: Daya Publishing House, 1990), 87.

8. Ibid., 133.

9. P. Barua and T. Tripathi, "Library Legislation in West Bengal: An Appraisal," in A.A.N. Raju et al., ed., *New Vistas in Library and Information Science* (New Delhi: Vikas, 1995), 535.

10. "Kerala Public Libraries (Kerala Granthashala Sanghom) Act 1989 Presents a New Model of Library Legislation," *RRRLF Newsletter* 10 (3) (July 1990), 2.

11. Ibid., 3.

12. Nagar, *Foundation of Library Movement*, 4.

13. Ibid., 120.

14. Kumar, *Library Organization*, 148.

15. Raja Rammohun Roy Library Foundation, *Annual Report*, 1991–92 (Calcutta: Raja Rammohun Roy Library Foundation, 1993), 1.

16. Ibid., 3.

17. *IASLIC Newsletter* (May 1995), 3.

18. *AIUN*, 12 January 1993, 201.

19. *ILA Constitution* (effective from January 5, 1987) (Delhi: Indian Library Association, 1987), 1.

20. Krishan Kumar, *Library Organization*, 144.

21. *ILA Newsletter* 11 (April 1995), 8.

22. Ibid.

23. Ibid.

24. Arun Roy, "Bengal Library Association" in R. Saha, ed., *Souvenir* (Calcutta: Bengal Library Association, 1988), 149.

25. D. R. Kalia et al., "Guidelines for Public Library Systems and Services," *Granthana* 2 (1) (January 1991), 51.

26. India, Advisory Committee for Libraries, Report (Delhi: Manager of Publications, 1959).

27. *National Policy on Library and Information System—A Presentation* (New Delhi: Committee on NAPLIS, 1986), 5–7.

28. NAPLIS Report on Public Libraries as Accepted by the Empowered Committee (mimeograph document), 1–2.

29. R. Kannan, *Salient Features of the Department of Public Libraries in Tamil Nadu*, 2 (mimeograph).

30. K. C. Ramola and Arora Sanjay, "Computerization of Central State Library at Chandigarh," in CP Vashishth, ed., *Library Movement and Library Development in India* (Delhi: ILA, 1994), 420–425.

31. Delhi Public Library, *Annual Report, 1996–1997* (Delhi: Delhi Public Library, 1998), 5.

32. Ibid., 1.

33. Kalyan Chaudhuri, "A Treasure-Trove: The Khuda Bakhsh Library," *Frontline* (August 28, 1992), 63.

34. Kalia et al., "Guidelines for Public Library Systems and Services," 36–38.

35. A. Satyanarayana, *Status Report on Public Libraries in Andhra Pradesh*, 6 (mimeograph).

36. R. K. Barman, "Public Library Services in Assam: An Observation," *IASLIC Bulletin* 39 (3) (1994), 110.

37. Ibid., 112.

38. R.S.P. Singh, "Public Library Development in Bihar," *Granthana* 2 (2) (July 1991), 202–203.

39. Pia de Meneze Rodrigues, *Public Library Services in Goa*, 4–5 (mimeograph).

40. Kaushik Shah, *Status Report on the Development of Public Library Services in the State of Gujarat*, 9–12 (mimeograph).

41. H. J. Upadhyay, "Gujarat and its Libraries," *Granthana* 2 (2) (July 1991), 124–127, 133.

42. S. M. Shafi and Rufai Reyaz, "Public Libraries in Jammu and Kashmir: An Appraisal," *Granthana* 2 (2) (July 1991), 169–177.

43. T. Malleshappa, "Public Libraries in Karnataka" (unpublished manuscript).

44. M. Khurshid Ahmed, "Status Report on Public Libraries in Kerala and State Central Library," 5 (unpublished manuscript).

45. "Status Paper on Library Service in Lakshadweep," 1 (unpublished manuscript).

46. "Status Report on Development of Public Libraries in Maharashtra" (unpublished manuscript).

47. "A Brief History of the Development of Library Services in the State of Meghalaya" (unpublished manuscript).

48. Bidi Diana Lanong and J. C. Binwal, "Public Library Services in Meghalaya," *Library Herald* 30 (2–4) (July 1991–January 1992), 239–242.

49. Moses M. Naga and J. C. Binwal, "Public Library Services in Nagaland," *Library Herald* 30 (2–4) (July 1991–January 1992), 243–248.

50. R. Kannan, "Salient Features of the Department of Public Libraries in Tamil Nadu" (unpublished manuscript), 20.

51. N. C. Das, "Status Report of Public Libraries of Tripura" (unpublished manuscript), 2–3.

52. V. V. Venkatappiah, *Indian Library Legislation*, vol. 2 (Delhi: Daya, 1990), 207.

53. *National Policy on Education: Programme of Action* (New Delhi: Ministry of Human Resource Development, 1986), 135.

54. D. R. Kalia, "Public Libraries and Panchayati Raj," *CLIS Observer* 10 (1–2) (January–June 1993), 2. The *CLIS Observer* is a journal in the field of library and information science.

55. Neelesh Misra, "Villages Step on Info Highway with Video E-mail," *Times of India* (Delhi edition), October 4, 1998, 12.

56. Kumar, *Library Organization*, 152–153.

SELECTED BIBLIOGRAPHY

India, Advisory Committee for Libraries, *Report* (Delhi: Manager of Publications, 1959).

Kumar, Krishan. *Library Organization* (New Delhi: Vikas, 1987) chaps. 7 and 10.

Nagar, Murari Lal. *Foundation of Library Movement in India* (Ludhiana: Indian Library Institute and Bibliographical Centre, 1983).

Narayana Rao Kodati et al. *Rise and Growth of the Public Library Movement in India* (Eluru: Iyyanki Library Awards Committee, 1981).

National Policy on Library and Information System, A Presentation (New Delhi: Committee on NAPLIS, Department of Culture, Government of India).

Vashishth, C. P., ed. *Library Movement and Library Development in India* (Delhi: Indian Library Association, 1994).

Venkatappaiah, V. V. *Indian Library Legislation*. 2 vols. (Delhi: Daya Publishing House, 1990).

❦ 5 ❦

School Libraries

EDUCATIONAL SYSTEM

India has a long tradition of learning and education. Today it has a very large educational system. In terms of number of students, teachers, and institutions, the system is the second-largest school system in the world. The Indian school educational system is highly diversified.

The Indian school system has four stages, namely, primary, middle (upper primary), secondary, and senior secondary. The period of instruction for primary stage varies from four to five years. The period for middle consists of four years. For the secondary stage it is two years and another two years for the senior secondary stage.

According to the Sixth All India Educational Survey conducted in 1999 by the National Council of Educational Research and Training (NCERT),[1] there were 822,486 schools. These consisted of 570,455 primary, 162,805 upper primary, 65,564 secondary and 23,662 higher secondary schools. Thus the Indian school education system is fairly large.

Goals

The Indian constitution, promulgated in January 1950, provides the framework for a federal political system. It listed education in the state list. An amendment[2] in 1976 placed it in the concurrent list. Thus the responsibility for education rests essentially with the states. However, the central government's responsibility lies mainly with maintaining and coordinating standards of higher and technical education. Therefore it follows that it is the clear responsibility of the central government to maintain the quality and character of education. In addition, the Ministry of the Human Resource Development, Department of Education shares with the states the responsibility for educational planning.

Present Situation

The importance of literacy is universally recognized. Literacy can bring qualitative change in the life and environment of the people. But the task of providing literacy in a country like India is a daunting one. One March 1, 1991,[3] India's population stood on 816.30 million. The literacy rate was 52.21 percent, excluding Jammu and Kashmir. Although the literacy rate has certainly improved in recent years, the number of illiterates still remains very high. Due to lack of resources, even after fifty years of independence the country is not able to provide "free and compulsory education for children up to the age of 14," as mandated by the Directive Principle of the Constitution. "Education for all" has remained a mere dream. Today the situation is that only one child out of three children enrolled in class I reaches class III. (Classes I–IV cover primary, V–VIII middle/upper primary, IX–X secondary, and XI–XII upper secondary school.) Thus the dropout rate is very high. Therefore we may conclude that Indian School Educational System has failed to meet the overall objectives laid down in the country's socioeconomic development program.

NATIONAL EDUCATION POLICY

To bring improvements in the system of education, the government of India appointed the Education Commission[4] (1964–1966) under the chairmanship of D. S. Kothari. On the basis of the report submitted by the Education Commission, education policy was adopted by the government of India in 1968. As a consequence, a ten-plus-two educational system was introduced in schools. (Up to class X, students study all subjects plus two or three languages. After passing class X, the student has the option of continuing at school or joining a polytechnic to do a two-year vocational program. In classes XI and XII, students narrow their focus into specific subjects, for example, science or commerce. After completing class XII, the student can join a college or professional program.) The aim of the system was to help relate educational objectives to the "life, needs and aspirations of the people," so as to produce young men and women who are deeply committed to the national development and service to the nation. The policy that had been adopted in 1968 was imaginative and purposeful, but the resources made available for educational reform were totally inadequate and the steps undertaken to implement the policy were halfhearted. Therefore it is not surprising that desired improvement did not take place. India's Ministry of Education issued a document in 1985 titled *Challenge of Education: A Policy Perspective* as "a basis for a nation-wide debate which could facilitate the formulation of new education policy."[5] Early in

1985 the central government reviewed the educational situation. On the basis of the review, it decided to bring about a new education policy. The draft of a new education policy as well as a program of action for the implementation of the same were prepared in consultation with the state governments.

As a result of a debate, the new education policy and a program of action were adopted by the Parliament in 1986. The government of India announced the National Policy on Education in 1986. It recommended "a transformation of the system of education to relate it more closely to the life of the people; a continuous effort to expand educational opportunity; a sustained and intensive effort to raise the quality of education at all stages; an emphasis on the development of science and technology; and the cultivation of moral and social values."[6] The new educational policy envisaged "a national system of education which would take determined steps for the universalization of primary education and the spread of adult literacy, thereby becoming an instrument for the reduction of disparities. It is based on a national curricular framework which contains a common core along with other, flexible, region-specific components."[7]

According to the 1986 National Policy on Education (NPE),

The availability of books at low prices is indispensable for people's education. Effort will be made to secure easy accessibility to books for segments of the population. Measures will be taken to improve the quality of books, promote the reading habit and encourage creative writing. . . . Good translations of foreign books into Indian languages will be supported. Special attention will be paid to the production of quality books for children, including text books and work books. . . . Together with the development of books, a nation-wide movement for improvement of existing libraries and the establishment of new ones will be taken up. Provision will be made in all educational institutions for library facilities and the status of librarians improved.[8]

The new education policy presents a challenge to various components of the Indian educational system (such as teachers, educational administrators, and school librarians). School librarians are expected to accept the challenge and respond to the changing needs of the society and help the educational system to achieve the goals.

Accordingly, the Seventh Five-Year Plan (1985–1990) emphasized decentralized planning, organizational reforms, promotion of nonformal as well as open learning systems, achieving closer links with industry and development agencies, mobilization of resources of the community, and greater involvement of the society. It made a provision for the establishment of pace-setting residential schools called Navodaya Vidyalayas.

The 1986 National Policy on Education (NPE), a landmark in the educational development of the country, was reviewed by a committee chaired by A. Ramamurthi in 1990. The report was considered by the Committee on Policy of the Central Advisory Board of Education, which submitted its report on January 22, 1992. Based on the report, revised policy formulations were tabled in the Parliament on May 7, 1992. A revised 1992 program of action (POA) was placed in the Parliament on August 19, 1992, and emphasized the following aspects:

1. Provision of free and compulsory education of satisfactory quality to all children up to fourteen years of age before the end of the twentieth century, through various centrally sponsored schemes in elementary education to be initiated
2. A District Primary Education Programme to achieve universalization of elementary education
3. Vocationalization of education at the secondary stage
4. Provision of education about India's common cultural heritage
5. Extension of open learning facilities

In accordance with these objectives, the Eighth Five-Year Plan (1992–1997) laid emphasis on the universalization of primary education taking into consideration the three dimensions of enrollment, retention and achievement, and also eradication of illiteracy, particularly in the fifteen- to thirty-five-year age group.

Navodaya Experiment

It is universally recognized that children having special talent or aptitude need to be given special facilities, whereby they can proceed at a faster pace than that of normal children. In addition, they may also be provided opportunities to get high-quality education, whereby they can turn out to be future leaders in the society. In view of these considerations, the Education Commission (1964–1966) recommended the selection of a certain percentage of schools as pace-setter institutions. This recommendation was not implemented immediately. However, the National Education Policy (1986) envisaged the establishment of such schools, called Navodaya Vidyalayas, on an average one in each district. In the Seventh Five-Year Plan, an outlay of Rs. 500 crores was proposed for the purpose.

The scheme of Navodaya Vidyalayas is considered as one of the most innovative experiments in the field of school education undertaken by the government of India. The scheme was started with the establishment of two Vidyalayas on an experimental basis in 1985–1986. By the early 1990s 324 Vidyalayas had been established in thirty-one states and union territories, covering classes VI to XII. It has proved to be an exciting movement in the field of school education, aimed at improving the quality of education at all levels.[9]

Navodaya Vidyalayas aim to promote excellence along with equity and social justice. This is achieved by enrolling children largely from the rural areas and also from the backward sections of the society. In addition, one-third of the total seats are reserved for girls. The Vidyalayas are able to offer quality education because they have excellent facilities (including excellent libraries and laboratories and adequate equipment and finances) and capable teachers. They have succeeded in attracting talented students and been given full support by the central government.

ORGANIZATION OF SCHOOL EDUCATION

The government of India is responsible for educational planning and policy, co-ordination and maintenance of standards, research and training, and so on. The Ministry of Human Resource is the nodal ministry that has the principal responsibility with regard to education.

National Agencies

The central government has set up three national agencies to help in its work. The first, the Central Advisory Board of Education, was established in 1935. It has played an important role in the evolution and monitoring of educational policies and programs such as the 1986 NPE (updated in 1992) and the 1992 POA. The second agency, the National Institute of Educational Planning and Administration, provides programs of research, extension, training and consultancy. Finally, the National Council of Educational Research and Training (NCERT) was established in 1961. It is located in New Delhi and its major objectives include "qualitative improvement and excellence in school education and teacher education."[10] It maintains effective liaison with state education authorities for providing academic inputs to the school education system. Its main contribution has been toward curriculum design, production of textbooks, and examination reform. NCERT has played an important role in an effort to improve the quality of school education.

State Agencies

As the constitution of India includes education in the state list, the decisions regarding the organization and structure of education lie largely with the states. Thus, within the overall policy framework, each state determines the educational structure to be adopted by it.

In each state there is a secretariat for education and separate directorate for school education. The state-level administration lays down policy and regulates the educational system. At the head of the district education administration is a district education officer with deputies and subdeputies, who are supposed to inspect and supervise schools. Due to the 1986 NEP, emphasis is now on decentralized, microlevel planning and management of education. Thus the infrastructural and institutional support at the district level is being strengthened.

In each state, a state council has been established. In Delhi the State Council of Educational Research and Training has been set up. A state council is responsible for curriculum, design, production of textbooks, examination reform, and continuing education (for both teachers and librarians) at the state level.

In view of the changing philosophy of education and also to bring improvements in the system of education, the government of India appointed the Education Commission (1964–1966) under the chairmanship of D. S. Kothari. On the basis of the report, education policy was adopted by the government of India in 1968. Thus a ten plus two plus three educational pattern was introduced. The emphasis in this pattern is on a common school curriculum up to Class X throughout the country, with vocational and technical courses starting at the secondary stage. However, professional courses for primary teacher training, medicine, and engineering commence only after the two-year senior-secondary course.

Categories of Schools

Schools categorized according to level include:

1. Primary schools (five years of schooling) (Classes I–V)
2. Upper primary schools (eight years of schooling) (Classes VI–VIII)
3. Secondary schools (ten years of schooling) (Classes IX and X)
4. Senior secondary schools (twelve years of schooling) (Classes XI and XII)

To these four categories, we may add one more, namely, preprimary schools, although we should note that preprimary education has received little attention.
   Schools categorized according to management include:

Government schools
   State government schools
   Kendriya Vidyalayas (central schools)
   Navodaya Vidyalayas
Local schools
Private-aided schools
Private-unaided schools

State governments run a large number of schools. Navodaya Vidyalayas and Kendriya Vidyalayas are the schools administered by the central government. Kendriya Vidyalayas (central schools) are mainly for the children of central government employees.

DISPARITIES IN FACILITIES AND STANDARDS

   Wide disparities in facilities and standards exist among different types of schools, varying from rural to urban areas and even from state to state. At one extreme are the "'public schools,' so called after British models, and the newly established Navodaya Vidyalayas. At the other extreme are ill-equipped, insufficiently staffed, and poorly supervised government rural or municipal schools. In between these extremes are a variety of private schools, the well-funded 'central schools' mainly for the children of central government employees, and the basic and postbasic schools run by people inspired by Gandhi's ideas on education."[11] The above indicates that the public schools, Navodaya Vidyalayas and Kendriya Vidyalayas (also called central schools), have reasonably good facilities and provide better education. Schools run by the state or municipal committee or corporation are in a poor state.

On the whole, preprimary education has been greatly neglected. Although the Integrated Child Development Services Programme has given attention to this area, primary education has been given priority and receives considerably more attention.

ROLE OF SCHOOL LIBRARIES

The role of school libraries has been emphasized a great deal in the reports of national commissions. Their contribution in improving the quality of education is well recognized. According to the report of the Secondary Education Commission (1952), "the library will be the hub and centre of intellectual and literary life of the recognised school and play the same part vis-à-vis all the other subjects as a laboratory plays for science subjects or the workshop for technical subjects."[12] Further it adds:

(1) As the proper use of a well-equipped school library is absolutely essential for the efficient working of every educational institution and for encouraging literary and cultural interests in students, every secondary school should have such a library; class libraries and subject libraries should also be utilized for this purpose.

(2) Trained librarians, who have a love for books and an understanding of students' interests, should be provided in all Secondary Schools and all teachers should be given some training in the basic principles of library work, in the training Colleges as well as through the refresher courses.

(3) Where there are no separate public libraries, the school libraries should, as far as possible, make these facilities available to the local public and all existing public libraries should have special sections on children and adolescents.[13]

NUMBER OF LIBRARIES

The Fifty Survey treats a collection of merely fifty volumes as a library. This does not take into consideration the student enrollment. It may be mentioned that a collection of fifty volumes cannot constitute a library by any stretch of imagination. If we assume that a collection of this size constitutes a library, then 293,427 (39.88%) schools have libraries, which would appear quite impressive.[14] But, if it is assumed more realistically that a collection with five hundred volumes, one thousand volumes, five thousand volumes, and five thousand volumes constitute primary school, upper primary school, secondary school, and higher secondary school libraries, respectively, then only 23,743 (3.22%) schools have libraries. This is indeed the true situation, which gives a very dismal picture.[15]

The Fifty Survey shows that there are 735,771[16] schools at various stages of education. Of these, 39.88 percent have libraries, if we treat a mere collection of fifty volumes to constitute a library. In the Fourth Survey, it was mentioned that 42.35 percent of the schools had libraries. Thus it appears that there has been decline in the percentage of schools having libraries. This would mean that new schools are being set up without being provided with proper libraries.

Out of the 293,427 schools, 234,998 (80.09 percent) are in the rural areas and 58,429 (19.91 percent) are in the urban areas. However, only 37 percent rural schools and 58 percent urban schools have libraries.[17] This shows a wide disparity in the provision of school libraries in rural and urban areas.

Before recognition is given by the government or a local body, a private school is expected to possess a library. As a consequence, 68.81 percent of private-aided and 62.63 private-unaided schools have library facilities. On the other hand, 46.26 percent of government schools and 24.59 percent of local schools have library facilities.[18] Thus private schools are better off in terms of library facilities than government and local schools.

BOOK SELECTION

Usually in school libraries, there is no well-laid-down book selection policy. In Orissa, "mostly, the headmasters jointly with subject teachers or alone had to select and purchase books for their libraries. In all cases the schools had to select books only from among the list of books approved by the Director of Public Instruction (Schools) of Orissa."[19] In the National Union Territory of Delhi, in government schools, the principal/headmaster and subject teachers are required to select books only from among the list of books approved by the Director of the Directorate of Education of the government. This restricts the role of librarian and teachers in the collection development.

COLLECTION

A survey was carried out among government libraries in Delhi. According to the study, "more than half of the libraries have a collection of more than 10,000 documents, 15 percent of the libraries have around 15,000 documents, while about 30 percent libraries have less than 5,000 documents."[20] The size of these collections may be considered reasonable. But these collections are poor in quality as most of these contain outdated books and the collection of reference books is extremely poor.

The poor quality of collections is revealed in a survey of secondary schools in Orissa.

The minimum collection in a school library was 148 volumes whereas the maximum was 35,983 volumes. The total volumes in the schools were, however, impressive in comparison to those in other developing countries.... The text book collections were very poor in the schools. The collection of reference books in the schools were still worse. Almost half of the books in the collection belonged to the category fiction; one third belonged to non-fiction. The collection of non-book materials was also very poor in the schools. Except for a few maps and charts, most of the schools lacked teaching aids.[21]

The findings of the Fifth Survey of NCERT regarding collections include the following:[22]

1. Of the primary schools in rural areas, 2.25 percent have more than five hundred volumes per library. However, 15.25 percent in the urban areas possess more than five hundred volumes. Thus 4.09 percent of primary schools have more than five hundred volumes.
2. Of the upper primary schools in rural areas 9.26 percent have more than one thousand volumes. However, 17.94 percent in urban areas possess more than one thousand volumes. Thus 11.03 percent of upper primary schools have a library.
3. Of primary, upper primary, secondary and high secondary schools, 7.11 percent, 20.58 percent, 57.34 percent, and 76.55 percent, respectively, subscribe to magazines, the majority of them subscribing to a few magazines.

CLASSIFICATION

In government school libraries, 57 percent of the libraries use the Dewey Decimal Classification system and 14 percent use the Colon Classification system. Furthermore, "28 percent of libraries are arranging books according to their subjects in alphabetical sequence."[23]

CATALOGS

The survey of government libraries in Delhi shows that "a little less than half of the libraries have no catalogue. It was largely attributed to the shortage of funds and facilities. About a third of the libraries were using a classified catalogue while the rest have a dictionary catalogue."[24]

OPEN VERSUS CLOSED ACCESS

In government school libraries, "only about two-thirds of the libraries have open access to library collection for students."[25] The situation in Delhi is much better than elsewhere. Most of the school libraries in India have closed access. In the survey of secondary school libraries in Orissa, it was found that "in all the schools the books were kept in closed almirahs."[26] The librarians are forced to adopt closed access due to reasons beyond their control. In an open access, loss of books is found to take place. In the case of loss of books, the librarian is often penalized and asked to pay for the loss of books. In the case of Delhi, the situation is much better as two-thirds of the libraries have open access.

SERVICES

According to Sunil Kumar, "on the service aspects, performance of Government school libraries is not very promising. Excepting some reference service, the only other service provided is circulation. Library instruction to students is again not a common phenomenon."[27] This aptly sums up the kinds of services offered in school libraries in India.

STAFF

Most of the school libraries are run by untrained librarians. Often a teacher may be made a teacher-in-charge of the library in addition to his or her normal teaching duties. According to Das and Mahapatra, "There are very few schools in Orissa with trained professional school librarians. Most of the schools were managed by untrained teacher-librarians who work as full-time teachers in the various fields and part-time librarians. Even in some schools PETs [Physical Education Teachers], office assistants and headmasters also remained in charge of library."[28] On the other hand, each secondary school library in Delhi has a trained person in charge of the library, who may possess either a bachelor's degree in library science or a diploma or a certificate in library science.

Only 4,350 (8.28 percent) secondary schools have full-time librarians. The percentage of rural secondary schools that have full-time librarians is 5.15 percent. On the other hand, 17.13 percent of urban secondary schools possess full-time librarians. Thus urban secondary schools are much better placed than rural secondary schools. Out of the full-time librarians working in secondary schools, only 2,885 (66.32%) are trained ones.[29]

Only 5,951 (38.48%) higher secondary schools have full-time librarians. The percentage of rural schools with full-time librarians is 29.58 percent. On the other hand, 46.10 percent of schools in urban areas have full-time librarians. Out of 4,248 full-time librarians, only 71.38 percent are trained.[30]

CONTINUING EDUCATION

State councils have been established in each state. In Delhi the State Council of Educational Research and Training has been set up. It has designed a three-week in-service program for school librarians,[31] which is conducted during vacation period. The program consists of lectures, demonstration, group/panel discussion, practical work, assignments, and library visits. Similar continuing education programs are also conducted by other states. The number of school librarians is so large that such programs can cover only a small percentage of librarians.

FUNDING

In secondary school libraries in Orissa, "except the yearly library fee collected from the students, the schools had no other major source of finance to develop their libraries. Even the yearly fee collected from the students seemed to be too less to become useful."[32]

In government secondary schools in Delhi, the situation is much better, and the "annual budget provision for acquisition of books varies from Rs. 3,000 to 10,000 depending upon the number of students enrolled in the respective schools. Sometimes contingency grants are also provided by the administration."[33] Even this amount is meager, considering the high prices of books, periodicals and other reading materials.

PHYSICAL FACILITIES

A survey of secondary school libraries in Orissa shows that "very few schools had separate rooms for libraries. Most of the schools had kept their library books either in the class rooms, office room, teacher's common room or a few had been kept in the headmaster's room. In all the schools the books were kept in closed almirahs. Hardly, any schools possessed adequate tables and chairs for their libraries. Thus the schools of this state had few almirahs and books only in their libraries without having any reading facilities for students."[34] This shows deplorable physical facilities in Orissa.

In Delhi each secondary school library is "housed in a single room with a seating capacity that varies from 20 to 50."[35] Sometimes, it may happen that due to shortage of space, the same room may also be used to hold classes as well.

STANDARDS

In 1986 the director of education in Delhi issued instructions under Article 42 of the Delhi Schools Education Act, 1973, and the Delhi Schools Education Rules, 1973, regarding the maintenance and use of school libraries.[36] These instructions were meant to be followed by all heads of schools/institutions, under the Directorate of Education, Delhi. This may be considered a landmark in the history of school librarianship in India since this was the first time that standards for school libraries were formulated and instructions were given for their implementation. Although there is no doubt that the implementation of the instructions would have revolutionized school libraries run under Delhi's Directorate of Education, once the higher authorities realized its implications, such as more financial support, more library materials, more space for libraries, they withdrew the circular containing the instructions. Article 42 had some remarkable features:

1. Minimum size of collection in terms of books, magazines, and newspapers, with an emphasis on audiovisual aids
2. Book selection policy (previously the school librarian had no role in this)
3. Services to be provided
4. Funding based on number of students and teachers
5. Staffing for different categories of libraries
6. Status of the school librarian
7. Verification of stock and weeding policy (the librarian is often held responsible for loss of books/materials; this would avoid penalization for a reasonable loss)
8. Duties of the librarian

9. Role of the teachers

Keeping in mind the changing environment, the Central Board of Secondary Education constituted a Special Committee to develop a manual. The report of the committee was published in 1995, under the title *Organising School Libraries: Guidelines*.[37] This manual provides excellent guidelines for organizing a school library. It considers a library as a "learning resource center." A few guidelines for computerization have been given. A librarian who is supposed to organize a new library shall find the work extremely useful. It gives useful guidelines, for the day-to-day working of a school library.

CHILDREN'S LIBRARIES

In addition to school libraries, children are also served by children's libraries or by university and public libraries with children's sections. Some of these have been established to serve children exclusively. For instance, the Library of Children's Book Trust, New Delhi, is an excellent library established to be used exclusively by children. As a normal practice, each public library has a children's section, a practice that goes back to the early twentieth century. The Central Library of Baroda was a pioneer in this regard. This library, under the patronage of Sayaji Rao Gaikwar III, Maharaja of Baroda, was the first example to have a separate corner equipped with tables, chairs, and bookcases suited for children.

Until 1913, the Central Library catered to the needs of adults only. On account of the dearth of children's literature in Indian languages, a separate section for the children could not be started earlier. But a small collection of books, especially suited for children, was organized separately. The available books were set aside and formed an independent collection, which was used mostly by the boys and girls attending the high schools. However, need was felt to provide special facilities for the children as a separate wing of the Central Library. Books in English with beautiful illustrations were available in plenty. In order to attract the very young people, a special children's library with such books was started in 1913.[38]

This shows the farsightedness of persons responsible for library development.
Children's sections of the National Library (Calcutta) and Delhi Public Library are very popular. Some of the university libraries have established children's libraries. Rajasthan University Library (Jaipur) and Roorkee Engineering University Library have established children's libraries for the use of the children of their employees. Shreemati Nathibai Damodar Thackersey Women's University (Mumbai) has set up the J. Govindji Morarji Smarak Trust Children's Library and Materials Research Centre, open to all children. It has built up an excellent collection of books, magazines, audiocassettes, pictures, and so on, and provides a variety of services including storytelling.

PROFILES OF TYPICAL LIBRARIES

The following examples provide statistical profiles of different kinds of libraries.

Government School

Name of school: Government Girls Senior Secondary School Library, Rajouri Garden (New Delhi)

Classes: Classes I–XII

Location: The library is located in a big hall, a part of which is used as a classroom due to shortage of classrooms.

Physical environment: It is a noisy place with shabby surroundings.

Number of students and teachers: There are twelve hundred students and seventy-two teachers.

Staff: There is one full-time librarian who is a postgraduate teacher (PGT) possessing a bachelor's degree and Certificate in Library Science. There is no additional help. Sweeping of floors and dusting is carried out by the students.

Collection: The collection consists of 13,500 books and 192 maps and charts. The library subscribes to nineteen magazines and three newspapers. In addition, there are 1,014 textbooks belonging to the Book Bank, which are issued to poor students for one year.

Classification and cataloging: The books are divided into broad groups (such as physics, chemistry, political science, history, etc.) and placed in locked almirahs. There is no proper catalog.

Services: Each section from Class VI to Class XII is allowed one half-hour library period. During the library period, the whole class moves to the library. At that time the students can borrow and return books and also read magazines and newspapers. The librarian puts the list of books added to the library on the library notice board, along with jackets. Press cuttings from newspapers are sometimes displaced on the notice board.

Funds: Rs. 1,500 are allocated for purchase of books and Rs. 3,000 for purchase of magazines and newspapers. In addition, if need be, the consolidated fund of the school can be used to purchase textbooks for the students.

Working hours: The library is open only during school hours. The librarians get a vacation like teachers. Thus, during vacations, the library is kept closed.

Problems: Due to lack of additional staff and fear of loss of books beyond a permissible limit, the librarian is forced to adopt a closed-access policy. If there is a loss of books beyond the permissible limit, the librarian is penalized. If the librarian is on leave, then the library does not function. If a teacher is absent, then the librarian is asked to go to the class and keep the students engaged. During the examination period, the librarian is asked to proctor exams and also assist the teachers in the compilation of the results. The librarian may be required to carry out other odd jobs, from time to time. The maintenance of the library room is poor. The lighting is inadequate. For sweeping of the floor and dusting of furniture, no proper arrangement exists. There is a separate audiovisual section under charge of a teacher, possessing TV, audiocassettes, maps, charts etc. It would be desirable that audio-visual materials form part of the library. The directorate of education, who looks after the school, compiles a list of books and sends this to the school. The book budget may be spent only on those books that appear on the list. This is indeed a handicap.

Future Plans: To compile a proper catalog of the library; to merge audiovisual section (at present, it is a separate section under the charge of a teacher) into the school library; and to pursue authorities for better maintenance of the library room with adequate lighting and more chairs and tables.

Private School

Name of school: Andhra Education Society Senior Secondary School, New Delhi

Classes: Classes I–XII. Previously the library served the students from classes VI to XII; however, from the 1997–1998 session, students of primary classes have been extended the library facilities.

Location: The library is located in a small room, with racks on four sides. There is no space for seating the students.

Physical environment: Neat and clean

Number of students and teachers: There are one thousand, one hundred students and sixty teachers.

Staff: There is one full-time librarian in the trained teacher grade possessing a bachelor of science degree and bachelor of library and information science degree. There is no additional help.

Collection: The collection consists of three thousand, five hundred books and twenty maps and charts; three hundred books were added during 1996–1997. The library subscribes to fifteen magazines and three newspapers.

Classification and Cataloging: The books have been broadly classified. There is a catalog.

Services: Lending of books; some reference service; help to students in preparing projects, science models for science fairs and interschool competitions (debates, essay writing, quizzes, etc.)

Funds: Rs. 5,000 for books, Rs. 3,000 for magazines and Rs. 2,000 for newspapers.

Working hours: The same as those of the school

Problems: As the library is situated in a small room, there is no space for seating students. Due to lack of staff, the librarian is unable to provide better library services.

Future plans: The library has plans to computerize the library.

Public School

Name of school: Mira Model Senior Secondary School Library (New Delhi)

1. Senior Library (Classes VI–XII)

Location: The library is located in the center of the school in a spacious hall. It has sixty seats for students and twenty for teachers.

Physical environment: The library is extremely attractive, neat, and clean. The size of the library is 90 x 30 meters.

Number of teachers and students: There are seventy teachers and nine hundred and seventy-five students.

Staff: There is one full-time librarian in the trained graduate teacher (TGT) grade who possesses a master's degree and a master's of library and information science degree. In addition, there is one library assistant (assistant teacher grade) and one library attendant.

Collection: The collection consists of twenty thousand books. It subscribes to 150 magazines and 6 daily newspapers. Awards are given to cultivate reading habits.

Funds: Books: Rs. 50,000 per year, magazines: Rs. 35,000 per year

Working hours: The working hours of the school are 8 A.M.–2 P.M. However, the library remains open from 8 A.M. to 3 P.M. It is also open during summer vacation.

Probems: The librarian is well qualified but she has not been given a PGT grade.

Future plans: To computerize the library

2. Junior Library (Classes I–V)

Location: Center of primary section

Physical environment: Well decorated and well maintained with furniture especially designed for small children. The size of the library is 40 x 10 meters, with seats for fifty students.

Number of teachers and students: There are 70 teachers and 1,025 students.

Staff: There is one assistant librarian in the assistant teacher grade.

Collection: The collection consists of seven thousand books, one newspaper, and fifty magazines.

Classification and Cataloging: Books have been classified according to the Dewey Decimal Classification system. The catalog was prepared based on Anglo American Cataloging Rules, 2nd edition (AACR2).

Services: (1) lending of books, (2) storytelling, and (3) preparing students for competitions such as Poetry Recitation, Book Week, Best Class Award, Best Library Readers Award

Funds: Rs. 5,000 for books, Rs. 5,000 for magazines

Working hours: 8 A.M.–2 P.M.

Problem: Lack of staff

Future plans: Computerization of the library

Public School

Name of school: Delhi Public School, R. K. Puram, New Delhi.

1. Main Library (serving students and teachers of Classes IX–XII)

Location: The main library is located in the basement near the entrance.

Physical environment: The library is attractive. It occupies an area of approximately 464.5 square meters.

Staff: There is one senior librarian in the PGT grade who possesses a master's degree and a bachelor's of library science degree; two assistant librarians in TGT grade who possess a bachelor's degrees and a bachelor's of library science degree, and two clerical staff who possess bachelors' degrees and certificates in library sciences.

Collection: The library has a rich collection consisting of forty thousand books and subscribes to sixty magazines (fifty Indian and ten foreign) and ten newspapers. It has 1,486 videocassettes and 840 audiocassettes. The library follows an open-access system.

Classification and cataloging: The Dewey Decimal Classification system is used. The catalog has been designed on the basis of AACR2.

Services: The library possesses an HCL 486 computer. It has one server and two terminals with Windows Fox Pro. The library package was designed by the computer department of the school. The catalog has been computerized. All issue and return are on computer. Overdue notices, list of daily issues, and subject lists have also been computerized. Internet access is available for students to collect information for various projects, people, and any subject of their interest. A photocopying facility is also available.

Funds: Total budget for books, magazines, salaries, and so on is Rs. 8.1 lakhs.

Working hours: Both libraries remain open from 7 A.M. to 11 P.M. on all days. Afterschool hours, libraries are mainly used by hostel students.

Problems: There is lack of space and a need for another large reading room for the main library.

Future plans: The library would like to purchase a fast computer and be able to bar code all the books received so that charging and discharging of books can be done faster and more accurately.

LIBRARY SCIENCE AS A SUBJECT OF STUDY

In some schools, library science has been introduced as one of the subjects of study under Socially Useful and Productive Work (SUPW) at secondary stage. The subject is taught by the school librarian. The students who complete this course are supposed to become effective and efficient users of libraries. This has certainly helped in popularizing librarianship. In some schools students pursuing an SUPW course help librarians by carrying out routine jobs (making entries in accession register, shelving, issuing books, etc.). This may form part of practical training.

LIBRARY AND RESOURCE LEARNING CENTER

Some schools have established separate units: (1) Library and (2) the Resource Learning Center or Audio-Visual Department. Library is confined to printed material, and nonprint media are the concern of the center. The interests of the users would be better served if both were run as a single unit under the supervision of the librarian. As a consequence, the library would be able to get more funds, staff, and space. In addition, nonbook materials would enable the library to attract more students and teachers to use its resources.

PROBLEMS AND PROSPECTS

Education in India has received low priority. School libraries also have been a low priority. Thus these have received inadequate funding. This is clear from the Fifth All- India Education Survey, mentioned earlier, which paints a dismal picture.

Wide disparities may be observed in terms of provision of facilities, collection, staff and services. On one extreme, public schools such as Navodaya Vidyalayas and Central Schools have well-equipped libraries. On the other extreme, there are schools run by government/local bodies/private bodies, especially in rural areas, that have ill-equipped libraries with inadequate staff, dismal collections, and poor supervision. In between lie a variety of private and government/local body schools with so-called libraries.

There is no doubt that libraries attached to public schools are better organized than other school libraries. According to Trehan, "Some public school libraries in urban areas possess professionally trained whole-time librarians and well-equipped and well-organized libraries with a collection of over 10,000 books. These institutions endeavour to make the library an integrated part in their educational programmes."[39] These have also taken an initiative with respect to computer application.

Disparities exist between libraries in rural and urban areas. Libraries in rural areas are worse off than in urban areas. School libraries in metropolitan towns are certainly better equipped. Variations also exist from state to state. School libraries in the state of Delhi are much better off than Bihar or Madhya Pradesh or Uttar Pradesh or Orissa.

The major problems facing libraries may be summed up as follows:

Lack of adequate and qualified staff. In most of the school libraries, the teacher in charge of the library may open the library at his or her convenience. If there is a full-time librarian, then he or she may be the *only* library staff person. During the period of his or her absence, the library would remain closed.

Lack of funds. There is usually a lack of funds to purchase books, periodicals, and other reading materials; equipment and furniture; and stationery, etc. In a large majority of school libraries, authorities are not in a position to provide funds for purchase of catalog cabinet and catalog cards. As a consequence, even a professional employed by the library would be unable to provide a proper library catalog for its users.

Misuse of library room. A library may be located in a multipurpose room that also serves as a TV or meeting room.

Loss of books. If a library is to be used reasonably well, then open access to the collection is a must. In such a library, book losses are bound to take place (losses take place even in a closed access library). In an Indian situation, a school librarian is very often penalized or harassed for loss of books even if he or she has taken reasonable care to prevent losses and also the loss may be within a permissible limit. This discourages a school librarian to implement open access.

Librarian as a teacher. It is usually in many schools that in the absence of a teacher, a librarian is asked to take a class. Sometimes he or she may be asked to assist the office of the school, in addition to his or her normal duties in the library.

Lack of recognition. The status of a librarian has improved during the recent years, but in some states or situations, the status is not comparable with the librarian's qualifications and nature of the work. There is a long way to go before librarians will get the recognition that they deserve.

The Indian Library Association (ILA) has been making some efforts to give impetus to the school library movement. It has a separate Central Sectional Committee on School and Children Libraries, which organizes activities related to school libraries. It has instituted the S. M. Ganguly Best School Librarian Award, which is awarded every year at the time of the All India Library Conference.

The ILA from time to time holds seminars on school libraries to draw attention of authorities to the lack of growth and development of school libraries. In 1986 it organized the All-India Seminar on School Library Development[40] to review Article 42 of the 1973 Delhi Schools Education Act and the 1973 Delhi School Education Rules. The participants expressed appreciation of the efforts of the state government and requested implementation at an early stage. It also recommended similar standards to be passed and implemented by other states and union territories.

On February 6, 1994, a seminar was organized by the ILA on the theme of improvement of the school libraries at Pragati Maidan. There was wide participation from school libraries. On August 17, 1996, the National Convention of School Libraries was organized by the ILA on the theme of the role of school libraries in the present-day education.

Governments at both the state and national levels have been taking steps to encourage school libraries. However, not enough has been done to improve the situation. In 1995 the government of National Capital Territory of Delhi instituted the Best Librarian award to be given annually. This is certainly a positive step.

CONCLUSION

Although efforts have been made to improve quality of education at all levels, the picture of the school educational system is dismal. The number of students in most of the schools is large; physical facilities are inadequate, and teachers are not well paid. Education is largely textbook oriented. There is a great deal of dissatisfaction with the existing system, mainly due to the fact that school education has not been given the high priority it deserved. The resources made available to achieve a high quality of education have been totally inadequate and the steps undertaken to implement the policy have been halfhearted. Therefore it is not surprising that the desired improvement has not taken place.

A school library is an essential part of an academic institution. As long as India's educational system remains in bad shape, so too will its school libraries. A report of the Secondary Education Commission (1952–53) states:

In a large majority of schools, there are at present no libraries worth the name. The books are usually [outdated], unsuitable and usually selected without reference to the student's tastes and interests. They are stocked in few bookshelves, which are housed in an inadequate and unattractive room. The person in charge is often a clerk or an indifferent teacher who does this work on a part time basis and has no love for books. What makes this situation particularly difficult is the fact that most teachers and administrators and authorities do not realize how unsatisfactory this position is and, therefore, they have no sense of urgency in the matter.[41]

The situation described by the report refers to the early 1950s, but the same situation holds true even today in many areas, especially in the states of Bihar, Madhya pradesh, Manipur, Orissa, and Uttar Pradesh. According to Das and Mahapatra,

"In India, particularly in Orissa, school libraries are in a very neglected and deplorable condition."[42] Collections are generally inadequate and out of date. There is a lack of well laid down book selection policy. Physical facilities are extremely poor.

The government and its agencies have made an effort to implement policies and programs to improve the library situation but the results have not been up to the expectations. According to Lahiri,

The "Operation Black Board" of the New Education Policy has proudly recorded the list of "Essential Facilities at the Primary Stage" which includes "Reference Books–Dictionaries, Encyclopaedias; children's books (at least 200), Magazines, Journals and Newspapers for teachers and children" under the "Books for Library" heading. The number of schools providing such facilities in the state are yet to be known. But the stark reality is that the school children sitting [in an] improper classroom with impoverishment dare to dream for a library with encyclopaedias, dictionaries, magazines, new fresh books and newspapers. Thus, Chattopadhyaya Committee's slogan for "no library no school" which echoes the "recommendations of the Secondary Education Commission (1952–1953), remains still unattended and unimplemented in many of the cases, not only in Manipur but in other parts of the country as well."[43]

Over the years, the situation has improved. There are certain bright spots. Public schools and schools run by central government are one. Schools in the National Territory of Delhi and in metropolitan towns have better libraries.

What are the reasons for the poor state of school libraries? There are multiple factors for this state of affairs. The "meagre allocation of funds, poor conception and imagination of the administrative machinery of these educational institutions, the non-appreciation of the value and importance of the library, the rigid book selection policy are mostly the contributing factors for the sorrowful plight of the school libraries in Orissa."[44] These factors are by and large equally applicable to other regions of India.

Luthra points out that "the major drawback is that there is no agency in the country to monitor development of school libraries, like UGC. The Planning Commission provides Funds for education including school libraries, without fixing the minimum percentage of total outlay to be spent on school libraries."[45] This is indeed a useful suggestion. The government of India and the state governments should create such agencies or identify existing organizations for the purpose.

A large majority of schools are run by the government (central, state and local bodies), but the government is not in a position to provide adequate funding for school education including school libraries. Therefore the government should encourage nongovernment organizations with a good reputation to come forward and run schools. However, the government should lay down standards, norms, and guidelines (including those for libraries) and enforce them strictly. Guidelines are already in place, but they are not being adhered to. The slogan should be "no library, no school." It is understood that if the school provides quality education, then the library is likely to be a good one. Both go together hand in hand.

NOTES

1. National Council of Educational Research and Training, *Sixth All India Educational Survey* Vol. 1 (New Delhi: 1999), 117.

2. *India, 1995: A Reference Annual* (New Delhi: Publications Division, Ministry of Information and Broadcasting, Government of India 1996), 66.

3. *India, 1996: A Reference Annual* (New Delhi: Publications Division, Ministry of Information and Broadcasting, Government of India, 1977), 6.

4. India, Education Commission (1964–1966), *Education and National Development: Report* (New Delhi: Ministry of Education, Government of India, 1966).

5. India, Ministry of Education, *Challenge of Education: A Policy Perspective* (New Delhi, Ministry of Education, Government of India, 1985), ii.

6. *India, 1995: A Reference Annual*, 66.

7. A Bordia, "India," in *International Encyclopedia of National Systems of Education*, 2d ed., edited by T. N. Postlethwaite (Oxford: Pergamon, 1995), 431.

8. India, Ministry of Human Resource Development, Department of Education, *National Policy on Education—1986* (New Delhi, Department of Education, Ministry of Human Resource Development, Government of India, 1986), 21–22.

9. S. K. Narang, *The Bright and Their Education* (New Delhi: Prime Publishers, 1994), 150, 164.

10. *India, 1995: A Reference Annual*, 87.

11. Bordia, "India," 433.

12. India, Ministry of Education, Secondary Education Commission (1952–1953), *A Report* (Delhi: The Manager of Publications, 1953), 232.

13. Ibid.

14. *Fifth All India Educational Survey*, 135.

15. Ibid., 137–139.

16. Ibid.

17. Ibid.

18. Ibid., 136.

19. Kailash Chandra Das and M. Mahapatra, "Development of Secondary School Libraries in Orissa: A Proposal" in C. P. Vashishth, ed., *Library Movement and Library Development* (Delhi: Indian Library Association, 1994), 251.

20. Sunil Kumar, *School Libraries in Delhi: A Study* (mimeograph), 2.

21. Das and Mahapatra, "Development of Secondary School Libraries in Orissa," 251.

22. *Fifth All India Educational Survey*, 137–145.

23. Kumar, *School Libraries in Delhi*, 2.

24. Ibid., 3.

25. Ibid.

26. Das and Mahapatra, "Development of Secondary School Libraries in Orissa," 251.

27. Kumar, *School Libraries in Delhi*, 3.

28. Das and Mahapatra, "Development of Secondary School Libraries in Orissa," 252.

29. *Fifth All India Educational Survey*, 140.

30. Ibid., 141.

31. Sunil Kumar, *In-Service Training Programme for School Librarians: Course Design* (New Delhi: State Council of Educational Research & Training) (mimeograph), 1.

32. Das and Mahapatra, "Development of Secondary School Libraries in Orissa," 252.

33. Kumar, *School Libraries in Delhi*, 4.

34. Das and Mahapatra, "Development of Secondary School Libraries in Orissa," 251.

35. *Kumar, School Libraries in Delhi*, 3.

36. Delhi Schools Education Act, 1973 (Article 42), and Delhi Schools Education Rules, 1973. *Regarding Maintenance and Use of School Libraries* (Delhi: Delhi Administration, Directorate of Education, 1986) (mimeograph).

37. *Organizing School Libraries: Guidelines* (New Delhi: Central Board of Secondary Education, 1995).

38. M. L. Nagar, *Foundation of Library Movement in India* (Ludhiana: Indian Library Institute and Bibliographical Centre, 1983), 66.

39. G. L. Trehan, "School Libraries in India," in *Handbook of Libraries, Archives and Information Centres in India*, vol. 1, edited by B. M. Gupta et al. (New Delhi: Information Industry, 1984–1985), 93.

40. C. P. Vashishth, ed., *School Library Development* (Delhi: Indian Library Association, 1986).

41. India, Secondary Education Commission (1952–1953), *A Report*, 232.

42. Das and Mahapatra, "Development of Secondary School Libraries in Orissa," 250.

43. Ramansu Lahiri, "Library Development and the School Phenomenon: A Highlight on Manipur," in C. P. Vashishth, ed., *Library Movement and Library Development in India* (Delhi: Indian Library Association, 1994), 247.

44. Das and Mahapatra, "Development of Secondary School Libraries in Orissa," 250.

45. K. L. Luthra, "School Library Development in India: A Survey Report," *CLIS Observer* 10 (1–2) (January–June 1993), 7.

SELECTED BIBLIOGRAPHY

Das, Kailash Chandra and Mahapatra M. "Development of Secondary School Libraries in Orissa; a Proposal." In C. P. Vashishth, ed., *Library Movement and Library Development* (Delhi: Indian Library Association, 1994), 250–256.

Delhi Schools Education Act 1973 (Article 42) and Delhi Schools Education Rules, 1973. *Regarding Maintenance and Use of School Libraries* (Delhi: Delhi Administration, Directorate of Education, 1986) (mimeograph).

Fifth All India Education Survey, vol. 1. National Council of Educational Research and Training, (New Delhi: 1993).

Kumar, Krishan. *Library Organization* (New Delhi: Vikas, 1987), chap. 3.

Lahiri, Ramansu. "Library Development and the School Phenomenon: A Highlight on Manipur." In C. P. Vashishth, ed., *Library Movement and Library Development in India* (Delhi: Indian Library Association, 1994), 242–247.

Luthra, K. L., "School Library Development in India: A Survey Report." *CLIS Observer* 10 (1–2) (January–June 1993), 4–16.

Organizing School Libraries: Guidelines (New Delhi: Central Board of Secondary Education, 1995).

Trehan, G. L. "School Libraries in India." In B. M. Gupta et al., ed., *Handbook of Libraries, Archives and Information Centres in India*, vol. 1 (New Delhi: Information Industry 1984–1985), 92–104.

Vashishth, C. P., ed., *School Library Development* (Delhi: Indian Library Association, 1986).

❧ 6 ❧

Special Libraries

BACKGROUND

The history of special libraries in India is interrelated with the growth of research institutions, which stimulated the setting up of such libraries in the country. Scientific and industrial research was greatly neglected by the British. It was only after the First World War, with the formation of learned societies and establishment of research institutions, that research activities received an impetus. Since independence in 1947, there has been a steady expansion of research activities due to the formation of scientific laboratories, installations, and organizations. In addition, there has been rapid industrialization. To meet the demand for improved library facilities, special libraries were set up.

Due to the efforts of Sir William Jones, a scholar and a judge of the Supreme Court, the Asiatic Society of Bengal was established in 1784. The society, "during the first century of its existence provided a house for meetings, a library, and a collection of ancient coins and medals as well as archaeological, technological and geological collections. *The Journal of the Royal Asiatic Society of Bengal* (started in 1832) was the first periodical in India for dissemination of the results of the scientific work in the country."[1] This journal played an important role in the advancement of science in India. The library attached to the society was established in 1784 and is considered "the first library in modern India."[2]

A medical college was established in Calcutta in 1835. It provided training in physics, chemistry, botany, anatomy, and clinical subjects. The Museum of the Asiatic Society was set up in 1841 and the Indian Museum in 1856. These merged to form a new organization in 1916, the Zoological Survey of India.

The first engineering college was established in Roorkee in 1847, under the name of Sir Thomson College. Later on it was converted into an engineering university.

Since 1818 the government had been employing geologists for the purpose of performing survey work. It was only in 1851 that the Geological Survey of India could be set up. The Meteorological Department of the Government of India came into being in 1875. Prior to it, meteorological observations and stations had been set up in Madras (1796), Calcutta (1824), and Bombay (1841).

The Survey of India was formed in 1878 and the Botanical Survey of India was founded in Calcutta in 1889.

The government established the Haffikine Institute in Bombay in 1899. Initially, it was meant to serve as a plague research laboratory, but later it developed into a leading center of research on preventive medicine.

According to T. S. Rajagopalan, and S. I. Islam,[3] there were thirty-five scientific libraries by the end of the nineteenth century. The resources developed very slowly. The literature published in western countries, especially in England, formed the major portion of the total collection. Due to lack of funds, the collections were inadequate.

The Indian Institute of Science, Bangalore, was founded by the Tatas in 1909 and is considered the first school of advanced research. It has played a pioneering role in advancing science in India. In 1913 the Indian Science Congress Association came into being. It is a leading organization of Indian scientists. The Indian Research Fund Association was formed in 1922 and has enjoyed a long and impressive history.

The Imperial Institute of Animal Husbandry and Dairying was established in Bangalore in 1923. In 1936 it was expanded and renamed the Imperial Dairy Institute. Subsequently, in 1955, the National Dairy Research Institute (NDRI)[4] came into being at Karnal. The institute at Bangalore was converted into a regional station. In addition, there is a regional station at Kalyani. The NDRI was conferred deemed university status by the UGC in 1969. It is fully supported by the Indian Council of Agricultural Research and functions as one of the National Institutes under its aegis.

The Indian Council of Agricultural (ICAR) was established in 1929 along with several associated committees for research.

The Indian Statistical Institute, Calcutta, came into being in 1932. This has been a landmark in advanced research. The Indian Industrial Research bureau was formed in 1934.

On January 3, 1935, the National Institute of Sciences of India was formed. In 1970 its name was changed to Indian National Science Academy (INSA). It is a coordinating body similar to the Royal Society of London. It is a premier scientific organization in India.

The Second World War provided a great impetus to the development of research activities. In 1942 the Council of Scientific and Industrial Research (CSIR) was formed. This was a turning point in the history of scientific research in India. Today the CSIR has a network of 43 national laboratories/institutes, 138 field stations/extension centers and 2 industrial research associations spread all over the country to carry out research and development (R&D) in various areas and disciplines.[5] All these institutions have very good special libraries attached to them. CSIR established the Indian National Scientific Documentation Center (INSDOC) in 1952. INSDOC is a modern documentation center, well equipped with the latest information technology and well qualified staff. It is a good example of a national documentation center in the field of science and technology, providing a wide range of documentation services.

The Atomic Energy Commission was set up in 1948. It is indeed a landmark. This was followed by the establishment of leading R&D organizations in the field of atomic research, such as Bhabha Atomic Research Centre, Trombay; Reactor Research Centre, Kalpakkam; and Variable Energy Cyclotron Centre, Calcutta, among others.

The Defence Science Organization was established in 1949. The year 1950 is quite significant because many important organizations were set up including the National Chemical Laboratory, Pune; National Physical Laboratory, New Delhi; National Metallurgical Laboratory, Jamshedpur; Central Fuel Research Institute, Jadavpur; and Central Food Technological Research Institute, Mysore.

The Indian Research Fund Association was formed in 1922. It was renamed Indian Council of Medical Research in 1950. Other leading organizations established in the 1950s[6] included the Central Drug Research Institute, Lucknow (1951); Central Electro-Chemical Research Institute, Karaikudi (1953); Central Leather Research Institute, Madras (1953); Central Building Research Institute, Roorkee (1953); and Central Salt Research Institute, Jaipur (1954).

The Indian Association for Special Libraries and Information Centres (IASLIC) was established in 1955 along the lines of Aslib of the United Kingdom. Since 1955 it has played an important role in the development of special libraries.

Formation of the Indian Council of Social Science Research (ICSSR) in 1969 is a landmark in the field of social sciences. The ICSSR set up the Social Science Documentation Centre in 1970, which was renamed in 1986 the National Social Science Documentation Centre (NASSDOC). The NASSDOC has played an active role in carrying out documentation activities in the field of social sciences.

With the assistance of UNESCO, the National Information System in Science and Technology (NISSAT) was launched in September 1977. NISSAT has given a push to special libraries, through establishment of sectoral information centers and the regional information centers.

As illustrated by the examples above, special libraries are primarily a twentieth-century phenomenon in India. Although a handful existed in the nineteenth century, the majority of these libraries came into being only during the last five decades or so. They are largely concentrated in major towns like Bangalore, Calcutta, Delhi, Hyderabad, Mumbai, and Madras. On the whole, special libraries have succeeded in building a better image than academic and public libraries. They have shown initiative and done better than other types of libraries. They have been forerunners in computer application in Indian libraries. India has succeeded in developing some excellent libraries in different fields of specialization which are comparable with libraries in the developed countries.

PRESENT STATUS

Humanities

India has a large number of libraries in the field of the humanities, forming a rich source of information for research scholars. Very often, in recent years due to lack of funds, these are not in a position to build up adequate collections to meet the needs of their users. For the same reason, they have also been slow in the matter of computerization. A brief description about the leading libraries follows.[7]

The Asiatic Society (Calcutta) Library is an institution of national importance. Formed in 1784, it is the oldest institution of learning in science and humanities in India today. It is also the oldest academic publisher in India. The society made a tremendous contribution to the growth and development of antiquarian, scientific and literary institutions in India. The Library of the Asiatic Society is the oldest of its kind in modern India. It holds about 200,000 books and journals (receives 457 journals), monographs, and pamphlets in European and Indian languages in humanities (particularly oriental studies), life sciences, and earth sciences. Many of the books are rare. It has about sixty thousand manuscripts.

The Bhandarkar Oriental Research Institute Library, Pune, has an excellent collection in the field of Indology, oriental studies and Sanskrit. It has a manuscript collection of forty thousand.

The Central Institute of English and Foreign Languages Library, Hyderabad, has a rich collection in linguistics, English language teaching and literature. The collection in linguistics is comprehensive. It provides current awareness service (CAS) and selective dissemination of information (SDI) to its users.

The Central Institute of Indian Languages (CIIL), Mysore, is a research organization under the Ministry of Human Resource Development, Government of India, established in 1969. The Library of CIIL has 50,000 volumes (books) in linguistics and Indian languages and subscribes to 350 journals. It has brought out a number of bibliographies.

The Dar-ul-Uloom Deoband Library, Deoband, was founded in 1867. It has the largest collection among Madrasah libraries in India, having a collection of 133,077 volumes including 1,563 manuscripts.

The Indira Gandhi National Centre for Arts (IGNCA), New Delhi, is a multilingual, multimedia, and multidisciplinary organization. The library of IGNCA has two wings, one for its reference library and the other for its visual library. The visual library consists of nonprint material. The library has created a number of databases. It has computerized its in-house activities. An OPAC of its collection is available. The reprographic unit is well equipped to supply duplicate copies of slides, microfilms and microfiches.

The Khuda Bakhsh Oriental Public Library, Patna, was established in 1875 by Md. Khuda Bakhsh. In 1891 it was opened to the public. In 1969 the Parliament passed the Khuda Bakhsh Oriental Public Library Act, which declared the library to be an Institution of National Importance. It has a collection of more than 80,000 volumes (books), 19,736 manuscripts, 200 palm leaves and 914 microfilms. The library has a staff of fifty-nine, out of which nineteen are qualified library professionals. It is being computerized. It has published a descriptive catalog of manuscripts available in the library in thirty-four volumes. The library conducts a one-year associateship in oriental librarianship and manuscriptology to prepare manpower for oriental libraries.

The National Archives of India (NAI), New Delhi, along with its state units acquires public and private records of permanent historical importance. The NAI has acquired noncurrent records including public records, private papers, manuscripts, maps, banned literature, Indian language newspapers of the nineteenth century, and so on. These are valuable sources of research to scholars in the humanities. The library emphasizes its collection of rare books and documents (reports, parliamentary papers, gazettes, etc.).

The National Library, Calcutta,[8] has a rich collection on humanities. It possesses some important personal collections gifted to it including personal collections of Sir Asutosh Mukhopadhya, Prof. Vaiyapuri Pillai, Sir Jadunath Sarkar, and Munshi Sayyid Sadruddin Ahmad-al-Musawi (i.e., the Buhar collection).

The Rampur Raza Library, Rampur, was founded in 1794. It is one of the oldest existing libraries in India. It has fifty-five thousand books and manuscripts in Arabic, Persian, Urdu, and Hindi. There are fifteen thousand manuscripts in the collection.

The Sahitya Akademi, New Delhi, was formally inaugurated in 1954. Sahitya Akademi Library is a library rich in Indian literature. It has brought out the following important bibliographies:

National Bibliography of Indian Literature

Cumulative Index to Indian Literature (bimonthly)

Catalogue of Indian-English Literature

Catalogue of Tagore Literature

Catalogue of Ramayana and Mahabharata Literature

Catalogue of Bhagvad Gita in the Library Holdings

Indian Literary Index (1988–)

The Thanjavur Maharaja Serfoji Saraswati Mahal Library was founded in 1918. It is an old and traditional library well known for its collection of rare books, manuscripts, and scholarly journals. It is a storehouse of ancient manuscripts numbering 42,996 covering arts, culture and literature. The manuscripts are written in Sanskrit, Tamil, Telugu, and Marathi.

The book collection as a whole (36,299 volumes) contains books written in Tamil, English, Telugu, Sanskrit, Marathi, and Hindi. The books cover the humanities. It also has a personal collection of Serfoji's, comprising books in English, French, and Latin. In addition, it possesses old records of Maratha kings. It has a special collection of old hand-printed albums, engravings, and photographs. The

holdings of its library are listed in the Descriptive Catalogue of Sanskrit Manuscripts in 22 volumes, the Catalogue of Tamil Manuscripts in 3 volumes, and the
Marathi Catalogue in 4 volumes. Due to its rare collection, it has been recognized
by the government of India as an Institution of National Importance.

Indology

Indology is a vast subject, which covers all about India, covering its languages,
literature, history, philosophy, religion, customs, and fine arts. By and large
Indological libraries are in bad shape due to lack of funds and proper management.
Some are fighting to survive.

Bibliographic control for manuscripts, which is considered the backbone of research in indology, is rather inadequate. Manuscript collections in the humanities
are scattered in different places all over the country. They are found in academic,
special, and public libraries; Jain Bhandaras; maths (monasteries); temples;
gurudwaras; mosques, madrassas, and so on. It is estimated that there are over three
million manuscripts. To strengthen bibliographical services, there is an urgent
need to bring out a comprehensive directory of indological collections found scattered all over the country and also abroad. At present there is no national policy.
The situation requires the setting up of the Indian Council of Humanities
Research[9] (ICHUR) along the lines of the Indian Council of Social Science Research (ICSSR).

Indological libraries had their origin as manuscript libraries started by princely
states. After 1947 these libraries were taken over by the state or central government. Many of them belong to philanthropist trusts. Some of these form part of academic libraries especially at the university level. A select list of the prominent
libraries includes the following:

Adyar Sanskrit Library, Madras
Akhil Bharatiya Sanskrit Parishad Library, Lucknow
Asiatic Society Library, Bombay
Asiatic Society Library, Calcutta
Bhandarkar Oriental Research Institute, Pune
Bharatiya Vidya Bhawan Library, Bombay
Bihar Research Society Library, Patna
Central Institute of Indian Languages Library, New Delhi
Central Sanskrit Vidya Peeth, Allahabad, Turupathi, Delhi
Government Oriental Manuscript Library, Madras
Indira Gandhi National Centre for the Arts, New Delhi
K. P. Jayaswal Research Institute, Patna
Khuda Baksh Oriental Public Library, Patna
Mithila Sanskrit Shodha Samsthana, Darbhanga
Raghunath Temple Library, Jammu

Raza Rampur Library, Rampur
Saraswati Bhawan Library, Varanasi

Social Sciences

It was only after the Second World War that the government of India realized the importance of research in the social sciences. Since 1947 steady expansion has taken place in the field of research activities. There are estimated to be six hundred social science libraries in India. An average social science library has a collection of twenty-five thousand to thirty thousand volumes and subscribes to around two hundred current purnals.[10] These are attached to universities, government departments, and research institutions and are mainly concentrated in New Delhi.

A brief description of leading social science libraries follows.

The A. N. Sinha Institute of Social Sciences is a prestigious research institute. It was formally inaugurated in 1958. The Library and Documentation Division had 45,294 volumes in 1988–1989. It has two special collections, namely, the collection on Bihar and J. P. collection. It receives 412 periodicals. It brings out a bibliographical series, covering different topics.

The Gokhle Institute of Politics and Economics Library, Pune, is an excellent library. It has succeeded in building up an outstanding collection. It possesses a strong collection of old parliamentary blue books of the East India Company period and a complete run of legislative volumes, both central and provincial. The library is considered an excellent source of materials on modern India and the study of international organizations.

The Indian Council of World Affairs Library was founded in 1943. At one time until the 1960s it was considered as one of the finest special libraries, but due to lack of funds the library has fallen on hard times. It has a special collection of press clippings and UN documents including those from its specialized agencies.

The Indian Institute of Mass Communication Library, New Delhi, was established in 1965. It has a strong collection on mass communication. It maintains newspaper clippings, provides CAS, and publishes *Digest of Mass Media* bimonthly. It has created a database of its collection.

The Indian Institute of Public Administration was established in 1954. The collection of the library consists of one hundred fifty-five thousand volumes. The library has an excellent collection in public administration and allied areas. It subscribes to over five hundred periodicals. It brings out *Documentation in Public Administration* (quarterly, current awareness service) and *News Index*.

The Institute of Economic Growth Library specializes in social sciences with emphasis on economic development and planning. The library brings out bibliographies on different topics. An excellent bibliography compiled by its staff is the *Asian Social Science Bibliography*.

The National Council of Applied Economic Research,[11] *New Delhi*, was set up in 1956. The library has a collection of fifty-two thousand volumes consisting of books, periodicals, maps, annual reports, statistical publications, and microforms. It possesses seven thousand, eight hundred bound volumes of periodicals and subscribes to six hundred current periodicals. It has a rich collection of statistical publications of the central and state governments and other agencies. It has created a database of reports and articles. Using MINISIS software, it brings out Artha Suchi, a quarterly computerized index to government reports, journal articles, and newspaper write-ups. The same is available online and in printed forms.

The National Institute of Public Finance and Policy Library, New Delhi, has an excellent collection on public finance and policy in the form of books, periodicals, and reports. The special collection on central government and state government budgets is a notable feature. The library has computerized its catalog, acquisition, and circulation.

The Nehru Memorial Museum and Library, New Delhi, was established by the government of India. The museum was inaugurated in 1964. The library has been developed as a research center on the history of modern India. It is basically a reference library having a collection of 118,862 books, pamphlets, and bound volumes of periodicals. The library is particularly rich in "subjects like Indian biographies, freedom movement of India, Indian political parties, regional history of India, economic history of India, trade union movement, peasant studies, women studies, social reform, Indian culture, demography, social change, social stratification and ethology."[12] It is one of the best libraries serving the needs of social scientists.

The Parliament Library, New Delhi, was founded in 1921. It has a strong collection of books (700,000 volumes), subscribes to one thousand periodicals. It has developed a strong collection of central, state, and foreign government reports; publications of the United Nations and its agencies; gazettes; debates; acts; rules, and bills. The library operations and services have been computerized. The Parliamentary Library Information System (PARLIS) has been developed. A number of databases (e.g., statistical tables on different areas of economy, presidential elections, etc.) have been created, which are accessible online. A modern massive building for the library is under construction.

The Ratan Tata Library (RTL) is a part of the Delhi University Library System. The RTL is regarded as one of the best libraries in the country in the field of economics. It specializes in social sciences including economics, commerce, sociology, and geography. It has built a strong collection of international labor office (ILO) publications. It possesses rare materials on economic history including the East India Company reports. It has a strong collection of company reports. The library has created a database of its books and periodicals.

The Sardar Patel Institute of Economics and Social Research Library, Ahmedabad, was established in 1969. It has a strong collection in economics.

The Tata Institute of Social Sciences Library, Mumbai, was established in 1936. It has a well-developed collection on social sciences, consisting of 61,000 volumes (books), and subscribes to 630 periodicals. In-house activities, bibliographic and SDI services have been computerized. It also provides newspaper clippings and referral services. Further, it brings out *Index to Indian Journals of Social Work*. It has developed a special collection of rare books and journals on economics.

Science

A few scientific libraries were established in the nineteenth century. The Second World War gave impetus to pushing R&D activities in the country. As a consequence, in 1942 the Council of Scientific and Industrial Research (CSIR) was formed. It has proved to be a turning point. The CSIR set up a chain of national laboratories, field stations/extension centers/regional centers. Other organizations that have played an important role include the Defence Research and Development Organization (DRDO), the Indian Space Research Organization (ISRO), the Atomic Energy Commission, the Electronics Commission, the Anthropological Survey of India, the Botanical Survey of India, the Geological Survey of India, and the Zoological Survey of India. It may be noted that these are government supported organizations. Nongovernment agencies have not given much attention to scientific research. The number of science and technology libraries is estimated to be one thousand, with an average library having thirty to forty thousand volumes, adding about five hundred volumes per year, receiving three hundred to five hundred current periodicals, and having staff strength of ten to fifteen, serving fifty to five hundred specialist users.[13]

A brief description of some of the leading scientific libraries follows.

The Anthropological Survey of India Library, Calcutta, was established in 1946. Regional libraries are located at Dehradun, Mysore, and Nagpur. These libraries are rich in maps, reprints, and reports related to the subject of anthropology.

The Bhabha Atomic Research Centre, Library and Information Services, Trombay, was founded in 1954. It is the best library in India in the field of atomic energy. It has 70,000 volumes (books) and 500,000 microfilms, and subscribes to 1,650 periodicals. The collection is rich in research reports. The library is fully computerized and uses the latest information technology. It has excellent facilities in terms of reprographic, translation, CD-ROM database search and online access services. It provides CAS, SDI, and retrospective search services.

The Botanical Survey of India Library, Calcutta, was established in 1911. It has a collection of 27,606 volumes (books) and subscribes to 50 periodicals. It is rich in survey reports.

The Bureau of Indian Standards, New Delhi, was established in 1947. The library of the Bureau of Indian Standards (BIS) has built up an excellent library on standards. The in-house functions of the bureau and also information services have been computerized. The computer is also used to produce the *BIS Handbook, Current Published Information on Standards, Standards Worldover, Manak Sandarbhika,* and *Buyers Guide.* The library also has reprographic and translation facilities (from the Russian, French, Italian, and German languages).

The Forest Research Institute and College Library, Dehradun, was established in 1906. It has 110,000 volumes (books), subscribes to 623 periodicals. It provides current awareness services.

The Geological Survey of India Library, Calcutta, was established in 1856. It has a strong collection of published and unpublished reports.

The *Indian Institute of Science Library, Bangalore*, was established in 1911. It has 120,000 volumes (books) and subscribes to 1,800 periodicals, with a special collection on history of science. The library has computerized its in-house operations and information retrieval. For online information service, it depends on the National Centre for Science Information of UGC, housed in the library building itself.

The *Indian National Science Academy (INSA) Library, New Delhi*, uses CDS/ISIS and FoxPro. For computerization of in-house library operations, modules have been developed on FoxPro Platform. It has a collection of 41,914 volumes (books) and subscribes to 1,200 periodicals. Reports and newsletters of Indian scientific institutions form a special collection.

The *Indian Space Research Organization, Space Applications Centre Library, Ahmedabad*, was set up in 1973. The collection consists of thirty thousand volumes (books), five hundred periodicals and five hundred microfilms. The special collection consists of technical and scientific reports consisting of twenty-five thousand items. The library has computerized in-house activities and reader's services.

The *Indian Space Research Organization, Satellite Centre Library, Bangalore*, was established in 1972. It has 14,125 volumes (books) and subscribes to 618 periodicals. The special collection consists of technical reports (5,947), trade catalogs (850), reprints (840), and audiovisual materials (104). The library operations have been computerized and it brings out *Satellite Technology Abstracts*.

The *Indian Statistical Institute Library, Calcutta*, was founded in 1931. The library is fairly large having eight branches in different cities. The collection consists of 150,000 volumes (books) and subscribes to 2,400 periodicals. The library at Calcutta and its branches are well equipped with modern technology.

The *National Aeronautical Laboratory, Library and Information Centre for Aeronautics, Bangalore*, was established in 1960. The center has built up a specialized collection on aeronautics. It is a fully computerized library and has computerized circulation, acquisition and serial control. It provides CAS, SDI, bibliographical research through the Dialog network, CD-ROM searches, e-mail, and Internet facilities. The center renders translation service in all European languages except Czech.

The *National Chemical Laboratory, Library and Documentation Services, Pune*, was established in 1949. The collection consists of 66,538 volumes (books) and subscribes to 667 periodicals. *Chemical Abstracts* (1907–1981) is available on microfiche. It is a highly computerized library that uses the latest information technology.

The *National Physical Laboratory Library, New Delhi*, was founded in 1950. The collection consists of 91,800 volumes (books) and subscribes to 309 periodicals, with a special collection of Indian patents and Indian and British standards. The library has computerized its in-house operations and information retrieval.

The *Physical Research Laboratory Library, Ahmedabad*, was set up in 1948. The collection consists of twelve thousand volumes (books) and thirty thousand bound volumes of periodicals and subscribes to three hundred periodicals. It has five thousand national and international reports. The library has computerized acquisition, cataloguing, serial control, and information retrieval. Also provided are reprographic and translation services.

The Tata Institute of Fundamental Research Library was founded in 1945. The institute is a prestigious one. The library has an excellent collection in the field of fundamental sciences, consisting of 40,000 volumes (books) and 650 periodicals subscriptions. It is a modern library, fully computerized. Acquisition, circulation, cataloguing, stock verification, and information services (CAS and SDI) have all been computerized. It has provision for online searching of databases and CD-ROM search facility. It is one of the best science libraries in the country.

The Wildlife Institute of India Library, Dehradun, is a well-equipped modern library.[14] In December 1992 it had twelve thousand books, five thousand research papers, two thousand volumes of journals, and seven thousand maps. It was subscribing to 210 journals. The library is fully computerized. It has created databases of its collection. It has facilities for CD-ROM database searches and online access to databases. The library building itself is unique, the top being in the form of a dome.

The Zoological Survey of India Library, Calcutta, was formed in 1916. It has a collection of seventy five thousand volumes (books) and subscribes to eight hundred periodicals.

Engineering and Technology

The engineering and technological libraries can be grouped mainly into the following three types:

1. Six Indian Institute of Technology (IIT) libraries situated at Bombay, Delhi, Guwahati, Kanpur, Kharagpur, and Madras
2. Fifteen REC (Regional Engineering College) libraries located in different states
3. 142 Engineering college libraries

A questionnaire was sent to 162 engineering and technological libraries, out of which 87 (53.7 percent) responded. Some of the findings are given below:[15]

1. About 55 percent of the total book stock, 61 percent of the total current periodicals and 90 percent of the total bound periodicals are available only with the high group (IIT and regional college libraries) of libraries.
2. The low group (those not in the high group) of libraries is facing the problem of shortage of staff.
3. Forty-five engineering and technological libraries have sixty-two photocopying machines.
4. Of the total staff, 13.4 percent and 8.3 percent are working in acquisition and technical processing, respectively.
5. No formal cooperative activity exists among engineering and technological libraries. The activities such as interlibrary loan and exchange of the lists of new editions to the library are maintained informally.

The six IIT libraries are the centers of excellence for teaching, training, and re-search, especially in the field of engineering and technology. The libraries have excellent collections and have been the leaders in the application of computer. They have computerized in-house activities, reader's services, and management functions. These have created databases of books, periodicals, and so on. Each has facilities for e-mailing, faxing, and Internet access. Online access to databases and CD-ROM database searches are available in each library. They are taking steps to transfer their libraries into digital libraries. The IIT libraries are comparable to the best libraries in the advanced countries.

Agriculture

Agriculture was given

attention by the Government, when the Department of Agriculture was opened in April, 1873. The Britishers, in the beginning, opened veterinary institutions for taking care of their military farms and animals e.g. College of Veterinary Science, Hissar (1882), and IVRI, Izatnagar (1889), and Mukteswar (1893). Later on Imperial Agricultural Research Institute (IARI) (1905) at Pusa, Bihar, five Government agricultural colleges (1906) at Coimbatore, Kanpur, Lyallpur, Akola and Sabhaur; and agricultural Institute (1910) at Naini were opened. Up to 1947 there were only 25 agricultural colleges and 2 research insti-tutes, namely IARI and IVRI.[16]

Today there are 61 ICAR institutes (4 deemed universities, 42 institutes, 4 na-tional bureaus, 10 project directorates, 1 National Research Centre in Agriculture for Women) and 28 state agricultural universities and 172 agricultural colleges. This shows the tremendous progress that has taken place during the last fifty years or so.[17]

Agricultural research in India is well organized,

having necessary infrastructure and well equipped with labs, libraries, manpower, etc. It also has the largest scientific manpower. It is estimated that the country today has over 60,000 scientists under various government and non-government organizations engaged in active research, excluding technical, administrative and supporting personnel. The scientific manpower-management staff, scientists and teachers engaged in research, education & ex-tension work in agricultural sector have been estimated to be about 31,000. All 28 SAUs [state agricultural universities] comprising 172 agricultural colleges and 4 deemed universi-ties under ICAR annually enroll about 16,500 students at various level courses under hu-man resource development programmes.[18]

The Indian Agricultural Research Institute (IARI) Library has the largest col-lection in the field of agriculture and is the apex library in the field of agriculture. India is participating in AGRIS and CARIS as an input center. The Agriculture Research Information Centre of ICAR feeds data to AGRIS and CARIS data-bases. ICAR, in collaboration with the International Services for National Agri-cultural Research (ISNAR), The Hague, is developing a computer network to link more than twenty-five thousand scientists and managers for improving management of information for the National Agricultural Research System (NARS).[19]

Health Science

There are more than 744 health science libraries[20] in existence that cover such diverse areas as allopathy, homeopathy, unani, ayurveda, yoga, and naturopathy. These libraries provide various information services to over ten to fifteen million health workers of different categories spread over fourteen thousand institutions, in both modern as well as indigenous systems of health care.

Steps have been taken to develop the Health Literature Library and Information Service (HELLIS) Network. Under the NISSAT plan, two sectoral information centers in health sciences–related fields have been developed. These are NICDAP (National Information Centre for Drugs and Pharmaceutical) at CDRI, Lucknow, and NICFOS (National Information Centre for Food Science and Technology) at CFTRI, Mysore. CFTRI feeds data to *Food Science and Technology Abstracts* (FSTA).

There are three leading libraries in the field of health sciences, located in New Delhi. These are the National Library of Medicine, the All India Institute of Medical Sciences Library, and the National Documentation Center of National Institute of Health and Family Welfare.

The National Medical Library is the apex library in the field of health sciences. It serves as a national focal point of the HELLIS Network (a regional network of the Health Literature Library and Information Service in South-East Asia).

The Library of the All India Institute of Medical Sciences has a rich collection of literature in the fields of biomedical and health sciences. It is well equipped with photocopiers, microfilm/microfiche reader-printer, audiovisual aids, e-mail, computers, CD-ROM drives, and CD-Networking. The library also possesses CD-Net System, which allows searching of desired information with speed and efficiency. It has the capacity to run more than one CD-ROM disk simultaneously in the multiuser environment. The library also has automated its housekeeping activities (such as acquisition of books, serial control, etc.) using the LIBSYS software package.

The library has a strong database search facility. Some of the databases available in the library include MEDLINE, POPLINE, CANCER, PSYCHIATRY, LISA, World Atlas, Encyclopedia of Library and Information Science, and so forth. These databases are being used extensively by the users for retrieving information.

The National Documentation Centre of National Institute of Health and Family Welfare was established in 1977. It is a national focal point for the primary health care network in India. It also acts as the national focal point for the Population Information Network (POPIN). It provides CAS, SDI, reprographic, and micrographic services. It has created a bibliographic database using CDS/ISIS. The library activities have been computerized. The library has built up an excellent collection.

Industry

An industry is considered an organized system of production. The emergence of industrial libraries in India is of recent origin compared with other kinds of special libraries. Most of these came into being from 1950 onward due to the impetus provided to industries by the Five-Year Plans of the government of India, the first of which commenced in 1951. Industrial libraries are usually small but well managed. Many of these are well equipped with the latest information technology. These are usually well supported by their parent bodies but the library and information professionals are expected to deliver goods.

A brief description of the leading industrial libraries follows.

The Bharat Heavy Electrical Ltd, Technical Information Centre, Hyderabad, was established in 1976. The collection consists of 12,000 volumes (books), subscribes to 560 periodicals, and possesses 35,000 microfilms. The library is strong in reports. It provides various services including CAS, SDI, literature searching and so on. The library has been computerized.

The Hindustan Aeronautics Ltd Library, Bangalore, was set up in 1945. The library has fifty thousand volumes (books) and subscribes to 165 periodicals. The special collection consists of standards and specifications. It provides CAS, SDI, reprographic services, and so on.

The Hindustan Machine Tools Ltd, Technical Information Centre, Bangalore, was founded in 1961. The collection consists of five thousand volumes (books), subscribes to two hundred periodicals and has fifty thousand microfilms. The special collection includes forty thousand trade catalogs, two thousand reports, fourteen thousand reprints, ten thousand standards, and five thousand slides and tapes. It provides various services including CAS and SDI. The library has been computerized.

The Indian Telephone Industries Ltd. Library, Bangalore, was set up in 1948. The collection consists of 12,187 volumes (books) and 200 periodicals subscriptions. It has a special collection on specifications.

The Tata Chemicals Library, Mithapur, was established in 1939. The library has a collection of 6,000 books. It subscribes to 150 periodicals and has 150 microfilms. It is a pioneer library in the chemical industry[21] sector.

The Tata Engineering and Locomotive Company Library, Jamshedpur, came into being in 1947. It has fifteen thousand volumes (books) and subscribes to two hundred periodicals. The special collections include standards and technical reports. It provides various services including CAS and SDI.

The Tata Iron and Steel Company, Technical and Central Libraries, Jamshedpur, was set up in 1938. The technical library has a collection of thirty-six hundred books on metallurgy, mathematics, physics, chemistry, ceramics, and other related subjects; eighty-five hundred standards and specifications and patents; two thousand technical documents; seven thousand technical translations and about fifty technical reference books and indexes. The central library has 4,800 books, 3,500 standards and specifications, 1,500 documents and 3,000 bound volumes of journals, 150 nontechnical reference books, and 100 technical reference books.[22]

Law

There are three types of law libraries: academic, judicial, and research. Academic law libraries predominate. There are 349[23] educational institutions imparting legal education. Of these, 234 are private colleges and 115 are publicly funded.

The leading academic law libraries include Bangalore University College of Law Library, Government Law College (Bombay), Bombay University Library, Calcutta University Law Library, Delhi University Law Library, Kashmir University Law Library, and Madras Law College Library. Delhi University is regarded as "one of the best law libraries in India"[24] and has a collection of over two hundred thousand volumes. The libraries attached to publicly funded institutions are better than their privately managed counterparts.

Judicial libraries consist of the Supreme Court Library (New Delhi) and High Court Libraries in eighteen states. In addition there are bar association libraries attached to the Supreme Court and the High Courts. The Supreme Court Library is one of the largest libraries with over three hundred thousand volumes.[25] Other leading judicial libraries include Calcutta High Court Library, Karnataka High Court Library (Bangalore) and Madras High Court Library. Each bar association has its own library. These are located at Bombay, Delhi, Calcutta, and Madras and serve their lawyer-members. These are usually financed by membership subscription.

Organizations engaged in legal research have their own libraries. The major such organization is the Indian Law Institute (New Delhi). It has a rich collection of over fifty thousand volumes consisting of documents, reports, and so on. The library brings out *Index to Indian Legal Periodicals*, which is a useful indexing service.

The growth and development of law libraries and information centers has been rather slow. Lack of finance and trained manpower are the major problems faced by them. There is a need for specialized training for law librarians; courses at the master's of library science and master's of philosophy levels would be useful in this training. To improve services and collections, college and university law libraries should follow seriously the library standards laid down by Bar Council of India.

Management

The growth of formal management education and training in India has been quite impressive, particularly during the last two decades. There are now "more than 250 institutions (4 Indian Institute of Management (IIMs), more than 50 universities and nearly 200 other types of institutions offer formal management education and training."[26]

The leading institutions are:

Administrative Staff College of India, Hyderabad

Indian Institute of Management, Ahmedabad

Indian Institute of Management, Bangalore

Indian Institute of Management, Calcutta

Indian Institute of Management, Lucknow

Indian Institute of Public Administration, New Delhi

Institute of Rural Management, Anand

Management Development Institute, Gurgaon

National Institute of Industrial Engineering, Bombay

Small Industry Extension Training Institute, Hyderabad

XLRI, Jamshedpur

The libraries of the four national-level management education institutions, the Indian Institutes of Management (IIM) have, over the years, developed a learning resource base in the fields of management and related areas, covering books, periodicals, reports, nonprint materials (microforms) and audiovisual materials (databases on CD-ROM and machine-readable media). The collection of these consist of 164,436 volumes, 142,121 volumes, 131,842 volumes, and 42,336 volumes at Ahmedabad, Bangalore, Calcutta, and Lucknow, respectively.[27]

The libraries of the management schools have succeeded in developing balanced and up to date collections. They are by and large well equipped with latest technological devices like computers and photocopying machines. These are rendering a variety of information services along a modern line.

NATIONAL SUBJECT LIBRARIES

There are a number of national subject libraries in India that have grown out of departmental libraries. These are special libraries, sponsored and maintained by the government of India or councils set up by it, to serve the specific subject needs. The National Science Library, New Delhi, is a part of the Indian National Scientific Documentation Centre. It was modeled on the National Science Library of the United Kingdom before its merger into the British Library. The National Medical Library, New Delhi, grew out of the departmental library of Ministry of Health and Family Welfare. The Indian Agricultural Research Institute Library is a library of the Indian Council of Agricultural Research. The National Medical Library, New Delhi, and the Indian Agricultural Research Institute Library, New Delhi, are modeled on the National Medical Library and National Agricultural Library in the United States. Indian national subject libraries are considered national due to their nature of collection and kinds of services; however, they do not perform other essential functions that are expected from national libraries.

The National Science Library

The Indian National Scientific Documentation Centre (INSDOC) was established in 1952. During the first phase, INSDOC did not build up a library of its own; instead, the Library of National Physical Laboratory (NPL) served as a base for the operation of its services. During the second phase in 1964, the National

Science Library was conceived as an integral part of INSDOC. It was meant to serve

as a cooperative acquisition facility for building up a balanced collection relevant to the requirements of the country. It would survey the holdings of scientific institutions and supplement the lacunae in their collection by itself acquiring them. As far as possible duplication would be avoided. It would also make a special effort to collect books by Indian authors and books and periodicals in Indian languages. In addition to scientific periodicals including cover-to-cover translated periodicals, the National Science Library will also acquire other scientific publications like reference works, research reports, conference proceedings, theses, state-of-art publications, certain costly publications, etc.[28]

The National Science Library has built up a collection with emphasis as just mentioned. The acquisition policy is based on the concept of resource sharing within the scientific and technical libraries in the country. The library has more than 136,000 bound volumes of books and periodicals. Currently, it receives more than thirty-five hundred serial titles both in hard copy and electronic form. The library has a rich collection of Russian S&T documents.[29]

The different activities of the National Science Library have been computerized. In-house operations (such as circulation control, cataloguing, and serial control) have been computerized on the basis of their own developed software CATMAN. For other purposes, various software packages are being used. These include CDS/ISIS, ver. 2.3; dBase III and dBase IV; LIBSYS, and CATMAN. The following services/products are being produced by the National Science Library.[30]

1. Recent additions to the Library: This is being brought out using CDS/ISIS version 2.3 (a software developed by UNESCO for libraries)

2. National Science Library catalog online

3. Contents Abstracts and Photocopies Service (CAPS): Under this service, one can get on a yearly subscription the contents of forty journals selected by one from five thousand core Indian and foreign periodicals.

4. Express CAPS: Documentation services, including document copy supply service, are being provided based on five hundred foreign periodicals on CD-ROM.

5. Central Acquisition of Periodicals (CAP): The National Science Library assists CSIR laboratories in the acquisition of foreign scientific and technical periodicals under the CAP project.

6. Standing order abstracts service

7. Chemical abstracts keyword index service (CAKIS)

8. International Serials Data System (ISDS): The ISDS center has been in operation since 1986 at INSDOC. It assigns International Standard Serial Number (ISSN) to Indian serials.

The National Medical Library

A departmental library was established in 1926 under the director-general of Indian Medical Services. In 1961 this library was named Central Medical Library, and it was designated the National Medical Library (NML) on April 7, 1966. The functions of NML are:[31]

1. The procurement of the costly and infrequently available publications and manuscripts to supplement the library collections of various biomedical institutions of India
2. To prepare and maintain up-to-date union catalogs of medical libraries in the country
3. To develop documentation services in the medical disciplines
4. To prepare bibliographies in anticipation of or on demand
5. To introduce computer application toward the information work and services of the NML
6. To function as a focal point for collecting, processing and supplying of biomedical information generated within and outside the country

The NML serves as a national library. It has a fairly large collection of books and periodicals and serves all categories of users in the field of health sciences. It uses LIBSYS for the cataloguing and acquisition of books, serial control and information storage and retrieval. It uses CDS/ISIS for indexing services.

The NML serves as a national focal point of the HELLIS Network. As a coordinator of the network, it has supplied microcomputers, CD-ROM drives, MEDLINE databases, and so forth to its various regional and resource libraries in the country.

It brings out the following bibliographical services:

Library Bulletin (bimonthly)

Selective Dissemination of Information (fortnightly, 1982–)

Index to Indian Medical Periodicals (quarterly, 1959–)

Highlights from Current Health Literature (monthly)

Chetna (quarterly, 1982–)

ADISDOC

Union Catalogue of Medical Periodicals in India

Directory of Medical Libraries in India

The NML also provides a literature search service using MEDLINE and POPLINE databases on CD-ROM.

The Indian Agricultural Research Institute Library

The Indian Agricultural Research Institute Library (IARI) is a focal point for collecting, organizing and disseminating of agrobiological information generated within the country and abroad. It may be regarded as a national library in the field of agriculture, though it is not designated as such. It is one of the largest and finest agrobiological libraries in southeast Asia, having about 3.5 lakh volumes, and receives 4,800 current periodicals. It is a depository of the Food and Agricultural Organization (FAO), International Development Research Center (IDRC), and

Asian Vegetable Research and Development (Taiwan) (AVRDC), among others, as well as a depository for CGIAR Institute's publications. The library has created an Indian agriculture database, the *Bibliography of Indian Agriculture*, created in 1944 in card form, and it has 161,500 references.[32]

The IARI library has the following facilities:

1. Online Public Access Catalogue (OPAC).
2. A database in machine-readable form of forty thousand records consisting of books, special research bulletins, theses, and so on.
3. CD-ROM databases from AGRIS (FAO); AGRICOLA; CAB CDS; CAB Spectrum CDs; and Derwent Biotechnology Abstracts.
4. E-mail and Internet capabilities and is a member of DELNET.

NATIONAL DOCUMENTATION CENTERS

There are a number of national documentation centers in different fields. These include the Indian National Scientific Documentation Centre (INSDOC), the National Social Science Documentation Centre (NASSDOC) and the Small Enterprises National Documentation Centre (SENDOC). We may also include the Defence Science Information and Documentation Centre (DESIDOC), which is a documentation center at the national level. The INSDOC, NASSDOC, and DESIDOC have been established mainly to serve the fields of science, social sciences, and defense science. The SENDOC was set up to meet the requirements of small scale industries.

The Indian National Scientific Documentation Centre

The Indian National Scientific Documentation Centre (INSDOC) was established in 1952. INSDOC is a premier institution of information science engaged in dissemination of information. In its first phase it was under the administrative control of the director of National Physical Laboratory. In 1963 it became a center and was given the status of a full-fledged independent laboratory within the CSIR complex. This was the start of the second phase. The functions of the INSDOC are given below:

1. To receive and retain all scientific periodicals which may be of use to the country;
2. To inform scientists and engineers of articles which may be of value to them by issuing a monthly bulletin of abstracts;
3. To answer specific enquiries from information available in the center;
4. To supply photo-copies or translations of articles required by individual workers;
5. To be a national depository for reports of the scientific work of the nation, both published and unpublished; and
6. To be a channel through which the scientific work of the nation is made known and available to the rest of the world.[33]

The center is located at New Delhi. It has three regional centers located at Bangalore, Calcutta, and Madras. It has two other outlets, namely, INSDOC-WRIC Information Services, Bombay and INSDOC-Communication Research Consultants Centre, Calcutta. The INSDOC provides the following services/products:[34]

1. Document copy supply
2. Literature search from national/international databases
3. Foreign language translation/interpretation
4. Bibliometric service
5. Retrospective conversion of catalog or library automation
6. Contents, abstracts, photocopies services (CAPS)
7. Short-term training courses
8. Microfilming and slide making
9. Desktop publishing
10. Compilation and publication of *Indian Science Abstracts*
11. Publication of *Annals of Library Science and Documentation*
12. Compilation of databases and directories
13. Consultancy and sponsored projects
14. Electronic imaging of archival records
15. Electronic mail services
16. Associateship in Information Science

The Computer Services Division handles the Scientific and Industrial Research Network (SIRNET), which provides computerized linking up of S&T institutions and facilitates e-mail, and database services.

The Data Services Division procures and supplies S&T documents, publishes *Indian Science Abstracts*, and provides bibliographic and reprographic services.

The Education and Training Division provides courses in information science, short-term training courses, the National Centre for Bibliometrics, and the *Indian Science Citation Index*.

Marketing and customer services are responsible for customer services related to products/services, sales promotion, and publicity. The Programme Management Division handles printing, consultancy projects, and so on. The Translation Services Division handles translation and interpretation jobs. The National Science Library provides documentation and information services as described earlier.

Online access to the following ten indigenous databases is available for public access on request from users both online and offline on a subscription basis:

1. Polymer Science Literature Database
2. Material Science Bibliographic Database
3. Medicinal & Aromatic Plants Abstracts (MAPA) Database

4. Indian Patents (INPAT) Database
5. Experts Database
6. Database of Standards
7. INSDOC's Serials Contents on Multi Media (ISCOMM) Database
8. National Union Catalogue of Scientific Serials in India (NUCSSI) Database
9. Metallurgy Database
10. National Science Library Catalogue

The INSDOC has been involved in computer application since the late 1960s. It has taken a key role in computer application for in-house functions, reader's services, and management functions. Furthermore, by holding training courses, especially in computer application, it has spread computer culture.

The INSDOC initially used to provide subsidized services to scientists and others. Now it has become highly commercialized. The quality of services has improved but at the same time, the charges have become highly comparable with commercial agencies. During 1993–1994, the INSDOC had external cash flow of the order of Rs. 105,458 lakhs,[35] the aim being to achieve self-sustenance. Today the INSDOC has achieved expertise in library automation, database design and development, and networking. The services have been streamlined, using modern information technology. However, charges on services are quite high.

The National Social Science Documentation Centre

The Indian Council of Social Science Research (ICSSR) was set up in 1969 as an autonomous organization to promote research in social sciences in the country by creating documentation and bibliographical services for research scholars in the field of social sciences, covering the fields of economics, education, geography, history, public administration, sociology, international relations, and all other subjects of an interdisciplinary nature. The ICSSR set up the Social Science Documentation Centre (SSDC) in 1970, which was renamed in 1986 as the National Social Science Documentation Centre (NASSDOC). It provides the following library and information services:

1. Literature search including bibliography compilation
2. Document delivery
3. Referral services to social scientists
4. Short-term training courses

The NASSDOC is a member of DELNET. It uses e-mail to communicate with other users of the Education Research Network (ERNET). It has acquired a number of databases on CD-ROM, such as POPLINE, AUSTROM, UNESCO CD-ROM, CD-DIS, the *Social Science Index*, the *Singapore National Bibliography*, the *Distance Education Bibliography*, the *Dissertation Abstracts of Disc*, and ERIC.

The NASSDOC uses dBase III, CDS/ISIS and ISMAS, Wordstar and Akshar. The major products are as follows:[36]

1. Area study bibliographies
2. APINESS Newsletter (biannually)
3. Bibliography on India in 2000 A.D.
4. Conference alert (quarterly)
5. Current contents of Indian Social Science Journals (quarterly)
6. Directory of Training and Research Institutions in Social Sciences, Peace Research, Human Rights, and International Law
7. Directory of learned periodicals in social sciences
8. Retrospective index of Indian social science journals
9. Union catalog of social science periodicals in India, 32 volumes

The machine-readable products are as follows:

1. Area study bibliography
2. Current index to Indian social science journals
3. Conference alert
4. Database of ICSSR Research Project Reports
5. Directory of Social Science Research and Training Institutions in India (*Note:* Similar directories on Peace Research, Human Research and International Law have been produced.)
6. Database of North-East Region
7. List of social science periodicals
8. Union catalog of social science periodicals

The NASSDOC is well equipped with information technology, but due to lack of support from the government of India, it has lagged behind: The reference collection of the Library of NASSDOC is inadequate to serve the needs of the patrons; the bibliographical services brought out by it have not kept pace with the growing demands of Indian social scientists; and, as a national documentation center, it has not succeeded in building a strong network of social science libraries/information centers, which would be a great advantage for Indian social scientists.

The Defence Scientific Information and Documentation Centre

In 1958, the Defence Research and Development Organization (DRDO) created the Scientific Information Bureau (SIB) to serve the information needs of the concerned R&D scientists and other agencies of the Ministry of Defence. In 1967 the SIB was recognized and its name changed to the Defence Scientific Information and Documentation Centre (DESIDOC), with wider scope and responsibilities. In 1970 it was upgraded into one of the DRDO establishments headed by a director. At present the DESIDOC is a unit of DRDO and serves as a central agency of the DRDO to collect, process and disseminate scientific and technical information to about forty DRDO laboratories and other establishments of the Ministry of Defence. It also provides S&T information to the Ministry of Defence. The DESIDOC performs the following functions:

1. Collection, processing and dissemination of information
2. Literature searches
3. Compilation of union catalogs of DRDO libraries
4. Translation bank
5. Training and consultancy
6. Reprography and printing

The Defence Science Library under the DESIDOC has about forty thousand books, forty thousand technical reports and fourteen thousand back volumes of periodicals. It is a repository of DRDO reports. It has an excellent collection of NASA and RAND reports. In addition, it has a collection of patents and standards. This library serves the needs of various laboratories/establishments of the DRDO and organizations of the Ministry of Defence. It also organizes short-term courses in computerized information services, indexing, and abstracting.

The DESIDOC brings out the following publications:[37]

Patents Information Alert (bimonthly)
Defence Reports Abstracts (bimonthly)
DESIDOC list (bimonthly)
Popular Science and Technology (biannually)
Science Abstracts from Foreign Language Journals (quarterly)
DESIDOC Bulletin (bimonthly)
Defence Technology Alert (a weekly CAS)

It collaborates with DRDO in the publishing of the following journals:

Defence Science Journal (quarterly)
R&D Bulletin (bimonthly)
DRDO Newsletter (bimonthly)

In computerization, the DESIDOC has achieved the following:

1. Developed a library automation software called the Defence Libraries Management System (DELMS) in-house that is useful for designing a database for scientific information and also for online searching and information retrieval
2. Computerized library acquisition, circulation control, and serials control
3. Created a database for the holdings of DSL, using Common Communication Format

4. Brings out New Additions to DSL

5. Created a centralized database of the holdings of the libraries/Technical Information Centers of the DRDO, scattered all over India, using CCF and Ingress software, developed in-house

6. Provided e-mail service to twenty-five libraries of the DRDO libraries through ERNET e-mail service and also e-mail connectivity through the RENNIC e-mail service of NIC (as a consequence, libraries/TICs of the DRDO have access to information resources available worldwide, through the Internet)

7. Provides computer-based information services by searching CD-ROM databases (including full-text databases) available at DSL as well as searching the Dialog databases online

8. Computerized the union catalog of periodicals available in DRDO libraries/TICs, using CDS/ISIS software

9. Provides a weekly computer-based awareness service, *Defence Technology Alert*, using CDS/ISIS

10. Provides computer-based SDI service to DRDO scientists, using fifteen CD-ROM databases subscribed by DSL

11. Provides a facility to conduct online searches for information from databases in the United States and the United Kingdom

The DESIDOC is a pioneering organization which has succeeded in using information technology to serve the information needs of its users effectively.

The Small Enterprises National Documentation Centre

The Small Enterprises National Documentation Centre (SENDOC), Hyderabad, was set up in 1971 as an organ of the SIET Institute. The institute assists in the promotion and modernization of small industries by means of training, research, and consultancy services. The library has built up a strong collection in the fields of science and technology and social and behavioral sciences with special reference to management. The library serves as a national bibliographic center to meet the requirements of small-scale industries and provides services to small enterprises toward their technological and managerial advancement.

THE NATIONAL INFORMATION NETWORKS AND SYSTEMS

To serve the information needs of different sectors, national information networks and systems have emerged. The National Information System for Science and Technology (NISSAT) was designed as a program rather than a system. The Information and Library Network (INFLIBNET) is another program at the national level, which is basically meant to serve the needs of university and college libraries. The INFLIBNET aims to enable university and college libraries to share their resources through networking arrangements. This has also benefited special libraries as there is now better infrastructure for sharing resources between academic institutions of higher learning and special libraries.

The INFLIBNET program was initiated by the UGC in 1990 as a project. It was formally launched in May 1991. It is being implemented by INFLIBNET Centre, located at Ahmedabad. The major aim of the program is to modernize academic libraries and to establish a national network of libraries and information centers in universities, institutes of higher learning and R&D institutes in India. So far the emphasis is on institutes of higher learning. University and college libraries are in the process of modernization; networking facilities and databases are being created. The situation is improving.

The UGC has established three national information centers at Bangalore, Mumbai, and Baroda. The National Centre for Science Information, Bangalore, covers science and technology. The National Information Centre at Mumbai takes care of sociology, women's studies, home science, special education and library science. The Social Science Information Center at Baroda covers economics, political science, education, and psychology.

At present there are no separate national systems for libraries in social sciences and the humanities, but these have also benefited from programs of the NISSAT and INFLIBNET. For instance, in local networks like CALIBNET and DELNET, initiated by the NISSAT, social science and humanities libraries are also participants and have taken advantage of their services.

In the field of health sciences, the Health Literature Library and Information Services (HELLIS) network has come up. In addition, two national information centers were developed by NISSAT, which have directly benefited health science libraries. These are the National Information Centre for Drugs and Pharmaceuticals at CDRI, the Lucknow, and the National Information Centre for Food Science and Technology at CFTRI, Mysore. A national information system is in the process of being set up in agriculture.

The National Information System for Science and Technology (NISSAT) is a program that was launched in September 1977. The National Focal Point of NISSAT is located in the Department of Scientific and Industrial Research. The NISSAT headquarters serves as the national focal point in the field of S&T information. It aims to promote and support a compatible set of information systems on science.[38] The NISSAT network consists of sectoral information centers (SICs); regional information centers (RICs); and other specialized services.

The objectives of the NISSAT are as follows:[39]

1. To develop national information services
2. To promote the existing information systems and services
3. To introduce modern information handling tools and techniques
4. To promote national and international cooperation in information
5. To develop indigenous products and services
6. To support education, training, and R&D in information

The basic guidelines followed by the NISSAT have been to make maximum exploitation of the existing resources and facilities. Toward this aim, it has taken necessary steps to integrate and coordinate the existing sources and facilities. It has filled up gaps rather than create services and facilities to duplicate these. Wherever required, existing information centers and services have been upgraded by means of additional support from NISSAT. NISSAT has established twelve sectoral information centers as shown in Table 6.1.

Sectoral information centers meet the information needs of a particular discipline, mission, or product. A sectoral information center coordinates its activities with other local information units in the same field. From their inception, the SICs have been provided financial support by the NISSAT to strengthen equipment, facilities, information resources, and the publication program. They provide a wide range of services such as current awareness services (CAS) including selective dissemination of information (SDI), translation, and reprographic services.

Table 6.1
NISSAT Centers[40]

Subject Area	Acronym	Host Institution
1. Leather Technology	NICLAI	Central Leather Research Institute, Madras
2. Food Technology	NICFOS	Central Food Technological Reseacrch Institute, Mysore
3. Machine Tools & Production Engineering	NICMAP	Central Manufacturing Technology Institute, Bangalore
4. Drugs and Pharmaceuticals	NICDAP	Central Drug Research Institute, Lucknow
5. Textiles & Allied Subjects	NICTAS	Ahmedabad Textile Industry's Research Association, Ahmedabad
6. Chemicals & Allied Industries	NICHEM	National Chemical Laboratory, Pune
7. Advanced Ceramics	NICAC	Central Glass and Ceramics Research Institute, Calcutta
8. Bibliometrics	NCB	Indian National Scientific Documentation Centre, New Delhi
9. Crystallography	NICRYS	University of Madras, Madras
10. CD-ROM	NICDROM	National Aerospace Laboratory, Bangalore
11. Management Science	NICMAN	Indian Institute of Management, Ahmedabad
12. Marine Science	MICMAS	National Institute of Oceanography, Goa

Regional information centers were planned at NISSAT contact points for users of the concerned region for supply of documents and services from the sectoral information centers. Regional information centers at Calcutta, Bombay, and Madras were initiated. The Bombay center was never established due to lack of space. The centers at Calcutta and Madras were taken over by the INSDOC.

With the assistance from UNESCO, computerized SDI service was commenced in January 1976, using the computer center of the Indian Institute of Technology, Madras, based on *Chemical Abstracts Condensates*. Beginning in January 1977 INSPEC A and B and COMPENDEX databases were added for the SDI service. The NISSAT provided support for the project. The project was discontinued as the response was not found encouraging.

The NISSAT has provided support to INSDOC to develop databases such as (1) the current research projects on S&T, (2) the directory of testing facilities, and (3) the National Union Catalogue of Scientific Serials in India. The NISSAT provided support to the Indian Library Association for the creation of a database on Indian libraries.

The NISSAT has sponsored special studies and projects on information processing and dissemination, micrographs, manpower development, and so on.

The NISSAT has been playing an active role in bilateral cooperation programs in S&T information with different countries within the framework of various agreements in science and technology, signed by the government of India with other countries (e.g., Germany, United Kingdom, United States). It collaborates with several regional and international programs, such as the International Referral System for Sources of Environmental Information (INFOTERRA), the Commonwealth Regional Renewable Energy Resources Information System (CRRERIS), and so on. The NISSAT Advisory Committee serves as National Committee on UNISIST in India. NISSAT has sponsored the following networks:

ADINET (Ahmedabad Libraries Network)

BONET (Bombay Libraries Network)

CALIBNET (Calcutta Libraries Network)

DELNET (Delhi Libraries Network)

MYLIBNET (Mysore Libraries Network)

PUNENET (Pune Libraries Network)

The NISSAT assists the networks to set up general infrastructural facilities. However, the participating libraries in a network are supposed to arrange infrastructural facilities at their end on their own.

The NISSAT publishes the *Directory of Forthcoming Conferences/Symposia/Meetings/Workshops on Science and Technology in India* (August 1977–) and the *NISSAT Newsletter*, now named *Information Today and Tomorrow* (quarterly).

The NISSAT has supported training programs for training manpower in the application of CDS/ISIS. Over twenty-five hundred persons have been trained under these programs.

The NISSAT has also given financial support for the creation of computer facilities at INSDOC, DESIDOC, DRTC (Bangalore) and Pune University for training manpower.

The NISSAT supports UNESCO activities and products in India. These include CDS/ISIS (about twelve hundred installations); IDAMS; and CCF (the Common Communication Format). The first is for bibliographical information processing and retrieval, the second for statistical data processing, and the third prescribes format for bibliographic records. The NISSAT has established e-mail connectivity with its information centers, library network societies, and so forth through ERNET. To provide access to international databases, the NISSAT has established these nine access centers:

National Aerospace Laboratory, Bangalore

Indian Association for Cultivation of Science, Calcutta

Central Leather Research Institute, Madras

INSDOC, New Delhi

National Chemical Laboratory, Pune

Ahmedabad Textile Industry's Research Association, Ahmedabad

Victoria Jubilee Technical Institute

Centre for Cellular and Molecular Biology, Hyderabad

Kerala State Industrial Development Corporation, Thiruvananthapuram.

CD-ROM-based SDI services are being offered regularly to users on the basis of their information needs from eight institutions. The NISSAT established in 1986 a facility at the Foundation for Innovations and Technology Transfer at the Indian Institute of Technology, Delhi, as a depository center for all CD-ROM databases on and about India.

The NISSAT has played a very important role in the introduction of modern information handling tools and techniques. The development of national sectoral centers has given a boost to R&D in science and technology. The NISSAT needs to be given higher financial support so that information systems in science and technology in the country can be further strengthened to meet the information needs of scientists and technologists adequately.

THE ROLE OF PROFESSIONAL ORGANIZATIONS

Professional organizations like the Indian Library Association (ILA), the Indian Association of Special Libraries and Information Centres (IASLIC), the Society for Information Science (SIS), Medical Library Association of India (MLAI), the Association of Agricultural Librarians, and the Documentalists of India (AALDI) have played an important role in the cause of special librarianship including special libraries.

The ILA is a major national body. There are seven central sectional committees that look after the interests of special libraries and librarians. These are Agricultural Libraries, Health Science Libraries, Special Libraries, Library and Information Technology, Documentation and Information Services, Oriental Libraries, and Engineering and Technology Libraries.

The Indian Association of Special Libraries and Information Centres (IASLIC) was formed in 1955.[41] There were 1,569 members in 1997. It is a national association that looks after the interests of special libraries and information centers. It organizes seminars and conferences, study circles, and education and training programs, and brings out different publications. The publications include *Iaslic Bulletin* (quarterly), *Iaslic Newsletter* (monthly), and *Indian Library Science Abstracts*. Apart from these, the Association brings out special publications covering papers and proceedings of the conferences and symposia as well as ad hoc publications. It has already completed forty-three years of fruitful existence. The success of the IASLIC is due to the dedicated efforts of a core group of voluntary workers.[42]

The Society for Information Science (SIS) is an association dominated by people from information science who are mainly interested in information technology. SIS holds its annual convention and conference every year. The Seventeenth Annual Convention and Conference was held in March 1998 on the topic of virtual libraries.

The need was felt to organize professional health science librarians. Thus on August 18, 1980, a number of prominent medical librarians/information scientists met in New Delhi. They resolved to form the Medical Library Association of India (MLAI). The MLAI was registered in 1981 as a professional body under the Societies Registration Act (India), 1860, with the following objectives:[43]

1. To facilitate professional development for effective health sciences information and library systems and services through mutual cooperation

2. To build up a body of professional experience that could be utilized in the smooth and effective functioning of the libraries in the field of biomedical and allied sciences

3. To help libraries provide effective service to students and trainees, practicing physicians, fieldworkers, research workers, teachers, and administrators in the biomedical and allied fields

4. To devise methods and techniques for the improvement in quality of collection, storage and dissemination of information

5. To foster mutual cooperation and assistance among the various biomedical libraries in the country and the library personnel working therein

6. To serve as an institution for the exchange of professional knowledge and experience by organizing training courses, seminars, conferences, lectures, workshops, and so on and by publishing reports, monographs, bulletins, catalogs, bibliographies, journals, and so on; also to promote the interests of the biomedical and allied sciences, libraries, and librarianship.

7. To cooperate with learned institutions and interested bodies national and international in the furtherance of these objectives

8. To issue appeals and applications for money and funds in the furtherance of the said objectives and to accept gifts, donations, subscriptions of cash and securities and of any property movable or immovable

The association has brought out the *MLAI Bulletin*, a quarterly, since 1983, and the *MLAI News*, also a quarterly. The association organizes national seminars and workshops whereby proceedings and papers are presented and published. Six publications have been published so far. The Sixth International Congress on Medical Librarianship was hosted by the MLAI in New Delhi in 1990.

The Association of Agricultural Librarians and Documentalists of India (AALDI) is an association of agricultural librarians. However, it is not active.

The Joint Council of Library Associations of India (JOCLAI) is a voluntary and informal body. The JOCLAI aims to promote, foster, and establish coordination and cooperation among professional associations of India in the field of library and information science.

PROBLEMS AND PROSPECTS

For many reasons it is becoming increasingly difficult for special libraries to meet the information needs of their users. Budget cuts, growing demands from users, and the rising costs of ever-growing reading materials all conspire against the libraries.

Information technology is bringing its own problems. In its initial application, there are often problems related to hardware and software, telecommunication, lack of trained staff, and so on. The staff must adjust to the changing environment, which is not always easy.

Bibliographic databases are in the process of being created. It takes considerable effort to achieve retrospective conversion of bibliographic data. The available union catalogs and lists are still inadequate and the backup services to procure an item via interlibrary loan or to get reproduction of an item are still weak.

The special libraries have started the application of information technology on a large scale only in late 1990s. Within another few years, the situation is likely to improve a great deal. Day by day information technology is improving and becoming more versatile. This is a good sign. Although special libraries have gotten a late start, they will have the latest information technologies available to them. They also need not repeat the mistakes made in developed countries.

CONCLUSION

Special libraries in India number over three thousand. They exist in great variety and have done quite well compared with other kinds of libraries. The strong impact of information technology has enabled them to achieve a high degree of modernization. Many are now in the process of converting themselves into digital libraries.

NOTES

1. J. Saha, *Special Libraries and Information Services in India and in the USA* (Metuchen, N.J.: Scarecrow Press, 1969), 5.

2. Ibid., 21.

3. T. S. Rajagopalan and S. I. Islam, "National Grid of Scientific Libraries," in *Documentation and Its Facets*, edited by S. R. Ranganathan (Delhi: 1963), 166–175.

4. National Dairy Research Institute (ICAR), *Annual Report, 1991–1992* (Karnal, 1993), 1.

5. *India, 1996: A Reference Annual* (New Delhi: Publications Division, Ministry of Information and Broadcasting, Government of India, 1997).

6. C. Sasikala, *Industrial Library Systems* (New Delhi: Reliance, 1994), 35.

7. The data in this section have been taken primarily from two directories: Joginder Singh and A. R. Sethi, ed. and comp., *Indian Library Directory*, 4th ed. (Delhi: Indian Library Association, 1985); and P. Dhyani, comp., *Directory of Information Services and Computer Application—Indian Libraries* (Jaipur: University Book House, 1994).

8. Sk. Mazharul Islam, "Buhar Collection in the National Library: Important information Source in Humanities," in L. S. Ramaiah and M. Kanakachary, ed., *Documentation and Bibliographic Control of the Humanities in India* (New Delhi: Aditya Prakashan, 1992), 145.

9. Krishan Kumar, "Bibliographic Control in Indology: Scope and Importance of the Humanities," in L. S. Ramaiah and M. Kanakachary, ed., *Documentation and Bibliographic Control of the Humanities in India* (New Delhi: Aditya Prakashan, 1992), 101.

10. P. B. Mangla, "Libraries and Information Systems in India," in C. P. Vashishth et al., ed., *New Horizons in Library and Information Science* (Madras: T. R. Publications, 1994), 492.

11. N. J. Sebaston, "National Council of Applied Economic Research (Library & Information Activities)," *Handbook of Libraries, Archives and Information Centres*, vol. 8 (Delhi: Aditya Prakashan, 1990), 161–163.

12. Kanwal Verma, "Nehru Museum and Library," in C.P. Vashishth et al., *Handbook of Libraries, Archives and Information Centres*, vol. 8 (Delhi: Aditya Prakashan, 1990), 150.

13. Mangla, "Libraries and Information Systems in India," 492.

14. M. S. Rana, "Changing Face of the WII Library," *WII Newsletter* 7 (3–4) (July–December 1992), 20.

15. P. Barua and B. Saibaba, "A Plan for Cooperation and Networking among Engineering and Technological Libraries in India," *Annals of Library Science and Documentation* 39(3) (1992), 162.

16. Chhotey Lal, "Development of Agricultural Libraries in India in the Post-Independence Era," *Library Herald*, 33 (1–2) (April–September 1995), 22.

17. Ibid., 23–26.

18. Ibid., 24

19. "Accessing Agricultural Research Information," *University News* 32 (24) (1994), 22–23.

20. R. P. Dixit, "Assessment of Health Literature Information Services in Indian Health Science Libraries," *International Information and Library Review* 25 (1993), 167–168.

21. IASLIC, *Directory of Special and Research Libraries in India* (Calcutta, 1962).

22. TISCO, *Library Manual* (Tatanagar: Tata Iron and Steel Company, 1989).

23. Theodore A. Mahr, "An Introduction to Law and Law Libraries in India," *Law Library Journal* 82 (1990), 111.

24. Ibid.

25. Ibid., 119.

26. Roshan Raina, "Library Resource Sharing among IIMs: Periodicals as the Thrust Area." *Annals of Library Science and Documentation*, 43 (4) (1996), 140.

27. Ibid., 140–152.

28. B. Guha, *Documentation and Information: Services Techniques and Systems* (Calcutta: World Press, 1983), 161.

29. *Annual Report, 1993–94* (New Delhi: INSDOC), 30.

30. Ibid., 31–34.

31. India, Ministry of Health and Family Welfare, *Annual Report, 1993–94* (New Delhi: Manager of Publications, 1994).

32. *Annual Work Report of IARI Library, 1994–95* (New Delhi: IARI Library, 1995).

33. B.S. Kesavan, Documentation in India (Delhi: INSDOC, 1968), 12.

34. *Annual Report, 1993–94* (New Delhi: INSDOC), 7.

35. Ibid., 9.

36. S.P. Agrawal and Manohar Lal, "Documentation Activities and Services in Social Science: Role of NASSDOC and ICSSR Regional Centre." In B. M. Gupta and V. K. Jain, et al., eds. *Handbook of Libraries, Archives and Information Centres in India*, vol. 8 (New Delhi: Aditya Prakashan, 1990), 78–108.

37. *Defence Scientific Information and Documentation Centre* (brochure dated August 28, 1995) (mimeograph), 3–4.

38. A. Lahiri, "National Information System for Science and Technology," in B.M. Gupta, V. K. Jain, et al., eds., *Handbook of Libraries, Archives and Information Centres in India*, vol. 3 (New Delhi: Information Industry Publications, 1986), 59.

39. *National Information System for Science and Technology* (NISSAT) (brochure), 1.

40. Ibid., 2.

41. Krishan Kumar, *Library Organization* (New Delhi: Vikas, 1989), 213.

42. Ibid., 214–215.

43. MLAI National Symposium and Workshop (New Delhi) *Souvenir* (New Delhi: Medical Library Association of India, 1995), 21.

SELECTED BIBLIOGRAPHY

Barua, P., and B. Saibaba. "A Plan for Cooperation and Networking Among Engineering and Technological Libraries in India." *Annals of Library Science and Documentation* 39 (3) (1992), 160–164.

Dixit, R. P. "Assessment of Health Literature Information Services in Indian Health Science Libraries." *International Information and Library Review* 25 (1993), 165–182.

Gupta, B. M., and V. K. Jain, et al., eds. *Handbook of Libraries, Archives and Information Centres*, vol. 3 (Delhi: Information Industry, 1986).

————. *Handbook of Libraries, Archives, and Information Centres in India.* Vol. 8. New Delhi: Aditya Prakashan, 1990.

Kesavan, B. S. *Documentation in India* (Delhi: INSDOC, 1968).

Kumar, Krishan. *Library Organization* (New Delhi: Vikas, 1989), chap. 6.

Lal, Chhotey. "Development of Agricultural Libraries in India in the Post-Independence Era." *Library Herald* 33 (1–2) (April–September 1995), 22–33.

Mahr, Theodore A. "An Introduction to Law and Law Libraries in India." *Law Library Journal* 82 (1990), 111–119.

Rama, Roshar. "Library Resource Sharing among IIMS: Periodicals as the Thrust Area." *Annals of Library Science and Documentation* 43 (4) (1996), 140–152.

Ramaiah, L. S., and Kanakachary, M., ed., *Documentation and Bibliographic Control of Humanities in India* (New Delhi: Aditya Prakashan, 1992).

Saha, J. *Special Libraries and Information Services in India and in the U.S.A.* (Metuchen, N.J.: Scarecrow Press, 1969).

Sasikala, C. *Industrial Library Systems* (New Delhi: Reliance, 1994).

Scholberg, Henry. "The Indian National Bibliography (INB): Its Origin, History and Accomplishments." *ILA Bulletin* 14 (1–4) (1978), 64–69.

Seminar on the Role of the National Library of India. Seminar papers of the Platinum Jubilee Celebration of the Library, Calcutta, November 22–23, 1978. Calcutta: National Library Employees' Association, 1979.

Singh, Gurnek. "Genesis of India's National Library." In R. N. Sharma, ed., *Indian Librarianship: Perspectives and Prospects.* New Delhi: Kalyani Publishers, 1981, 217–225.

Viswanathan, C. G. "What Ails the Indian National Bibliography." *Library Association Records* 81 (7) (July 1979), 333.

❧ 7 ❧

The State of Bibliographic Control and Services

Bibliographic control is a topic concerned with a vast amount of published and unpublished sources of information with problems. These sources include printed catalogs, bibliography of bibliographies, guides to periodical literature, government publications, guides to theses and dissertations, biographies, union catalogs of periodicals, archives, indexing and abstracting services, directories, and other bibliographic sources.

The term *bibliographic control* covers a wide range of activities related to a nation's recording and maintaining of bibliographic descriptions of published materials. It generally refers to the procedures designed to identify book and nonbook materials so that they may be easily retrieved. Since the beginning of librarianship, access to the recorded information has been available through bibliographic control. World librarianship has given the historical background for effective control of and access to recorded knowledge. The editor of AACR2, Michael Gorman, argued that "Bibliographic control is the heart of librarianship."[1] He continued, "Bibliographic control is central to librarianship in a realistic and functional manner. It is impossible to imagine anything called 'librarianship' without the structures and patterns of thought that we find in bibliographic control."[2]

For the purposes of this chapter, various activities from cataloging a library collection and developing electronic databases of available information in a country (or on an international scale for area studies) will be called bibliographic control. Bibliographic control is important for several reasons. It provides records of materials that are intended for research in a given area; that is, the materials are arranged systematically by place or origin (publication, printing), by date or period of publication, by language, or by subject. Bibliographical control is facilitated by the entry, which is sometimes followed by annotation, abstract, descriptive notes, or critical commentary. Another purpose of bibliographic control is that "books are for use" (Ranganathan's first law of library science). International researchers Timo Kuronen and Paivi Pekkarinen wrote that if the first law is taken by intuition, indeed, books are meant for use. Yet the reader's right to have access to the books he or she wants is a global issue.[3] In the context of the virtual library, Kuronen and Pekkarinen believe that books per se are no longer the issue, but *information* is. Everyone should be able to benefit from access to information to realize his or her knowledge potential and his or her plan of life.[4]

Ranganathan's five laws, according to Martin Kesselman, head of Reference and Instructional Services at the Library of Science and Medicine at Rutgers University, "still have much relevance for libraries and electronic information resources today, especially if one replaces the term book with information."[5]

This chapter covers the state of bibliographic control and services since India's independence in 1947. According to Jagdish S. Sharma, the postindependence period (1948–1974) "can appropriately be named as the golden age of bibliographical renaissance in India."[6] Libraries and documentation centers experienced notable growth after independence, and there was evidence of bibliographic control of published materials with the *Indian National Bibliography* (INB), first published in 1958. Bibliographic controls in India are increasing each year. The attention in this chapter is restricted to bibliographic controls for English-language materials. The titles consist of selected lists of writings and are produced in the country. A comprehensive coverage of bibliographic control and services is not provided in this chapter.

Issues in the field of bibliographic control include bibliographic organization and library catalogs. The dean of a library school, Jesse H. Shera (1903–1982), wrote in 1976 on the issue of bibliographic organization, "Librarians, like the legendary shoemakers whose children were supposed to have gone unshod, have been so pre-occupied with classifying, cataloging and indexing the writings of others that they have, at least until recent years neglected the bibliographic organization of their own professional literature."[7]

What is bibliographic organization? It may be defined as, "the pattern of effective arrangements which results from the systematic listing of the records of human communication. Such listings are themselves called bibliographies, and the art of making them is bibliography."[8] Bibliographic organization includes "the study of the organization and operation of the recording, interlibrary co-operation and of the improvement of the methods of educating bibliographers."[9]

Library catalogs include such diverse materials as books, pamphlets, serials, maps, reports, conference papers, patents, computer files, music, microforms, and a variety of audiovisual materials. The activities relating to these different forms result in bibliographic control. The demand for cooperative libraries and electronic conversions for these different types of materials cause difficulties for librarians.

To summarize bibliographic control theory, Doralyn J. Hickey has written, "The task of a contemporary theory of bibliographic control is to discover which aspects of bibliographic communication are transcendent of cultural biases—and thus can be regularized—as opposed to those which are reflective of the rich cultural heritage of a people—and thus should be understood but not eradicated."[10] Cultural biases are important to consider when new programs are being developed for use in international bibliographic control. If some trends on universal bibliographic control, such as journals being replaced by electronic article access come to light, the advocates of libraries must stand by to monitor proper procedures. Pauline Cochrane has observed, "By the turn of the century we may see our work at description more and more in the hands of the electronic publishers and their catalogers, who will provide both the description and the full-text online."[11] The goal of universal bibliographic control is becoming a completed reality. However, being able to access materials will not happen if the opportunity is not available to the library patron. A consideration of user availability must be taken into account. This problem will be most prominent in some developing countries. Without technical equipment and training the library users will be at a disadvantage.[12]

The use of bibliographic control is to provide the library users with access to their required materials; therefore the activities related to bibliographic control and services in a country are dependent upon the publications of the country, the information needs of different people in society, and the country's willingness to serve those information needs.

As far as the number of books published in India are concerned, there have been no great fluctuations from 1950 to 1981. For example, the number of titles published in the country in the year 1950 was 12,698. In 1960 the number was 10,741; in 1970, 14,145; and in 1981, 11,562.[13] In 1991, the number of titles published was 14,438; in 1992, 15,778; and in 1993, 12,768. The total number of daily newspapers published in 1992 was 27,500.[14] According to *Information India 1998 Global View*, "India is the third largest producer of books in English," after the United States and the United Kingdom.

Most of the bibliographic control activities in India have been attempted by individual libraries, types of libraries, and government organizations. The needs for bibliographic devices are generally generated from scholars, researchers, and specialists.

The most active roles in bibliographic control in the country are played by the national libraries, government organizations, scientific and technical documentation centers, and other organizations. One of the major functions of bibliographic control is to provide the complete bibliographic records of all the available publications, and in this context the national libraries of the country have been playing key roles: "A . . . national bibliography should reflect the interests and unique characteristics of a country much as a mirror reflects the uniqueness of an individual."[15]

7

BIBLIOGRAPHIES

The INB has been a significant bibliographical tool in providing bibliographic records of the materials published in the country. Published by the National Library, Calcutta, since 1958, it lists the books published after 1953 in the fourteen regional languages of the country with their basic bibliographic descriptions under classifications of subjects with an author index. The INB "was modeled to a very large extent on the British National Bibliography, using the Dewey Decimal Classification as the basis of arrangement, and providing a single classified sequence of entries transliterated into a common Roman script."[16] A. J. Wells, then editor of *British National Bibliography* in the early 1970s, wrote, "As a result of being based upon the British National Bibliography, the Indian National Bibliography reimported some of Ranganathan's ideas. It provided a classified arrangement with "features," and it had a chain index."[17]

The *ALA Cataloging Rules for Author and Title Entries*, published in 1949, incorporated some of the rules of the Classified Catalog Code (CCC) of Ranganathan. The impact of CCC on AACR of 1967 continued.[18] Another important bibliography has been the *National Bibliography of Indian Literature* published by the National Library since 1962, which lists books published during 1901–1953 under classifications of broad subjects such as fiction, drama, history or biography with an author and subject index.

The series of printed retrospective bibliographies, known as the *Bibliography of Indology* was also started by the Indian National Library in the 1950s. The fifty-six-volume bibliography covers all aspects of Indian life and culture, for example, as evidenced by these volume titles: *Bibliography of Anthropology*, *Bibliography of Indian Botany*, and *Bengali Language and Literature*. This last volume was brought out in 1964.

Jagdish Saran Sharma has compiled the various lengthy descriptive bibliographies on the Indian National Congress and its leaders, for example, Mahatma Gandhi, Jawaharlal Nehru, and Vinoba Bhave. His descriptive bibliographies are valuable tools for the Indo-British period. Some of his other bibliographies and reference works include *Chronology of India*, *Encyclopaedia Indica*, *Encyclopedia of India's Struggle for Freedom*, *The National Biographical Dictionary of India*, and *The National Geographical Dictionary of India*.

The *Impex Reference Catalogue of Indian Books*, published since 1960 by the India Book Export & Import Company (New Delhi), lists books in print under authors and subjects with an index.

The *Early Indian Imprints: An Exhibition from William Carey Historical Library of Serampore*, compiled by Katherine Smith Diehl in 1962, lists 330 rare books printed in India with their basic bibliographic information.[19]

The *Primary Sources for 16th-19th Century Studies in Bengal, Orissa and Bihar Libraries* was edited by Katherine Smith Diehl and published by the American Institute of Indian Studies in Calcutta in 1971.

The *PL 480 Accessions Lists* (The Library of Congress, Public Law 480 Program) has been prepared monthly by professional personnel in the Library of Congress field office in New Delhi for India since 1962 and is published for distribution without charge to libraries and interested individuals worldwide. These lists played a large role for bibliographical purposes. Entries include price and description. Entries have been arranged alphabetically by author within each Indic language. Cumulative annual author indexes as well as annual lists of serials of these lists have been published. *Accessions List, South Asia* (Library of Congress), prepared monthly by the Library of Congress Office of New Delhi since 1981, is a record of all publications published in India and Islamabad (Pakistan) acquired for distribution to the Library of Congress and other research libraries in the United States, participating in one or more of the Cooperative Acquisitions Programs. *BEPI: A Bibliography of English Publications* begun in 1976 was an annual that listed scholarly and significant English-language publications from the country. It has since stopped printing. The main section of this source was the author part which provides the full bibliographic information. The *Indian Books in Print* (IBP), compiled by Sher Singh in three volumes, lists books in print in the English language under their author, subject, and title. It is published annually. IBP, 1998, covers eighty-five thousand Indian books published up to December 1997. There are also other ventures like *Reference Catalogue of Indian Books in Print*, in three volumes from 1973 to 1997, and *Recent Indian Books*.

The following titles give some idea of the range of the many other subject and specialized bibliographies. *Gandhiana: A Bibliography of Gandhiana Literature* of Deshpande lists material in various languages such as Hindi, Gujarati, Marathi, Bengali, Urdu, Kannada, Sanskrit, and English. A *Bibliography of Indian Agricultural Economics*, published by the Ministry of Food and Agriculture in 1952, provides bibliographic information on the country's agricultural economics. A *Bibliography of Bibliographies on India*, compiled by D. R. Kalia and M. K. Jain in 1975, lists most of the items for English-language publications. Among these items, eight are for library science. *Indiana: A Bibliography of Bibliographical Sources*, by M. K. Jain and published in 1989, lists bibliographical material on India published in English. Entries have been classified under different subject headings with bibliographical details. An index is provided. The 1972 *Bibliography of Census Publications in India*, compiled by C. G. Jadhav, edited by B. K. Roy, lists all census publications up until the 1961 census. A *Guide to Reference Materials on India*, compiled and edited by N. N. Gidwani and K. Navalani in two volumes and published in 1974, is a source for reference materials on every aspect of the country. *Indian Library Literature: An Annotated Bibliography*, by Ram Gopal Prasher and published in 1971, covers the period 1955–1970, providing listings of about 3,550 articles and books on the Indian library science. It is a useful introduction to the country's library science. A work by Sewa Singh, I. V. Malhan, and R. L. Arora, has updated Prasher's bibliography for the 1971–1980 period and was published in 1986. A second work by Sewa Singh has been updated for the 1981–1985 period, published in 1988. *Indian Library and Information Science Literature*, also by Sewa Singh and published in 1991, covers the period 1986–1989. This 1991 published source is "an attempt at bibliographic control of the publications (English language) pertaining to the Indian librarians, library and information science teachers, and other scholars, of different aspects of library and information science."[20] It provides listings of 2,662 items. During 1981 to 1989, the author provided a total of about 4,650 entries.[21] Part V of this source includes subject and author indexes. The 1991 source by Singh provides listings of 1,322 items for 1990–1991.[22] The series *Handbook of Libraries, Archives, and Information Centers in India*, vols. 11 and 12, edited by B. M. Gupta and published in 1991 and 1992, includes a comprehensive annotated bibliography in the field of library and information science, covering the 1970–1990 period. The two volumes provide total listings of 5,892 entries, which have been arranged alphabetically and are classified under different subject headings. Volumes 11 and 12, an annotated bibliography by Gupta, are comprehensive items on the literature of library and information science in India. In the production of literature of librarianship in English, India ranks after the United States and the United Kingdom.

PRINTED LIBRARY CATALOGS

The catalog of the National Library in Calcutta has been published in over twenty volumes. This catalog has ten volumes of printed entries in Western languages, two volumes of entries in Sanskrit, and four volumes of entries in Bengali. It gives the basic bibliographic information of the deposited books, which are listed under the author, with a mixture of original script and transliteration.[23] This catalog also has three volumes of the Asutosh collection containing subject catalogs of fine arts, literature: American and European, history, geography, travel, and biography in European languages. Volume 4 of the Asutosh collection catalog in science and technology in the European languages was published in 1983. The supplements of several author catalogs have been published by the National Library in Calcutta since 1964. The *Catalog of Civil Publications* of the government of India since 1948 has listed documents that are sold by the Controller of Publications, the Department of Publication (Ministry of Works and Housing), and it is the largest publisher of official documents in the country.[24]

A few catalogs of books in specialized libraries have been published. The *Catalog of Books in the Library of the High Court of Madras, brought up to July, 1961*, by the Madras High Court Library, was published in 1964. The *Author Catalog, 1955 and 1956*, by the Indian Institute of Public Administration Library in New Delhi, was published in 1959. It has been a common practice for many libraries to publish their own lists of additions.

The catalogs of Sanskrit language manuscripts in Indian libraries have been published. The *Catalog of Sanskrit Manuscripts in the Nagpur University Library*, edited by V. W. Karambelkar and published in 1958, lists twenty-five hundred manuscripts with bibliographic details in English.[25]

In the early 1990s, according to S. P. Agrawal, former Director of the National Social Science Documentation Center ICSSR, New Delhi, "The Ministry of Human Resource Development, Government of India, is considering the setting up of a Central Microfilm Library and Documentation Center to locate, preserve, and mobilize judicious use of rare manuscripts in the country. The Ministry already has a program of providing financial assistance to the institutions for converting old documents into microfilm."[26]

GUIDES TO PERIODICAL AND NEWSPAPER LITERATURE

In 1955 the first effort was made in publishing the *Nifor Guide to Indian Periodicals, 1955–56*. It was a very useful source of information for Indian periodicals which were classified by language, subject, and geographic location. *Indian Periodicals: An Annotated Guide*, by N. N. Gidwani and K. Navlani and published in 1969, is another effort for Indian periodicals in the English language. *Indian Periodicals in Print*, compiled by H.N.D. Gandhi and others in two volumes and published in 1973, is also a useful source for Indian periodicals. The three-volume *Quinquennial Serials Cumulation*, published by the Library of Congress field office in New Delhi in 1977, is another useful source in this connection. The *Indian Periodicals Record*, formerly *Indian Periodicals*, published from 1966 to 1972, was a useful subject guide to periodicals. *Directory of Periodicals* published in India (1994) was compiled by Susheel Kaur and P. Sapra. The second edition published in 1994 covers seventy-two hundred periodicals. This is an excellent directory of Indian periodicals.

Newspaper indexing provides some assistance in the bibliographical control of Indian serials. The *Press in India*, published by the government, is issued annually in two parts from 1957. Part 1 covers the Report of the Registrar of Newspapers. Part 2 covers catalog of Newspapers. The *Indian News Index* in 1963, 1965, and 1970 covered "news items, editorials, leading articles, letters to the editors, statements, sports, profiles, obituaries, supplements, magazine sections, book reviews, contemporary events at the national and international levels in all fields of human activity and is arranged under specific and related subject headings word by word"[27] (e.g., Agricultural Administration—India; Agriculture—India). The *Indian Press Index* (IPI) published by the Delhi Library Association since 1968 indexes articles, special features, editorials and some important statements and letters in seventeen daily newspapers published in the country. An introduction, alphabetical index, author index and geographic index are contained in each issue of IPI.[28] The IPI was published as a monthly from 1968 to 1983. Later on it stopped. The *Social Science News: Index to Select Indian Newspapers in English*, published by the Center for Research in Library and Information Studies, National Social Science Documentation Center, in New Delhi since 1986, is a comprehensive guide to the country's daily newspapers in the social sciences. *Abstracts and Index of Reports and Articles*, a quarterly from 1963, is useful for economics and public administration. Indian, selected foreign government and UN reports, and the articles are chosen from Indian periodicals and newspapers. The *Directory of Periodicals Published in India: A Classified Guide, 1986–87*, was published in New Delhi. The *Press and Advertisers Yearbook* is a source that gives information about Indian newspapers.

INDEXES AND ABSTRACTS TO PERIODICAL LITERATURE

The *Guide to Indian Periodical Literature: Social Sciences and Humanities* since 1964 is a quarterly publication, which was modeled after the American *Social Sciences and Humanities Index*. The guide is a subject-author index to articles in the social sciences and humanities in the English language periodicals published in India.

Index India: A Quarterly Documentation List on India of Material in English, Combining in One Sequence, Indian Newspaper Index, Index to Indian Periodicals, Index to Composite Publications, Index to Biographical Profiles, Index to Book Reviews, Index to Theses and Dissertations, with Separate Author and Subject Indexes. The title *Index India* describes the broad scope of this index. It lists worldwide materials on India. The cumulative indexes of some Indian library science journals have been published. Two examples are: *33 Years of Annals of Library Science & Documentation: Cumulative Index, 1954–86*, compiled by A. Tejomurthy and K. H. Shukla and published in 1988, records about 588 articles. *20 Years of Library Herald: A Cumulative Index*, vol. 1–20 (1958/59–1981/82), published by Delhi Library Association in 1983, lists 369 articles with author, title, subject, book reviews, and reviewer indexes. The *National Index of Translations*, published since 1977 by the Indian National Scientific Documentation Center, has been a valuable index for English translations of foreign language scientific and technical publications. *Indian Dissertation Abstracts*, published since 1973 by the Indian Council of Social Science Research, is a quarterly journal for summaries of doctoral dissertations mainly in the social sciences approved by Indian universities. *Indian Library Science Abstracts*, published by the Indian Association of Special Libraries and Information Centers since 1967, lists articles with abstracts of the Indian library science periodicals in English and modern Indian languages.

Other indexes and abstracts that have been developed include *Abstracts of Books, Reports and Articles*, a quarterly published by the Parliament Library and Reference, Research, Documentation and Information Service in New Delhi; *Social Science Research Index*, published by the National Social Science Documentation Center in New Delhi; *Indian Science Abstracts*, published by the Indian National Scientific Documentation Center in New Delhi; and *Indian Psychological Abstracts*, published by the National Social Science Documentation Center in New Delhi. *The Index to the Indian Legal Periodicals*, published since 1963 by the Indian Law Institute, lists the legal articles appearing in Indian periodicals.

GOVERNMENT PUBLICATIONS IN INDIA

The *Indian National Bibliography*, published monthly, provides information about government documents in English and regional languages in India. The *P.L. 480; Accessions List, India*, published since 1962, is also useful. *Accession List: South Asia*, published monthly by the Library of Congress Office in New Delhi since 1981, is also valuable for current information about government documents. The *Parliament Library Bulletin* published weekly by the Parliament Library in New

Delhi is another bibliographical tool for current information about government documents. *The Catalog of Civil Publications of the Government of India* (later under the title *Catalog of Government of India Civil Publications*) is published irregularly by the Controller of Publications in New Delhi and provides reports and surveys by ministries and departments of the government of India. It had been the bibliographical tool since the early 1950s, giving information about the government publications. Some libraries attached to Ministries of the Central Government, such as Ministries of Education, Labor, Law, Information and Broadcasting, Finance, and Agriculture brought out the catalogs or their holding lists. *List of Publications*, issued by various ministries of the government of India, was published by Lok Sabha Secretariat in 1959. The price lists of government publications for sale have been published in India. Various ministries of the central government publications for sale are listed in the *Catalog of Civil Publications*. Indian government publications are sold through agents in the country and agencies worldwide. The Publications Department of the government of India is ranked as one of the largest publishers among people in the country. Mohinder Singh's *Government Publications of India: A Survey of Their Nature, Bibliographical Control and Distribution Systems, including over 1,500 Titles*, published in 1967, covers over fifteen hundred publications of about 250 government offices, ministries, and departments.

The second bibliographical tool by Singh is *Government of India Publications*, published in 1982. The publishing activities and the distribution system of the Government of India have been described by the author. Singh has also brought out *State Government Publications in India: 1947–82* in two volumes, published by Academic Publications (Delhi) in 1985, which is a select bibliography of the publications of the various state governments. The publications by Singh are very useful sources for bibliographical control of government publications in the country. The *Chronological Tables of Central Acts, Regulations and Ordinances* published in 1958 (Delhi) is a very useful tool for the control of laws and statutes. It contains central acts, regulations, ordinances, and acts of the president from 1934 to 1957.[29]

DISSERTATIONS AND THESES

There is adequate bibliographical control of dissertations and theses dealing with India and fields of interest relating to the country. There are bibliographies, abstracts, and lists of academic dissertations and theses submitted to universities in the country that are available to aid in the bibliographical control of dissertations and theses.

Social Sciences: A Bibliography of Doctoral Dissertations Accepted by Indian Universities, 1857–1970, published in 1974 (New Delhi), records about 2,820 entries, including 4 entries in library science.

Research in Library and Information Science in India: A Bibliography of Ph.D., M.Phil., M.Lib. Sci. Dissertations, compiled by P.S.G. Kumar in collaboration with A. Tejomurtby and H. R. Chopra, published in 1987, covers "1780 entries including 1641 M.Lib.Sci. dissertations, 74 Ph.D. dissertations, 13 M.Phil. dissertations and 52 Ph.D. research projects in progress, submitted or in progress from 1965 to 1985."[30] *Bibliography of Research in Library and Information Science in India,* compiled by Vijay Pathak and L. S. Ramaiah, published in 1986, lists 1,026 entries: 966 for M.Lib.Inf.Sc. and associateship dissertations, and 57 for Ph.D. theses. The publication of the University of Delhi, *Research in Library and Information Science: A Bibliographical Survey,* compiled by R. K. Sharma and published in 1987, lists 408 dissertations submitted to the University of Delhi for M.Lib.Sc., M.Phil. and Ph.D. degrees.[31] A number of other Indian library schools issue lists of dissertations and theses approved and accepted in their own institutions.

Educational Investigations in Indian Universities, 1939–1961: A List of Theses and Dissertations Approved for Doctorate and Master's Degrees in Education, published by the National Council of Educational Research and Training in Delhi (1966), records 2,941 theses, by the name of university with author and subject indexes.

Research in Progress: A Record of Subjects Taken by Scholars Registered for Doctoral Degrees with the Indian Universities during 1958–1966, was published by the Inter-University Board of India (1968–1972), in four volumes.

FESTSCHRIFTEN

Volumes of essays written by colleagues, friends, and former students in honor of a distinguished, well-respected prominent scholar or librarian have been published. Such a *Festschriften* volume is awarded on a suitable anniversary or on birthdays. One title in this category is *Index to Papers in Commemorative Volumes,* published by the Bhandarkar Oriental Research Institute, postgraduate and Research Department Series 5, in Poona (India) in 1963, with author and title index. It provides the contents of 129 of over 250 *Festschriften* published from 1888 to 1957. It includes 4,644 essays in Indian and European languages.

In the field of library and information science, *Festschrift* volumes of prominent librarians have also been published for, for example, S. R. Ranganathan, P. N. Kaula, D. N. Marshall, S. R. Bhatia, C. G. Vishwanathan, V. A. Kamath, S. N. Srivastava, J. S. Sharma, K. A. Isaac, K. S. Deshpande, B. S. Kesavan, P. B. Mangla, and B. Guha.

BIOGRAPHY

Biographical material is available in biography collections for India. The updated *India: Who's Who,* published annually since 1969, contains an alphabetical index of the biographies. The *National Biographical Dictionary of India,* compiled by Jagdish S. Sharma in 1972, notes about five thousand persons with a comprehensive index. *The Directory of Booksellers, Publishers, Libraries and Librarians in India (Who's Who),* 2d ed., edited by Raj K. Khosla, 1973, offers in the second section biographical entries for about eight hundred prominent Indian librarians. Other biographical directories include the 1980 *Handbook of Information Scientists and Librarians in India,* compiled by Neelima Kaul; the 1988 *Who's Who Among Library* and Information Science Teachers in India, compiled by H. R. Chopra and others; the 1989 Directory of Foreign Language Scientific and Technical Translators in India, compiled by the Indian Scientific Translators Association; and the 1985 Directory of Professors and Readers in Indian Universities, published by the UGC.

UNION CATALOGS AND LISTS

Union catalogs and union lists have been developed in the country. The Union Catalog of Learned Periodical Publications in South Asia, compiled by S. R. Ranganathan and others, vol. 1: Physical and Biological Sciences, 1953, published with the assistance of UNESCO, records about 6,000 periodical holdings of about 424 participating libraries. Entries contain full bibliographical information. The National Union Catalogue of Scientific Serials, compiled between 1965 and 1978 by the Indian National Scientific Documentation Center (INSDOC), published 17 volumes supplying information of holdings of about 30,000 scientific serials in 530 libraries of the country. The National Union Catalog of Scientific Serials in India, produced by INSDOC, is available in print and CD-ROM and is also accessible online. It covers thirty-six hundred titles. The Union Catalogue of Medical Periodicals in India was published by the National Medical Library in several editions. The Union Catalog of Social Science Serials, published by the National Social Documentation Center (NASSDOC), 1970–75 in 32 volumes, supplies the location of 31,125 serials in 535 different types of libraries in the country. The task of updating this union catalog has been carried out.[32] The Union List of Social Science Periodicals Currently Received in Libraries at Delhi, Mysore, Andhra Pradesh and Bombay, was compiled as the first phase by the Social Science Documentation Center of Indian Council of Social Science Research (ICSSR), starting in 1970. During 1971–1972, four volumes of the union list have been published, covering the number of periodicals currently received in Delhi libraries, libraries in Karnataka, libraries in Andhra Pradesh, and libraries in Bombay. The union list of Delhi has been kept updated. In 1985 it recorded 2,909 periodical titles in Delhi libraries.[33] Other catalogs and lists that have been developed in the country include the Holding List of Social Science Periodicals in Chandigarth, 1963–1984, published by the ICSSR; the Union Catalogue of Newspapers Available in Delhi Libraries, published by the NASSDOC; the Union Catalogue of Books on Library and Informatics Publications, published by the NASSDOC; The Union Catalogue of Serials in Fifty-Five Academic Libraries in the State of Rajasthan; and the Union List of Serials in Humanities and Social Sciences in the Libraries in Mysore City.[34]

REFERENCE BOOKS

Along with the increase of general publications, the numbers of valuable reference works have also increased. The field of library and information science has a variety of reference tools as a result of the development of degrees (M.Lib.Sc., M.Phil., Ph.D.) in librarianship at universities in the country. Some among other reference sources in the field of library and information science include the 1977 *Indian Library Chronology*, by P.S.G. Kumar, which supplies a chronological record of the published material on library science in the country through 1975. The *Handbook of Libraries, Archives, and Information Centers in India*, edited by B. M. Gupta and others, is a sixteen-volume set in the field of library and information science. Sixteen volumes of the set have been published. The contents of the sixteen volumes include *Libraries and Archives* (vol. 1); *Libraries and Archives* (vol. 2); *Information Policy, Systems and Networks* (vol. 3); *Asia-Pacific Cooperative Information Systems, Networks and Programs* (vol. 4); *Information Technology, Industry and Networks* (vol. 5); *International Cooperative Information Systems, Networks and Programs* (vol. 6); *Science and Technology Information Systems and Centers* (vol. 7); *Social Sciences Information Systems and Centers* (vol. 8); *Humanities Information Systems and Centers* (vol. 9); *Professional Organizations and Associations* (vol. 10); *Archives, Libraries and Information Technology: An Annotated Bibliography* (vol. 11–12); *Bibliometrics, Scientometrics and Informetrics* (vol. 13); *Social Science and Humanities Information Centers and Sources* (vol. 14); *Indian Languages Reference Sources, Bibliographical Control and Publishing Industry* (vol. 15); *Library Developments in India* (vol. 16). S. P. Agrawal, general editor of the series *Concepts in Communication, Informatics & Librarianship* (CICIL), has published sixty volumes. The first volume in the CICIL series is called *Development of Library Services in India: Social Science Information*, by S. P. Agrawal, and volume 60 is *Librarianship and Library Science in India: An Outline of Historical Perspectives*, by Mohamed Taher and Donald Gordon Davis, 1994.

The library associations have been publishing directories of libraries. The 1985 *Indian Library Directory*, 4th ed., compiled by Joginder Singh and A. R. Sethi, provides extensive coverage of 1,595 Indian libraries. The *Directory of Special and Research Libraries in India*, 2d ed., published by the Indian Association of Special Libraries and Information Centers (IASLIC), covers five hundred libraries. The 1983 *Directory of Government of India Libraries*, published by the government of India Librarians Association (now the Association of Government Librarians and Information Specialists), lists one hundred twenty-seven libraries.

Another type of publication is the annual review of progress in the country. Two examples are *Year's Work in Indian Librarianship, 1987*, compiled and edited by T. S. Rajagopalan, 1988, and *Advances in Library and Information Science*, in two volumes, edited by C. D. Sharma and D. C. Ojha, 1988–1989.

Dictionaries in the field have been published; only two are noted here: the 1989 four-volume *Encyclopaedic Dictionary of Library & Information Science*, compiled by P. P. Parmar and P. Bhuta, and the 1990 *Dictionary of Library Science*, by R. N. Chopra.

The Indian Standards Institution (now the Bureau of Indian Standards) plays a major role in standardizing bibliographic descriptions. In the areas of library and information science, the following standards, among others, have been compiled: (1) Recommendations for bibliographical references (IS 2381:1978); (2) Guide for the preparation for bibliographical description sheet for technical reports (IS 9400:1981); (3) Guide for preparation of abstracts (IS 795:1976).[35]

As for classifying books on Indian philosophy and Indian religions, the *Dewey Decimal Classification for Indology*, by Pandey Suraj Kant Sharma, was published in 1979; it is the expansion and modification of the Dewey Decimal Classification (18th ed.) for classifying Indological books with special reference to Indian philosophy and Indian religions. The AACR2 was adopted in 1987 by the National Library of India for cataloging books.

The *Statistical Abstract of the Indian Union*, published annually since 1950, is a statistical source for the country that provides various statistics on India's economy and society.

The *Directory of Publishers and Booksellers in India*, compiled and edited by Anand Sagar and published by New Light Publishers in 1986, provides information on the country's publishers and booksellers. The *Directory of S&T Information Systems*, published in 1990, provides about one hundred computerized databases developed in different types of Indian libraries and information centers.

Such Indian research institutions as the NISTADS, DRTC, and INSDOC, among others, have been active in publishing survey and research reports, directories, guides, and other sources. For example, the *Guide to Records Relating to Science and Technology in National Archives of India*, published by NISTADS in 1982, and the *Directory of Awards and Rewards in Science and Technology*, by INSDOC, supplies about three hundred entries in the directory.

DATABASES AND INFORMATION TECHNOLOGY

Some of the available bibliographic data are now available on computerized databases and can be retrieved online. INSDOC is an online institution, maintaining "various databases, such as those on polymer science, Indian patents, medicinal and aromatic plants, and materials science, as well as its *National Union Catalogue of Scientific Journals* and a table of contents database, which scans about one thousand sci-tech journals."[36] The *Library of Indian Agricultural Research Institute* has maintained a database of Indian Agricultural research in card form. The National Library has developed "a standardized chart of diacritics for automatic bibliographic services in Indian languages."[37]

Such Indian information centers as the Center for Development of Instructional Technology, New Delhi, NASSDOC, New Delhi, and National Informatics Center, New Delhi, among others, have automation facilities for documentation and other activities. The National Informatics Center, for example, has assisted Indian government departments in computerization of their data and has been successful in developing 150 databases. Even databases developed on an international scale are available by some libraries and institutes in the country. For example, the literature search services of INSDOC include access to various CD-ROM databases, such as *Applied Science and Technology Index* and *Science Citation Index*, and online DIALOG and STN.

INTERLIBRARY LOAN SERVICE

Users' physical access to the necessary materials is possible in certain libraries, through interlibrary loans, or by users' visit to the libraries holding those materials. The National Social Science Documentation Center (NASSDOC) supplies the copies of the requested documents (research reports, theses, and other documents). About eight hundred thousand copies were supplied to scholars and other users during 1991–1992.[38] There is a cooperation of library resources between NASSDOC and other libraries in New Delhi. NASSDOC has also acquired a copy of each Ph.D., M.Phil., and master's degree dissertation in the social sciences, including library and information science. These dissertations are available for consultation by users' visit to NASSDOC. India's National Library also provides interlibrary and international loan facilities, and INSDOC, through satellite communications, is connected to networks worldwide.

The status of bibliographic control in the country has developed remarkably and has achieved a certain standard. The country has been producing enough original and important primary sources to require bibliographic control.

BIBLIOGRAPHIC CONTROL PROBLEMS

With respect to bibliographic control and services, there are problems that require careful consideration. The Seminar on Bibliographical Organization and Control was sponsored and financed by the government of India's Ministry of Education in 1962. The scope of the seminar was, "library resources of various forms (particularly in the English language) relating to India and/or of interest to Indian scholars and research workers, as available in libraries and other institutions in India, and techniques and tools for locating, retrieving and preserving library materials."[39]

The National Seminar on Bibliographical Control in India was organized by India's National Library in 1985. It discussed the problems and prospects of developing services for bibliographical control of the country's literary heritage with particular attention to the improvement of the INB.

Fundamental, too, are the problems set by classification and cataloging. Of the more widely used classification systems, an expansion of the Dewey schedule on Indian history has been provided by Bal Krishan in the *Herald of Library Science* 4(3) (1965), 220–228. John P. Comaromi and M. P. Satija, in their article, "History of the Indianization of the Decimal Classification," *Libri* 35(1) (March 1985), supply about eighty references on the problem of adaptation and amendments of the DDC on Indian subjects.

The study of the cataloging problems has been published; only four are noted here. Jashu Patel has published an article titled "International Problems in the South Asian Bibliographical Information Service," *International Library Review* 15 (1983), 95–103; references and a selected bibliography are provided on the problems of cataloging. A second contribution is C. P. Shukla, "Cataloguing Problems of Indic Names: A Commentary on Resolution of the Seminar on Indic Names," *Iaslic Special Publication* 2 (1961), 24–32. A third contribution is Virendra Kumar,

"Pseudonyms in Indian Literature: Some Problems in Cataloguing," *Library Herald* 7 (1964), 249–258. A fourth contribution is by Upinder Kumar Tikku, "Cataloguing Practices in India: Efforts for Standardization," *International Library Review* 16 (1984), 285–298.

EDUCATION FOR BIBLIOGRAPHIC CONTROL

For settling bibliographic control problems, the librarian's role will become an important factor as it is a responsibility of a librarian to assist library users to make the most of those tools, and it will be the librarians who will make the requested materials available to library users. To achieve the results, librarians should recognize the importance of bibliographic control and have enough knowledge about the related activities. In this context, Maureen Patterson, then bibliographic specialist for South Asia, University of Chicago Library, on the education of South Asian Bibliography, wrote:

There is great continuing need for interpretation of the existing tools for the individual reader, be he beginning student or advanced scholar. In this age of both increasing specialization and increasing interdisciplinary approach, it is the trained South Asian bibliographical specialist and reference librarian who is needed to supplement and interpret the available printed tools. And . . . he is needed to aid in the development of new tools.[40]

A course (i.e., paper) has been offered on "Bibliographical Control and Service" by the (British) Library Association for its professional examination in librarianship. Another relevant course has been offered on the librarianship and bibliography of South Asia by the (British) Library Association. In the United Kingdom developments in graduate programs have been reported at the University of London. The School of Librarianship and Archives has offered since 1966 a program on the bibliography of Asia and Africa leading to a graduate diploma, has offered programs leading to master's, master's of philosophy, and doctorate degrees in librarianship, all of which are providing an Asian specialization. The master's program provides an option on regional studies in bibliography and librarianship.

Gorman proposes an outline for a bibliographic control syllabus, which contains both traditional and newer technology oriented elements. Among the more current applications of cataloging reflected in Gorman's teaching plan are Bibliographic Control and Library Automation; Bibliographic Control and Databases/Networks; and Bibliographic Control in the Online Environment.[41]

NOTES

1. Michael Gorman, "How Cataloging and Classification Should Be Taught," *American Libraries* (September 1992), 694.

2. Ibid.

3. Timo Kuronen and Paivi Pekkarinen, "Ranganathan's Five Laws of Library Science Revisited—The Challenge of the Virtual Library," *Herald of Library Science* 35 (1–2) (January–April 1996), 5.

4. Timo Kuronen and Paivi Pekkarinen, "Equity and Information," *Library Herald* 32 (1–2) (April–September, 1994), 1–13.

5. Martin Kesselman, "Report from IFLA (1992) and the International Library Technology Fair," *Wilson Library Bulletin* (December 1992), 78.

6. Jagdish S. Sharma, "India's Contribution in the Field of Bibliography," *Library Herald* 16 (3–4) (October 1974–March 1975), 97.

7. Jesse H. Shera, *Introduction to Library Science* (Littleton, Colo.: Libraries Unlimited, 1976), 136.

8. Quoted in Donald Davinson, *Bibliographic Control*, 1st ed. (Hamden, Conn.: Linnet Books, 1975), 7–8.

9. Ibid., 8.

10. Doralyn J. Hickey, "Bibliographic Control in Theory," *IFLA Journal* 6 (3) (1980), 241.

11. Pauline A. Cochrane, "Universal Bibliographic Control: Its Role in the Availability of Information and Knowledge," *Library Resources* and *Technical Services* 31 (October 1990), 429.

12. Ibid., 428–429.

13. H. K. Kaul, "Publishing in India—The Challenges Ahead," in P. B. Mangla et al., eds., *Fifty Years of Librarianship in India, Past, Present and Future*. Twenty-ninth All India Library Conference, 1983, Mysore University (Delhi: Indian Library Association, 1983), 456–457.

14. *UNESCO Statistical Yearbook 1995* (Paris: UNESCO, 1995), 7–38, 7–103.

15. Barbara L. Bell, *An Annotated Guide to Current National Bibliographies* (Alexandria, Va.: Chadwyck-Healey, 1986), xix.

16. A. J. Wells, "Ranganathan's Influence on Bibliographical Services," in Edward Dudley, ed., *S. R. Ranganathan: 1892–1972* (London: Library Association, 1974), 13.

17. Ibid.

18. John T. Thomas, "India's Contribution to Library Science: A View from the Western World," in V. V. Venkatappaiah, ed., *March of Library Science: Kaula Festschrift* (New Delhi: Vikas, 1979), 106.

19. Benoyendra Sengupta, "Bibliographical Organization and Control: The Indian Scene," in N. B. Sen, ed., *Progress of Libraries in Free India*, 1st ed. (New Delhi: New Book Society of India, 1967), 119.

20. Sewa Singh, *Indian Library and Information Science Literature* (New Delhi: Ess Ess Publications, 1991), v–vi.

21. Ibid., vi–vii.

22. Sewa Singh, *Indian Library and Information Science Literature, 1990–1991* (New Delhi: Concept, 1994), 10.

23. Maureen L. P. Patterson, "Bibliographical Controls for South Asian Studies," *Library Quarterly* 41 (April 1971), 90.

24. Jagdish Saran Sharma and D. R. Grover. *Reference Service and Sources of Information* (New Delhi: Ess Ess Publications, 1987), 261.

25. M. K. Jain, *Indiana: A Bibliography of Bibliographical Sources* (Concepts in Communication, Informatics & Librarianship Series—4) (New Delhi-Concept Publishing, 1989), 213, item no. 1492.

26. S. P. Agrawal. *National Information Resources for Social Sciences in India: Mobilization, Dispersal and International Enhancement* (Concepts in Communication, Informatics & Librarianship Series—36) (New Delhi: Concept Publishing, 1992), 31.

27. C. P. Vashishth, "Bibliographical Control of Newspaper Contents in India," *Library Herald* 17 (1–4) (April 1975–March 1979), 109.

28. G. E. Gorman and J. J. Mills. *Guide to Current Indexing and Abstracting Services in the Third World* (New York: Hans Zell, 1992), 163.

29. Benoyendra Sengupta, "Indian Government Publications (Documents): Their Bibliographical Control," in K. K. Bhattacharjee, ed., *Modern Trends in Librarianship in India* (Calcutta: The World Press, 1979), 123.

30. E. M. Gupta, *Handbook of Libraries, Archives & Information Centers in India*, vol. 11 (New Delhi: Aditya Prakashan, 1991), xxv.

31. Ibid.

32. Agrawal, *National Information Resources for Social Sciences in India*, 35.

33. Ibid.

34. Ibid., 35–36.

35. Gupta, *Handbook of Libraries, Archives and Information Centers in India*, xx.

36. Kesselman, "Report from IFLA 1992, 78.

37. D. N. Banerjee, "India's National Library." *Herald of Library Science* 33 (3–4) (July–October 1994), 234.

38. Agrawal, *National Information Resources for Social Sciences in India*, 38–39.

39. J. C. Mehta and N. N. Mohanty, *50 Years of Indian Library Association: 1933–1983* (Delhi: Indian Library Association, 1983), 37.

40. Maureen Patterson, "Bibliographical Controls for South Asian Studies," *Library Quarterly* 41 (2) (April 1971), 100.

41. Gorman, "How Cataloging and Classification Should Be Taught," 697.

SELECTED BIBLIOGRAPHY

Babel, L. S. "The National Problem of Bibliographical Control." In N. B. Sen, ed., *Progress of Libraries in Free India*, 1st ed. New Delhi: New Book Society of India, 1967, 204–213.

Banerjee, S. R. "Bibliographic Control of Materials" (IASLIC Special Publication, No. 1). Calcutta: IASLIC, 1960, 181–199.

"Bibliographical Control: An Annotated Bibliography." In B. M. Gupta, ed., *Handbook of Libraries, Archives, and Information Centers in India*. Vol. 11. New Delhi: Aditya Prakashan, 1991, 64–77.

"Bibliographical Services and Databases." In T. S. Rajagopalan, ed., *Year's Work in Indian Librarianship, 1987*. Indian Library Association 1988, 169–179.

Biswas, Subhas C. "Bibliographical Control in Indian Libraries." In Albertine Gaur, ed., *South Asian Studies*. London: British Library, 1986, 190–195.

Ghosh, Arun. "Bibliographic Control of Social Science Literature in India." *IASLIC Bulletin* 36 (3) (September 1991), 111–120.

Gorman, G. E., and J. J. Mills. *Guide to Current Indexing and Abstracting Services in the Third World*. New York: Hans Zell, 1992.

Gorman, Michael. "How Cataloging and Classification Should be Taught." *American Libraries* (September 1992), 694–697.

Hickey, Doralyn. "Bibliographic Control in Theory." *IFLA Journal* 6 (3) (1980), 234–241.

Jain, M. K. *Indiana: A Bibliography of Bibliographical Sources*. New Delhi: Concept, 1989.

Johnson, Donald Clay. "The Bibliographical Heritage of the British Influenced Areas of Southern Asia." *Libri*. 23 (2) (1973), 109–121.

Kalia, D. R., and M. K. Jain. A *Bibliography of Bibliographies on India*. Delhi: Concept, 1975.

Kaul, H. K. "Publishing in India: The Challenges Ahead." In P. B. Mangla et al., eds., *Fifty Years of Librarianship in India, Past, Present and Future*. Twenty-ninth All India Library Conference, 1983, Mysore University. Delhi: Indian Library Association, 1983, 453–460.

Khurshid, Anis. "Problems of Bibliographical Accessibility of South Asian Collections." *International Library Review* 15 (1) (January 1983), 61–94.

Kuronen, Timo, and Paivi Pekkarinen. "Equity and Information." *Library Herald* 32 (1–2) (April–September 1994), 1–13.

———. "Ranganathan's Five Laws of Library Science Revisited—The Challenge of the Virtual Library." *Herald of Library Science* 35 (1–2) (January–April 1996), 3–17.

Patel, Jashu. "International Problems in South Asian Bibliographical Information Services." *International Library Review* 15 (1) (January 1983), 95–103.

Patterson, Maureen. "Bibliographical Controls for South Asian Studies." *Library Quarterly* 41 (2) (April 1971), 83–105.

Sarin, Ashok Kumar, and Janak Raj Sharma. "Bibliographical Services in India" (IASLIC Special Publication, No. 14, Parts 1–2). Calcutta: IASLIC, 1972, 309–328.

Satija, M. P. "Bibliographical Control of Indian Library and Information Science Literature." In B. M. Gupta et al., eds., *Handbook of Libraries, Archives, and Information Centers in India*. Vol. 2. New Delhi: Information Industry Publications, 1986, 645–656.

Sengupta, Benoyendra. "Bibliographical Organization and Control: The Indian Scene." In N. B. Sen, ed., *Progress of Libraries in Free India*, 1st ed. New Delhi: New Book Society of India, 1967, 115–121.

———. "Bibliographical Organization and Control of Government Documents and Technical Reports in India." In Sewa Singh, ed., *Librarianship and Library Science Education: A Collection of Essays in Honor of Dr. J. S. Sharma*. New Delhi: Ess Ess Publications, 1989, 319–333.

———. "Indian Government Publications (Documents): Their Bibliographical Control." In K. K. Bhattacharjee, ed., *Modern Trends in Librarianship in India*. Calcutta: The World Press, 1979, 121–126.

Sethi, A. R. "Bibliographical Control of Indian Publications in English: An Assessment." *ILA Bulletin* 17 (1–2) (April–September 1982), 14–23.

Sharma, Jagdish S. "India's Contribution in the Field of Bibliography." *Library Herald* 16 (3–4) (October 1974–March 1975), 87–138.

Taher, Mohamed, and A. Majeed Pangal. "Bibliographical Control of Islamic Literature in India: Perspectives. *Islamic Culture* 58 (April 1984), 161–169.

Thomas, John T. "India's Contribution to Library Science: A View from the Western World." In V. Venkatappaiah, ed., *March of Library Science: Kaula Festschrift*. New Delhi: Vikas, 1979.

Vashishth, C. P. "Bibliogrpahical Control of Newspaper Contents in India." *Library Herald* 17 (1–4) (April 1975–March 1979), 105–116.

Vyas, S. D. "Bibliographical Control of Social Sciences in India." *Indian Library Association Bulletin* 15 (1–2) (June 1979), 25–37.

Wells, A. J. "Ranganathan's Influence on Bibliographical Services." In Edward Dudley, ed., *S. R. Ranganathan: 1892–1972*. London: Library Association, 1974, 13–15.

❧ 8 ❧

Professional Organizations

There are a variety of professional organizations and associations (more than seventy) in India that are organized along national, state, and local levels. Some of the major organizations and associations are described below. Five topics with reference to these organizations are included: objectives, membership, organization, activities, and publications.

THE INDIAN LIBRARY ASSOCIATION (ILA)

The ILA was founded in 1933 during the first All-India Library Conference in Calcutta. The establishment of the ILA was achieved through the efforts of prominent librarians and others. Some of these individuals included K. M. Asadullah, R. C. Manchanda, A.M.R. Montague, S. R. Ranganathan, M. O. Thomas, and A. C. Woolner.

Objectives

The association set out the following objectives:

1. Promotion of library movement
2. Promotion of the training of librarians
3. Improvement of the status of librarians
4. Promotion of bibliographic study and research in library science
5. Cooperation with international organizations with similar objectives

6. Publication of bulletins, periodicals, and books

7. Establishment of libraries, documentation, and information centers

8. Promotion of library legislation

9. Provide a common forum to all persons engaged or interested in library and information work by holding conferences and meetings for discussion on professional, technical and organizational issues

10. Accreditation of institutions for library and information science education

11. Promotion and formulation of standards, norms, guidelines for management of library and information systems and services

12. Activities necessary to fulfill the objectives of the association[1]

During the 1944–1953 presidency of Ranganathan, the ILA was involved in several international projects. For example, compilation of the *Union Catalogue of Learned Periodicals in South and South East Asia* was undertaken with the help of a UNESCO grant. Ranganathan was invited to participate in International Federation of Library Associations (IFLA) and International Federation of Documentation (FID) conferences. A new era began under his presidency. In his presidential address to the librarians he presented "a thirty year library development plan" for the country. The original quarterly publication of the association, the *Library Bulletin* (1942–1946) was renamed by him *Annals, Bulletin, and Granthalaya* (ABGILA) with a wider scope in three parts. The first part (Annals) includes research articles, the second (Bulletin) reported news and notes, and the third (Granthalaya) contained articles in the national language of the country, Hindi. Books and directories were published between 1946 and 1953.

Membership

The memberships of the association are divided into the following seven categories: (1) institutional members, which include libraries, schools, and other institutions with library facilities, (2) patron members, (3) honorary members, (4) life members, (5) library association/members, (6) ordinary members, and (7) associate members. As of 1996 the number of membership holders reached 2,301, composed of 165 institutional members, 1,319 ordinary members, 843 lifelong members, and 33 member associations.[2]

Organization

The ILA has a president, six vice presidents, a general secretary, and an executive committee. It is organized to operate through these sectional committees: Library and Information Technology, Education in Library and Information Science, University and College Libraries, Special Libraries, School/Children's Libraries, Public Libraries, Oriental Libraries, Health Science Libraries, Engineering and Technology Libraries, Government Department Libraries, and Agricultural Libraries.

Activities

Major activities of the ILA include sponsoring conferences, seminars, conventions, and other activities on different aspects of librarianship. It has also been observing National Library Week during November since 1968.

The ILA held thirteen conferences between the years 1933 and 1963. Its main activities during the thirty-year period 1933–1963 were as follows:

1. It drafted a model library bill.
2. It started cooperation with the international organizations such as IFLA, UNESCO. The ILA president, Ranganathan, was associated with three UNESCO projects during the early 1950s. They were (a) Standardization of Rules for Rendering South Asian Names in Bibliographies and Catalogs, (b) Preparation of a Directory of Asian Learned Periodicals, and (c) Preparation of a Directory of Asian Reference Books. The ILA also formed a national committee to provide assistance to the 1961 IFLA International Conference on Cataloging Principles in Paris.
3. It arranged advanced training and internship for Indian librarians with the British Library Association in London.[3]

The ILA held twenty-three other conferences between the years 1964 and 1990. It conducted symposia/seminar on Library Legislation; School/Children Libraries; Library Cooperation/Resource Sharing; Library Personnel; Reading Materials/Collection Development; Marketing; Bibliography and Documentation; University Libraries, Their Functions and Problems; Research Libraries in the Country; National Pay Policy for Libraries and Information Centers; National Information System; Computerization and Library Networks; Library Research; Standards; and Library Education.[4] The ILA organized the International Conference on Ranganathan's Philosophy: Assessment, Impact and Relevance, at New Delhi in November 1985.

The ILA is a member of IFLA and the Commonwealth Library Association (COMLA). The ILA, in collaboration with Sarada Ranganathan Endowment for Library Science, organized the Second Regional FID Conference, "Classification and Communication" held in 1985 at New Delhi. The ILA also hosted the 1992 IFLA conference in New Delhi.

Publications

The ILA's publishing program started with the *Library Bulletin*. Although its title has been changed a few times, it has been published since 1942, though it was once suspended in 1946 and was published again as ABGILA from 1949 to 1953 under the editorship of Ranganathan. This title was changed to the *Journal of the Indian Library Association* in 1955, the *Indian Library Association Bulletin* in 1965, and the *ILA Bulletin* in 1975. The bulletin is a quarterly publication which carries not only professional articles on different aspects of library science and librarianship but also promotes the library movement. Another quarterly publication of the association is *ILA Newsletter*, which was started in the 1980s. Besides the bulletin and newsletter, the association has published professional tools, conference and seminar proceedings, and annual reports. The association publications include *Indian Library Directory*, *ILA Members Directory*, *Year's Work on Indian Librarianship*, *A Survey of Public Library Services in India*, and *50 Years of Indian Library Association: 1933–1983*, to name a few.

Since the first U.S. association of librarians in 1876, library associations in other countries of the world have made efforts to promote library services as well as their own status and recognition, and they have succeeded to some extent. The Indian Library Association, like the American Library Association (ALA), has many divisions. However, the ILA is not considered a very strong association in terms of membership. In 1989, for example, members numbered only 2,607. It has no accreditation power. The ALA's function of accrediting library schools has played a decisive role in controlling the standard of the quality of professional librarians. P. N. Kaula, on the future of ILA, in 1970 suggested that "the standardization of library science courses (i.e. programs) at the junior level should be taken up by the national organizations."[5] Another Indian library educator, U. A. Chavan, a decade later in 1981 on accreditation also observed, "Accrediting agency sets definite standards pertaining to all aspects of education which are to be followed by all the schools. If any national association in India sets forth such standards with due consideration to the present problem, certain levels of uniformity can be achieved in the field of library education.[6] One of the objectives of the ILA has been set out as accreditation of institutions for library and information science education. An unfortunate fact is that the accreditation objective has not been achieved.

The status of library development in each country is different from one to another, depending upon the power and influence of the national library association. The number of members and activities of the association, and their impact on the library profession and the society, will depend upon librarians' willingness to contribute to their profession, and their determination to promote their own status as well as their attitude to assist library users. In the context of the Indian library profession, D. N. Marshall, then librarian of the University of Bombay, commented:

The depressing picture of libraries in India is to be viewed as a measure of failure on the part of the profession, inasmuch as it has not built up its image and has no organizational strength to influence public opinion, it is evident that the profession as such has failed to realize its responsibilities toward the society it is called upon to serve. So far, the profession seems to have disregarded the comprehensive functions, which have devolved upon its members in the context of modern life. It is obvious, therefore, that it is time for an effort to be made to create a sense of occasion. . . . The situation demands a radical alteration in the outlook and approach of the members of the profession. Today, it must be admitted that there is little of dedication or devotion, so necessary for the solution of problems that face us (libraries).[7]

The task of comparing one country's library association with that of another country's is not easy. For example, compared to the two oldest library associations in the world, the ALA and the British Library Association, the ILA is not an accrediting agency for library schools. The ALA has great influence on qualifications of librarians, as evidenced by its advertisements of job positions. Candidates are required to have a master's degree in library science from an ALA-accredited institution for academic, public, special, and some other libraries. Candidates without such a degree are generally eliminated from the search process. Library employers in the United States are very strict about librarians' qualifications. There are roughly fifteen library schools without ALA-accredited graduate programs in the United States. Those who graduate from these unaccredited library schools with a master's degree in library science generally seek employment in elementary and secondary school libraries or other library media positions. The unaccredited degree limits them to holding certain library positions throughout their library careers. It is evident that the ALA-accredited degree has certain advantages.

The ILA does not have influence on librarians' qualifications in India. According to the statistics of the ALA membership department, the ALA had 56,688 members as of August 31, 1996, whereas the ILA had only 2,301 members in 1996. Although the ILA has not been an influential and powerful association, it still can benefit from other older associations, which have been powerful and are successful in fulfilling their responsibilities as national associations. To quote B. L. Bharadwaja, president of the ILA from 1978 to 1981:

The Indian Library Association has still to go a long way and has a lot to achieve and has to work consistently and persistently to fully justify its claim to be the premier library organization of the country and has to project the importance of libraries in the educational and cultural development of the nation.[8]

THE INDIAN ASSOCIATION OF SPECIAL LIBRARIES AND INFORMATION CENTRE (IASLIC)

The IASLIC is the second-oldest national library association in the country. It came into existence at a meeting held on September 3, 1955, at the lecture hall of the Indian Museum, Calcutta. Some of the founders of the association were J. Shah, A. K. Mukherjee, and G. B. Ghosh.

Objectives

The association has the following major objectives:

1. To promote library and information service
2. To improve the quality of library and information services
3. To coordinate activities and foster mutual cooperation among special libraries, scientific, technological and research institutions, learned societies, commercial organiza-

tions, and industrial research establishments, as well as other information and documentation centers in social sciences and humanities

4. To improve the technical efficiency of the workers in special libraries and information centers and to take care of their professional welfare
5. To act as a center of research and study in special library and documentation techniques
6. To act as a center of information in scientific, technical, and other fields
7. To undertake other activities that may be incidental and conducive to the attainment of the objectives of the association

Membership

The membership of the association are divided into the following four categories: (1) institutional members, (2) ordinary members, (3) honorary members, and (4) life members.

As of 1997 the number of membership holders reached 1,569, comprising 252 ordinary, 906 life, 405 institutional, 3 donor, and 3 honorary members.[9] The institutional members consist of large business enterprises, small private industries, financial and commercial banks, government departments, academic libraries, public libraries, and a variety of other special libraries. Compared with the numbers of libraries and individuals engaged in the various fields, the membership has expanded well beyond the concept of an association limited to special librarianship. Membership size has attracted the interest of the professionals in the field of librarianship.

Organization

The IASLIC has a president, six vice presidents, a general secretary, and other office bearers. It is organized in six divisions: Documentation Service, Education, Publications and Publicity, Library Services, Documentary Reproduction and Translation, and Cooperation and Coordination of Libraries.

The IASLIC council has created four special interest groups: Special Interest Group on Industrial Information, Special Interest Group on Social Science Information, Special Interest Group on Computer Applications, and Special Interest Group on Humanities.[10]

Activities

The IASLIC's major activities are as follows:

1. It provides bibliographical services on demand.
2. It conducts short-term continuing education programs.
3. It publishes the *IASLIC Bulletin* and the *IASLIC Newsletter*.
4. It advises on problems of libraries and information services.
5. It ensures cooperation among libraries and interlibrary loans.

6. It provides copies of documents to individual researchers and institutions and English translation of articles from foreign languages.
7. It provides an opportunity through a study circle to discuss local problems among professionals.

The IASLIC has been regularly holding seminars and conferences on topics of concern to librarians and senior Indian scientists in the country. Sixteen seminars were organized from 1956 to 1987, and fourteen conferences were organized from 1961 to 1990. The broad areas of issues dealing with the current problems of library science and documentation have been discussed at conferences and seminars, including Mechanization of Library Services; Documentation Problems in India; Industrial Planning and Information Services; Training of Special Librarianship in India; Rendering of Indic Names; Bibliographical Control of Special Libraries; Standardization of Indic Names for International Cataloguing Code; Methods of Scientific Communication; National Science Library for India; Decentralization of Library and Information Services; Users and Library and Information Services; Education for Librarianship in India; General versus Special Classification Schemes; Interlibrary Loan and Exchange of Materials; Dewey Decimal Classification; Library's Role in Research and Development in the Indian Context; Application of Management Techniques to Library and Information Systems; Organization of Data Services in India; User Education and Training Programs; Bibliometric Studies; Marketing of Library and Information Services in India; Financial Management in Library and Information Services; Document and Data Processing in Special Libraries in India; Problems and Prospects of Library Associations in India; Indexing and Abstracting Services in India; and Translation Services.

These seminars and conferences, which were organized by the association, have been held in many cities throughout the country and have attracted a great deal of interest and participation among librarians and scientists. As a result of these seminars and conferences, the IASLIC's contribution to the library profession was noticeable, and the IASLIC raised the status and image of librarians in society.

The association also provided a program titled "Training in Special Librarianship and Documentation" from 1964 to 1970. The association also conducted language courses in German, French, and Russian from 1958 to 1963 for translators for special libraries.

The association has invited Indian and international experts for lectures on different aspects of library and information services.[11] It is affiliated with the International Federation of Library Associations and Institutions (IFLA) and the International Federation for Information and Documentation (FID) and plays its role in international cooperation with IFLA and FID.

The IASLIC medal is awarded each year by the association for the best article published in its bulletin. The association has also undertaken special projects such as the Survey of Library and Information Needs in India.

Publications

The *IASLIC Bulletin*, its official journal, has been published quarterly since 1956 and carries articles in the field of library and information science and other related fields. It is available free to members. The *IASLIC Newsletter* has been a bimonthly publication since 1966 and carries brief news about the activities of librarians and institutions relating to library and information science. It is also free to members. The *Indian Library Science Abstracts* carries abstracts of articles from Indian library and information science journals and books. It started as a quarterly publication in 1967 and currently is published annually.

As of 1987 the association has published about thirty volumes containing papers presented in conferences and seminars on about fifty-two different issues. The association has also published professional tools and aids for librarians and library users. Publications include *Directory of Special and Research Libraries in India, Glossary of Cataloging Terms in (Indian) Regional Languages, Education for Librarianship in India: A Survey, Draft General Code for Interlibrary Loan, Development of Medical Societies and Medical Periodicals in India, 1780 to 1920, Methods of Scientific Communication, IASLIC: Perspective, Performance*, and *Promise—A Silver Jubilee Commemorative Volume, Indexing Systems*, and *Library Architecture*.

Based on the foregoing objectives, activities, and publications of the IASLIC, it can certainly be claimed that it has been an influential and vibrant association. M. N. Nagaraj's observations on the IASLIC provide an appropriate final note:

In spite of all financial or organizational difficulties . . . the Association (IASLIC) has been . . . expanding in different directions. The essential role of the Association has been that of a leader-coordinator, seeking to bringing about a harmonious development in the entire field of librarianship through development and co-ordination of professional thinking and performance of the individuals in the profession. The Association expects one and all interested in this total development to muster strong around the Association banner and help it fulfill its cherished aims and objectives.[12]

THE INDIAN ASSOCIATION OF TEACHERS OF LIBRARY AND INFORMATION SCIENCE (IATLIS)

The IATLIS was founded in 1969 at a meeting of library science teachers at the Documentation Research and Training Center, Bangalore. P. N. Kaula played a major role in founding the IATLIS.

Objectives

The association has the following major objectives:

1. To promote library science education and research
2. To promote the publication of library science education books and periodicals
3. To promote exchange of ideas on library science education

4. To hold conferences and seminars for the development of ideas on library science education
5. To provide consultation services on library science education
6. To promote the training of the library science educators in the country
7. To protect the interests and status of the library science educators in the country[13]

Membership

The number of membership of IATLIS in 1990 reached 112, composed of individual, lifelong, and associate members. The library educators in the United States, Canada, and other countries are encouraged to become life members of the IATLIS.

Organization

The IATLIS has a president, vice president, secretary, treasurer, and executive committee.

Activities

The IATLIS has been holding seminars and conferences on problems of library and information science education. Some topic titles discussed at conferences and seminars have included "Teaching Methods in Library Science"; "Graduate Library Science Education Program: Bachelor of Library Science (B.Lib.Sc.)"; "Relevance of Library and Information Science Education to the Changing Needs of the Country"; "Use of Audio-Visual Aids in LIS Teaching"; "Education for Academic Librarianship"; and "Reconstructing of Library and Information Science Curriculum." In 1981 one of these seminars attracted sixty delegates. Approximately forty-one papers were presented.[14] In 1973 the Graduate Library Science Education Programme was held. Some who contributed their papers were Ranganathan ("Observations on B.Lib.Sci. Course [Program]"), and Pauline Atherton, a professor at Syracuse University Library School ("Putting Knowledge to Work in Today's Library Schools").[15]

The association has promoted the separation of library science departments from the university libraries. It has also urged the UGC for provision of full-time teachers (professors, readers, and lecturers) in library science departments, provision for additional facilities for graduate education and research, and allocation of funds for research. It observes August 12, the birthday of Ranganathan, as Library Science Day.

The association's plans are to establish a clearinghouse on library and information science educational and training material and to maintain a register of specialization of library science teachers and other professionals interested in teaching in the country.[16]

Publications

The *IATLIS Communication*, its official journal, has been published quarterly since 1981 and contains information on library education in India. It is free to members. The association also issues an annual report.

The association has published professional tools and aids for librarians and library patrons. The publications include *Research in Library and Information Science in India: A Bibliography of Ph.D., M-Phil. and M.LIS. Dissertations, Who's Who among Library and Information Science Teachers in India, Directory of Library and Information Science Schools in India, and 33 Years of Annals of Library Science & Documentation: Cumulative Index, 1954–86.*

The history of the IATLIS illustrates the role it has played in education for librarianship. In some ways it has fulfilled its potential. However, when compared with the American Association for Library and Information Science Education (ALISE), the IATLIS has a lot to learn to fulfill its potential. The ALISE has had a long history, from 1915 to the present. As of February 29, 1996, ALISE had $179,718.91 in total assets. As of March 21, 1996, ALISE had a total personal membership of 658, composed of 394 full-time faculty of member library schools, 135 part-time faculty of member library schools, 81 at-large, full-time employed, and 48 at-large, part-time employed/retired persons.[17] The ALICE conferences include job interviewing and discussions about career issues for library and information science teachers and professionals who recently received their Ph.D. degrees or who are near completion of their doctoral dissertations.

ASSOCIATION OF GOVERNMENT LIBRARIANS AND INFORMATION SPECIALISTS (AGLIS)

The Government of India Libraries Association was founded in 1933. The name was changed to the Government of India Librarians Association in 1977 and changed again to the Association of Government Librarians and Information Specialists (AGLIS) in 1987.

Objectives

The association has the following major objectives:

1. To promote the application of information technologies in the library and information field
2. To develop methods of resource sharing among government libraries and information centers and establish cooperation between national and international organizations with similar interests
3. To educate and promote government librarians and information specialists in India
4. To hold conferences and seminars to improve the professional status of the library personnel

5. To publish the association's journal, along with other materials in the field of library and information work[18]

Membership

In the late 1980s the number of membership holders reached approximately 250, and were composed of ordinary, lifelong, fellow, affiliate, associate, and institutional members.

Organization

The AGLIS has a president, two vice presidents, secretary, treasurer, and council members. Some of the past presidents of the association have been A.M.R. Montague, a British engineer and the first president; Sir John Sargent, then educational commissioner in India; B. S. Kesavan, then librarian of the National Library of India, Calcutta; S. R. Ranganathan, then professor at the Delhi Library School; and V. K. Rangra, then deputy director of the Defense Scientific Information and Documentation Centre (DESIDOC, New Delhi).

The association's regional chapters have been located in many cities throughout the country.

Activities

Major activities of the AGLIS are grouped under the following programs:

1. Various Event Programs
   National Conventions and Seminars
   Study tour of libraries abroad
2. Education and Training Programs
   One-year graduate diploma program
   Short-term courses
   Lectures on practical library operations
3. Planning of Library Personnel Development Program
   Planning and promotion of library personnel development
   Status improvement of government librarians
4. Publishing Programs
   ACLIS journal
   Publications on library and information science[19]

The AGLIS has been regularly holding conventions and seminars on a variety of topics. As of 1990 the association has held fourteen seminars in many Indian cities. Some conventions and seminars organized by the former GILA and the present AGLIS have included: Role of Librarians in Socio-economic Development;

Documentation Services in Departmental Libraries; The Establishment of Central Library Service; Government Departmental Libraries: Evaluation of Their Service; The Challenges of New Technologies: (a) New Roles and New Goals for Information Handling; (b) Future Competencies Needed for Library/Information Science Professionals; Acquisition Problems Faced by Government Librarians; Information Technologies in the Management of Libraries and Information Centres; Management of Government Libraries and Information Centres; and Computerization of Government Libraries and Information Centres: Progress and Prospects. Study tours of libraries and information centers of Southeast Asian countries (Thailand, Malaysia, and Singapore) were arranged by the ACLIS in 1986 and 1989.

The association conducted a one-year graduate diploma program in library science. The graduate diploma was recognized as equivalent to the graduate degree (bachelor's of library science) awarded by the library schools of Indian universities for employment in government libraries. It has also been conducting short-term refresher courses for employed librarians.

The association has invited international and Indian experts for lectures on a variety of topics in library and information services. Some of these worldwide library leaders were Luther H. Evans, librarian of the Library of Congress; Milton Lord, president of the American Library Association; F. M. Gardner, UNESCO consultant in India; Ralph Shaw, president of the American Library Association, S. R. Ranganathan, then professor of Delhi Library School, Judith Baskin, principal librarian at the National Library of Australia, and David Cornelius, director of public libraries in Ghana.[20]

The AGLIS has been continuously making efforts for the improvement of salary, service conditions, and status of government librarians. The association's D. R. Kalia Award is awarded biennially to an individual and institution for recognizing outstanding performance.

Publications

The *AGLIS Journal*, the title of which was changed from *GILA Bulletin*, has been published since 1982. It is a quarterly publication that carries not only professional articles in the field of library and information science but also articles about government policy decisions impacting the profession of librarians in India. It is free to members.

Besides the journal, the association's other publications include the *AGLIS Focus* and *Current Library and Information Science Contents*. The *AGLIS Focus*, whose title was changed from the *GILA Newsletter*, has been published since 1987 and is a monthly publication that carries news about the association's activities. It is also free to members. *The Current Library and Information Science Contents* has been published since 1988. It is a monthly publication that includes contents of current professional journals in the field of library and information science. It has also published *The Directory of Government of India Libraries* and a supplement which list the total of 251 libraries.[21] At present the association brings *AGLIS Bullet* and *AGLIS Focus.*

Considering the financial and other resource problems faced by the association, the AGLIS has made efforts to improve the service conditions, salary, and the status of government librarians. In some ways it has achieved its objectives and its future potential looks promising.

OTHER NATIONAL ASSOCIATIONS

Many other national associations are available for those interested in specific aspects of librarianship in the country. Examples include the Indian Association of Academic Libraries, the Indian Association of Agricultural Librarians and Documentalists, the Indian Scientific Translators Association, the Society of Information Science, the Federation of Publishers and Booksellers Association of India, the Computer Society of India, the Association of Writers and Illustrators for Children, the Federation of Indian Publishers, the Association of Indian Archivists, the All-India Federation of Master Printers, and the Medical Library Association of India. The first national association in the country, the All-India Public Library Association, was founded in 1920, as a result of the first All-India Public Library Conference held in Madras in November 1919, and it was sponsored by the Andhradesa Library Association, the first state library association in the country, which was established in 1914. The first president of the All-India Public Library Association was J.S. Khudolkar, then curator of the state libraries of Baroda. The association provided service to progress the cause of the free public library movement in the country, published the *Indian Library Journal,* conducted a summer school of librarianship in 1934, represented as delegates to the annual conferences of the British and American library associations in 1928 and 1933, and the second International Congress of Libraries and Bibliography, held in Spain in 1935. The association also held public library conferences in different cities of the country. Unfortunately, it ceased to exist around 1934 and was replaced by the establishment of another association, the Indian Library Association.

Additional information on other national associations is available in volume 10 of the *Handbook of Libraries, Archives and Information Centers in India.*

STATE LIBRARY ASSOCIATIONS

There are seventeen states in India. All states have library associations and some states have more than one association. For example, the state of Andhra Pradesh has three associations: the Andhra Pradesh Library Association, the Andhra Pradesh Public Library Association, and the Andhra Desa Library Field Workers Association. Some state library associations were founded even earlier than the national associations. These include the Andhra Pradesh Library Association, 1914; the Bengal Library Association, 1925; the Madras Library Association, 1928; and the Punjab Library Association, 1929.

The Andhra Pradesh Library Association

Founded in 1914, the Andhra Pradesh Library Association is the first state library association of the country. Its objectives are to promote the library movement, Telugu language, and culture and to publish works in the field of librarianship. As of 1987 the number of membership was composed of 11 patrons, 456 lifelong individual and 17 lifelong institutional members, 312 ordinary individual, and 96 ordinary institutional members.[22] It has held state conferences, library conferences at the district (county), and the taluk (subdivision of a country) levels. It has also held seminars. Two such seminars held in 1986 were titled "AP (Andhra Pradesh) Public Libraries Act" and "Rural Libraries." The association has organized boat library service, bicycle library service, and even foot mobile service. It has conducted a program of short courses at the certificate level for librarians in the towns and villages. Its monthly periodical is the *Granthalaya Sarvaswamu* (in Telugu language), published since 1915. Besides the periodical, the association has also published a library directory, several pamphlets, and a few books on librarianship.[23]

The Bengal Library Association

Founded in 1925, under its first president, the Nobel Prize winner and poet Rabindranath Tagore, its foundation day is observed as Library Day throughout the state every year. Library Day has been declared by the state government as a holiday for the public library personnel. During this day and the following two weeks, meetings are held all over the state, special supplements to observe Library Day are published, and leaflets and posters describing and advertising the Library Day programs are circulated by the association to all libraries in the state.

In the early 1970s the association had a total membership of over two thousand. In the late 1980s it had a total membership of around three thousand, comprising honorary, donor, lifelong, personal, and institutional members. It has "the record of largest membership among library associations in the country."[24] In the early 1970s it received a state grant of over 50 percent of its income. The association has executive staff and the headquarters. It has a president, five vice presidents, a general secretary, a joint secretary, an assistant secretary, a treasurer, and an editor. The headquarters of the association has facilities for classrooms, lectures, office, and a library.

The association has been active in its library education program at the certificate level. It conducts the summer training courses of four months' duration and weekend courses of seven months' duration. Successful candidates receive certificates.

Since the early 1930s the association had been very persistent in its efforts to promote library legislation for the state. The first attempt was made in 1932 but without any success. Other attempts were made to promote library legislation. Finally, the state of West Bengal enacted a library law and the bill was passed by the state legislature in 1979.[25] The association was instrumental in its efforts in the enactment of library law.

As of 1988 the association has held forty-two all-Bengal library conferences in different locations of the state. The association has invited national and international experts for lectures in the field of library and information science. One of the international library leaders was George Chandler, then president of the International Association of Metropolitan City Libraries. He was one of the early visitors of the association in 1970, and when he lectured to the association there were only about eighty members.[26]

The association has published a monthly journal *Granthagar* (in Bengali language) with abstracts in English since 1961. It contains articles on library science, news of leading librarians, and news of the state and the central governments.

Besides the journal, the association has published professional tools and aids for librarians. The association publications include the *Directory of Libraries in West Bengal*, *Glossary of Library Science Terms in Bengali*, and *Dr. Ranganathan's Draft Library Bill*. It has also published a number of books and pamphlets, including a select list of books in Bengali to assist in book selection, a retrospective bibliography of children's books in Bengali, along with the proceedings of its seminars and conferences.

The Madras Library Association

Founded in 1928, the primary objective of this association is to promote the library movement. As of 1991 its membership numbered over six hundred. Ranganathan was one of its founders, its secretary in 1928, president in 1955 and president emeritus in 1967.[27] It moved to a new building in 1976, which has facilities for association meetings, library, and other activities.

The association's efforts in the enactment of the state library law, drafted by Ranganathan, brought successful results in 1948 when the state legislature passed the Madras Public Library Act, the first public library act in the country. The later library acts of the Indian states (Andhra Pradesh, 1960; Karnataka, 1965; and Maharashtra, 1967) were modeled on the Madras act.

The association founded a school of librarianship under the directorship of Ranganathan in 1929, which was taken over by the University of Madras in 1931. It also organized a course for teachers on school library service. In 1931 the association initiated a mobile library to promote library service in rural areas.

The association has held seminars on topics such as public library services and information networks, public library system library automation, curriculum development for information technology, and information for industry. It has arranged lectures for international experts on a variety of topics in the field of library and information science, including "Resource Sharing in Libraries," by Jean Plaister, president of the British Library Association; "Public Relations as a Management Tool," by Robert C. Usherwood, then senior lecturer, Department of Information Studies, University of Sheffield; "Changing Dimensions of Information Services: The Implications for Curriculum Development for the Future," by Kevin McGarry, College of Librarianship, Wales; "The Invention and Design of Information Products," by Paul Wasserman, professor, University of Maryland College of Library and Information Services; "Library User Education in Britain," by Ruth Alstor, University of Cambridge; "Libraries in the Year 2001," by Wilfred Lancaster, professor, University of Illinois Graduate School of Library and Information Science; "The Commonwealth Library Association," by K. C. Harrison, Westminister Public Library, London; "A Race against Time: Preserving Our Cultural Heritage," by John E. MacIntyre, National Library of Scotland; and "Libraries, Information and the Quality of Life," by D. J. Foskett, University of London Library, on the occasion of the association's golden jubilee in 1979.[28]

The association has organized workshops such as a Workshop on Computer Applications in Libraries and Workshop on Preservation of Documents. Placement and consultancy services are also available on request through the association.

The association introduced the hospital library service in the country for the first time in the late 1920s under the guidance of Ranganathan. It took gifts and voluntary service of young university students and ladies for library service to about forty hospitals in Madras. The association also provided library service to the School for the Deaf and Dumb, prisons, and other institutions.

The association has published a number of Ranganathan's earlier works. It has published professional tools and aids for librarians and some textbooks for library science students. The association's publications include *The Five Laws of Library Science; Library Administration; Prologomena to Library Classification; Theory of Library Catalogue; Reference Service and Bibliography*, vol. 1 and 2; *School and College Libraries; Library Classification: Fundamentals and Procedures; Library Catalogue: Fundamentals and Procedures; Colon Classification; Classified Catalogue Code (CCC); Dictionary Catalogue Code (DCC); Library Legislation;* and *Library Science in India,* to name a few. It has also published three annual volumes of *Memoirs of the Madras Library Association* (1940, 1941, 1944), along with the *Annual Reports of the MALA* (Madras Library Association) on the library development in the province. Additionally, the association has published the proceedings of its seminars, workshops, and a few lectures as occasional publications. The Madras Library Association *Newsletter* has been published quarterly by the a association since 1988.[29]

Punjab Library Association

The association was founded in 1929. The seventh All-India Public Library Conference was instrumental in its establishment. Two of the main objectives among others were "to further the establishment, extension, and development of libraries and to publish books or booklets concerning library development in India and particularly in Punjab."[30]

The association has held conferences. The second conference held in 1932 was attended by about one thousand delegates and visitors. The conference held in the YMCA hall during this occasion had many inspiring mottoes, including: "Libraries are not luxuries but necessities of life;" "The library is a took par excellence to hew down the tree of ignorance;" "A city without books is a city without light;" "The man who reads is the man who succeeds;" and "Reach much, think more, talk less."[31]

Seminars and book festivals are other activities of the association. It has held seminars on such topic titles as "How to Rebuild Libraries in East Punjab," "The Book in India," "Problems of College Librarians," "Library Legislation for Punjab State," "Development of Libraries in Punjab State," "Library in College Instruction," "National Planning and Libraries," "Reading Materials—Their Availability and Use," and "Libraries in the Life of the Nation." The conferences, seminars, and book festivals were "a great success and brought home to the public and the Government the importance of libraries for planned development of library service in the state."[32] One author noted, "The Book Festival organized at Ambala on October 3, 1959 was acclaimed as remarkable by Press and All India Radio."[33]

The association celebrated the library movement's first fifty years (1916–1966) in 1966. A book exhibition on "Punjab through the Ages" was organized during this golden jubilee celebration, and a conference was also held on the topic titled "Library Service and Its Future." Library Service Merit Awards were given to the secretary of the Punjab Library Association, G. L. Trehan, and to the senior librarians. The booklet *Fifty Years of Library Movement in Punjab*, by G. L. Trehan, was distributed to the librarians and visitors. Over one thousand people attended the golden jubilee celebrations.[34] The association has also celebrated the National Library Week every year since 1968.

The association published the *Modern Librarian* in 1931. It was a quarterly journal that carried not only professional articles in the field of librarianship, but also a bibliography of writings by and about Ranganathan, book reviews, and the proceedings of the first three conferences (1931, 1932, and 1933) held by the association. *Modern Librarian* published fifteen volumes before it was suspended in 1946. S. R. Bhatia assumed the association presidency in 1966 and replaced *Modern Librarian* with a quarterly journal, *Indian Librarian*. Its last issue came out in December 1981.

Apart from the journals, the association has also published the Library in India Series and thirty professional booklets in its tools for librarians. These publications include *Guide to Library Literature; Public Libraries in India; Expanded Dewey Decimal Classification of Indian Subjects; Non-Christian Religions, Hindustan, Muhamadanism, History of India; Colon (Classification) System and Its Working; Hints to School Libraries; Service of the Library in Adult Education; Great Books of India; Rudyard Kipling and His First India Editions; Importance of Publishers and Booksellers in India; The Human Elements in the Libraries; Special Libraries; Baroda Libraries; Preservation of Books from Insects; Classification of Urdu Literature; Library Service for Children; Current Trends in the Library Organization; A Directory of Libraries in Punjab*; and the *Punjab Library Service Yearbook*.

Delhi Library Association

Founded in 1953, as a result of the efforts by P. N. Kaula at a conference, the association's main objectives were to promote library movement in the Delhi state, promote training facilities in library science, publish in the field of library and information science, improve the status and working conditions of librarians, and cooperate with other organizations with similar objectives. As of 1990 the number of membership holders reached 517, comprising 295 lifelong, 219 ordinary, and 3 institutional members.[35]

The Delhi Library Association has a president, three vice presidents, a general secretary, a treasurer, two secretaries, and a public relations officer. The headquarters of the association has its own new building.

The association conducts a certificate program in library science of two terms in a year. Of over one thousand applications more than one hundred are selected for a certificate program.[36] The program is designed to train personnel for school librarianship and for junior or semiprofessional jobs in other large libraries of Delhi. The program has been very popular and is recognized by the Delhi administration for the purpose of jobs.

The association has also been conducting a one-year graduate diploma in library science since 1972. The diploma was equivalent to the bachelor's degree in library science for certain purposes. The association has held conferences on topics such as "Library Movement in India" and "Acquistion of Reading and Other Materials." The conference papers have been published by the association.

The association has held several seminars, such as Standardization of International Statistics Relating to Periodicals and Publications; Draft Model Public Libraries Bill; School Libraries: Problems and Prospects; and Reference Sources. The association also sponsored a study circle for discussing the topics of current interest in the field of library and information science until 1990.

The association has invited national and international library leaders and educationists to deliver lectures on a variety of topics. It has also held the Das Gupta Memorial Lectures. The first Das Gupta Memorial Lecture, held in 1967, was delivered by B. S. Kesavan on two topics: "University Libraries," and "Education for Librarianship in India."

The association has been urging the Delhi administration for improvement of school libraries in Delhi State. In the past, it organized an essay competition for school students toward promoting reading habits for a number of years and awarded prizes to the winners.

From time to time the association organizes book exhibitions in Delhi. One such exhibition held in 1953 was on Gandhiana. The other exhibition held in 1956 was on Indian Library Literature. According to N. N. Goil, "Over 250 publications in the English and the vernacular languages were exhibited. A map of India showing important libraries and charts showing the progress of libraries throughout India were also exhibited."[37]

The association has developed cooperation with various Delhi agencies and outside Delhi. The purchase of books by different types of Delhi libraries was negotiated through cooperation with the Delhi State Book-Suppliers Association.[38] The association has also provided technical assistance in organizing the libraries in Delhi.

The *Library Herald*, the association's quarterly publication since 1958, carries scholarly and professional articles in the field of library and information science. It also reviews library and information science materials. From time to time special issues of the *Library Herald* on some aspects of library and information science are published. Its cumulative index of the first twenty years has been published by the association. Edited by Professor Krishan Kumar, the journal is free to members. The association published the monthly *Indian Press Index* (1968–1983), which indexed seventeen daily English newspapers.

The association's professional tools and aids for librarians publications include *Directory of Libraries and Who's Who in Library Profession in Delhi; Indian Library Literature; Library Movement in India; University Libraries and Library Education in India; College Libraries in India: Needed a Policy for Development; Classification* and *Communication: Papers Presented at the Second Regional Conference of FID/CR; Dictionary of Pseudonyms in Indian Literature; Delhi Library Association: Fifteen Years of Activity, 1953–1967; Acquisition of Reading Materials;* and *20 Years of Library Herald: A Cumulative Index to vol. 1–20.*

OTHER STATE LIBRARY ASSOCIATIONS

There are other state associations that serve the interests of their geographic areas. A few states also have separate associations serving the needs of academic and public librarians. Examples include the Andhra Pradesh Public Library Association, the Andhra Desa Library Field Workers Association, the Bihar Rajya Pustaklaya Sangh, the Bombay Science Libraries Association, the Gomantak Graiithalaya Sangh, the Gujarat Granthalaya Sangh, the Gujarat Pushakalaya Mandal, the Haryana Library Association, the Karnataka Library Association, the Kerala Library Association, the Maharashtra Federation of the College Library Association, the Rajasthan Library Association, and the Uttar Pradesh Library Association.

Two American library pioneers in British India who inspired the establishment of state library associations were William A. Borden (1953–1931) and Asa Don Dickinson (1876–1960). Borden went to Baroda in 1910 at the invitation of the Maharaja Sayajirao Gaekwar (1862–1939) of Baroda. The first professional organization of librarians in the country, the Baroda Library Club, was founded in 1912. Borden was instrumental in its establishment. He wrote, "I have induced the members of my staff to start the Baroda Library Club, which meets monthly and which already has respectable membership."[39] The main objective of the club was to promote the library movement. The club published the *Library Miscellany* in 1912 in three languages of Baroda state: English, Gujarati, and Marathi.

Asa Don Dickinson, the second American library pioneer in India, was invited in 1915 by the University of Punjab to organize its library on modern American lines. The credit goes to Dickinson for founding the Punjab Library Association in the 1916 meeting of librarians. He wrote the *Punjab Library Primer* and was the founding father of modern librarianship in British India. His accomplishments in one year made a significant impact on the future development of libraries and librarianship in India. The accomplishments of these two American library pioneers in two major types of library systems (public and academic) in two types of state government was "so fundamental and deep-rooted that it became the permanent foundation for the growth and development of libraries and librarianship in the whole of South Asia."[40]

Other state associations of libraries and librarians and their details are included in volume 10 of the *Handbook of Libraries, Archives and Information Centers in India*.

PROBLEMS AND PROSPECTS

Some problems that require careful consideration have continued over the years. The IASLIC held a seminar in 1963 on the topic "Problems and Prospects of Library Association in India." It discussed the problems and prospects of library associations in the country. The IASLIC has published the proceedings of the 1963 seminar in *IASLIC Special Publication* 6 (part 2) (1966).

There are numerous library associations. In the early 1980s ILA president, B. L. Bharadwaj (1978–1981), commented on the number of library associations and their problems,

Although we have now a very large number of associations . . . there appears to be very little cooperation between their workers. The vastness of the country and the varied interests involved are no doubt an impediment in the way of this coordination. But, its absence has resulted in lopsided developments, duplication of efforts and even waste of energy and resources. There is, therefore, an urgent need for a concerted effort to bring about this coordination and cooperation. It has two aspects: (1) coordination between national all-India bodies and that between the states, and (ii) regional associations and the national associations.[41]

In the late 1980s another ILA president, T. S. Rajagopalan (1985–1988), observed on the problems of numerous library associations,

The proliferation of library associations causes frittering away capacity for collective efforts. Mortality, inactivity, groupism, etc. are not uncommon in the development of library associations in the country. . . . The profession had always felt that library associations should be more effective to plead its cause on issues of crucial importance. . . . The need for a unified approach in matters of establishing and running library associations to look after common interests of the profession is emphasized.[42]

Considering the role of library associations in society and the benefits derived by the profession from their existence, the importance and relevance of the library and its development and progress should be recognized by the society. Different types of libraries need to offer their communities many innovative programs and services. Programs of common concern and cooperation should exist and increase among national and state library associations.

Financial problems are the major cause for slow expansion of programs of library associations. However, through development of national and international conferences, seminars, and other library related activities, if library associations generate influence in the society, then the financial support might be available from the state and federal government. To persuade affluent parts of the society to work for favorable legislation, many library leaders may need to perfect appropriate lobbying techniques within their own states. Library legislation should be of concern to library associations, libraries, and librarians. For example, because legislation at the national level affects professional standards and the status of librarians, these and other issues demand the attention of library leaders. At the national level legislation, the ILA should lead other national library associations. School library legislation, if passed, will prove very useful in the future for establishing an Indian association of school librarians. For favorable library legislation, political efforts are necessary, for example, the ability to compromise when necessary or to express opinions strongly regardless of the consequences. The library associations' relations with state and federal governments may also be a part of a library legislative effort.

Cooperation with other national and state associations in other fields, such as Indian Medical Association and the Indian Education Association, is suggested. The important and substantial work already done at the federal level by associations in other fields may be beneficial to library associations; similarly, the associations in other fields may benefit from library associations.

Library associations in the country continue to be weak, although some have prospered. Depending upon the size of membership and library associations' efforts for the people of India in their search for quality library and information services, prospects remain hopeful.

NOTES

1. C. P. Vashishth, "Indian Library Association (ILA)," in H. M. Gupta et al., eds., *Handbook of Libraries, Archives and Information Centers in India*, vol. 10 (New Delhi: Aditya Prakashan, 1991), 97.

2. Indian Library Association, *Sixty-third Annual Report on the Working of the Association and Audited Statement for the Year 1995–96* (Delhi: ILA, 1996).

3. J. C. Mehta and N. N. Mohanty, *50 Years of Indian Library Association* (Delhi: Indian Library Association, 1983), 1–38.

4. Vashishth, "Indian Library Association (ILA)," 102.

5. P. N. Kaula, "Library Associations in India," *Unesco Bulletin for Libraries* 24 (6) (November–December 1970), 325.

6. U. A. Chavan, "Professional Associations: Their Role and Utility in the Development Programmes of Library Education," *Herald of Library Science* 20 (1–2) (January–April 1981), 67.

7. D. N. Marshall, "Eighth Conference of Indian Association of Special Libraries and Information Centers," in N. N. Gidwani, ed., *Comparative Librarianship* (Delhi: Vikas, 1973), 240.

8. B. L. Bharadwaja, "The Indian Library Association: Its Contribution to the Development of Libraries in India," in S. N. Agarwal et al., eds., *Perspectives in Library and Information Science: Viswanathan Festschrift*, vol. 1 (Lucknow: Print House, 1982), 155.

9. IASLIC, *Annual Report and Audited Statement of Accounts, 1996* (Calcutta: IASLIC, 1997), 3.

10. B. M. Gupta, "Indian Association of Special Libraries and Information Centers (IASLIC)," in B. M. Gupta et al., eds., *Handbook of Libraries, Archives, and Information Centers in India*, vol. 10 (New Delhi: Aditya Prakashan, 1991), 81.

11. Ibid., 82–86.

12. M. N. Nagaraj, "Indian Association of Special Libraries and Information Centers," in Ramkrishna Shah, ed., *Souvenir* (Calcutta: Bengal Library Association, 1988), 17.

13. P.S.G. Kumar, "Indian Association of Teachers of Library and Information Science (IATLIS)," in B. M. Gupta et al., eds., *Handbook of Libraries, Archives, and Information Centers in India*, vol. 10 (New Delhi: Aditya Prakashan, 1991), 92–93.

14. Ibid., 93.

15. P. N. Kaula, "Notes and News," *Herald of Library Science* 12 (2–3) (April–July 1973), 260.

16. Kumar, "Indian Association of Teachers of Library and Information Science," 94.

17. "Association (ALISE) News and Views—Treasurer's Report-Executive Director's Report," *Journal of Education for Library and Information Science* 37 (3) (summer 1996), 286.

18. V. K. Rangra, "Association of Government Librarians and Information Specialists (AGLIS)," in B. M. Gupta et al., eds., *Handbook of Libraries, Archives, and Information Centers in India*, vol. 10 (New Delhi: Aditya Prakashan, 1991), 20.

19. Ibid., 20–21.

20. Ibid., 21–22.

21. Ibid., 22.

22. T. S. Rajagopalan. *Year's Work in Indian Librarianship 1987* (Delhi: Indian Library Association, 1988), 204.

23. S. R. Ranganathan, "Andhra Pradesh Library Association," in *Encyclopedia of Library and Information Science*, vol. 1 (New York: Marcel Dekker, 1968), 416.

24. Rajagopalan, *Year's Work in Indian Librarianship 1987*, 204.

25. Arun Ray, "Bengal Library Association," in Ramkrishna Shah, ed. *Souvenir* (Calcutta: Bengal Library Association, 1988), 152.

26. George Chandler, *Libraries in the East; An International and Comparative Study* (London: Seminar Press, 1971), 04.

27. Suseela Kumar, "Madras Library Association," in B. M. Gupta et al., eds., *Handbook of Libraries, Archives, and Information Centers in India*, vol. 10 (New Delhi: Aditya Prakashan, 1991), 236–238.

28. Ibid., 242–244.

29. Ibid., 240–244.

30. Sant Ram Bhatia, "Punjab Library Association," in *Encyclopedia of Library and Information Science*, vol. 25 (New York: Marcel Dekker, 1978), 28.

31. Ibid.

32. B. M. Gupta, "Punjab Library Association," in B. M. Gupta et al., eds., *Handbook of Libraries, Archives, and Information Centers in India*, vol. 10 (New Delhi: Aditya Prakashan, 1991), 255.

33. M. L. Bliagi, "Library Movement in Punjab," *Herald of Library Science* 3 (1964), 205.

34. "Punjab Library Association," 31.

35. H. R. Chopra, "Delhi Library Association: A Living Monument of P. N. Kaula," in V. Venkatappaiah et al., eds., *Dimensions of Library and Information Science: Kaula Festschrift* (New Delhi: Concept, 1990), 437.

36. Rajwant Singh, "Delhi Library Association (An Appraisal)" in B. M. Gupta et al., eds., *Handbook of Libraries, Archives, and Information Centers in India*, vol. 10 (New Delhi: Aditya Prakashan, 1991), 203.

37. N. K. Goil, ed., *Delhi Library Association: Fifteen Years of Activity, 1953–1967* (Delhi Library Association, 1968), 28.

38. Chopra, "Delhi Library Association," 442.

39. W. A. Borden, "Baroda, India, and Its Libraries," *Library Journal* 38 (December, 1913), 663.

40. "Asa Don Dickinson: American Academic Library Pioneer in British India," *International Leads* 5 (summer 1991), 5.

41. B. L. Bharadwaja, "Library Associations in India," in B. M. Gupta et al., eds., *Handbook of Libraries, Archives, and Information Centers in India*, vol. 2 (New Delhi: Information Industry Publications, 1984–1985), 762–763.

42. Rajagopalan, *Year's Work in Indian Librarianship: 1987*, 199.

SELECTED BIBLIOGRAPHY

Bharadwaja, B. L. "The Government of India Libraries Association." *IASLIC Conference: Souvenir* (December 1967), 61–65.

———. "The Indian Library Association: Its Contribution to the Development of Libraries in India." In S. N. Agarwal et al., eds., *Perspectives in Library and Information Science: Viswanathan Festschrift*. Vol. 2. Lucknow: Print House, 1982, 149–56.

———. "Library Associations in India." In B. M. Gupta et al., eds., *Handbook of Libraries, Archives and Information Centers in India*. Vol. 2. New Delhi: Information Industry Publications, 1986, 755–66.

Bhatia, Sant Ram. "The Indian Library Association: Yesterday and Today." In R. N. Sharma, ed., *Indian Librarianship: Perspectives and Prospects*. New Delhi: Kalyani Publishers, 1981, 228–234.

———. "The Punjab Library Association: Its History, Aims, and Objectives." In *Encyclopedia of Library and Information Science*. Vol. 25. New York: Marcel Dekker, 1978, 27–31.

Chandler, George. "India—Delhi; India—Calcutta." In *Libraries in the East: An International and Comparative Study*. London and New York: Seminar Press, 1971, 67–68, 83–86.

Chavan, U. A. "Professional Associations: Their Role and Utility in the Development of Programmes of Library Education." *Herald of Library Science* 20 (1–2) (January–April 1981), 65–68.

Dixit, K. B. "Problems and Prospects of Library Associations in India." In. N. B. Sen, ed., *Progress of Libraries in Free India*. New Delhi: New Book Society of India, 1967, 71–74.

Ganguly, S. M. "Library Associations on National and State Level: A Critique." In S. K. Kapoor et al., eds., *Role of Information Centers in Technology Transfer and Role of State Level and National Library Associations in Library Development in India*. Calcutta: IASLIC, 1980, 107–116.

Goil, N. K., ed. *Delhi Library Association: Fifteen Years of Activity, 1953–1967*. Delhi: Delhi Library Association, 1968.

————. "Delhi Library Association: A Profile of Performance of the Main Activities during 1960's" *Library Herald* 13 (2) (July–September 1971), 124–139.

Gupta, B. M. "Indian Association of Special Libraries and Information Centers (IASLIC)." In B. M. Gupta et al., eds., *Handbook of Libraries, Archives, and Information Centers in India.* Vol. 10. New Delhi: Aditya Prakashan, 1991, 80–91.

Gupta, B. M., et al., eds., *Handbook of Libraries, Archives, and Information Centers in India.* vol. 10. *New Delhi: Aditya Prakashan, 1991.*

Jain, T. C. "Role and Functions of Library Associations." *Herald of Library Science* 2 (2) (April 1963), 86–92.

Kaula, P. N. "Library Associations in India." *UNESCO Bulletin for Libraries* 24 (6) (November–December 1970), 319–325.

Kesavan, B. S. "Bengal Library Association." In *Encyclopedia of Library and Information Science.* Vol. 2. New York: Marcel Dekker, 1969, 332–334.

Khurshid, Anis. "Library Associations in Asia." *Herald of Library Science* 8 (1–2) (January–April 1989), 3–15.

Kumar, P.S.G. "Indian Association of Teachers of Library and Information Science (IATLIS)." In B. M. Gupta et al., eds., *Handbook of Libraries, Archives, and Information Centers in India.* Vol. 10. New Delhi: Aditya Prakashan 1991, 92–95.

Mehta, J. C., and N. N. Mohanty. *50 Years of Indian Library Association.* Delhi: Indian Library Association, 1983.

Nagaraj, M. N. "Indian Association of Special Libraries and Information Centers." In Ramkrishna Shah, ed., *Souvenir.* Calcutta: Bengal Library Association, 1988, 12–17.

Problems and Prospects of Library Associations in India (IASLIC Special Publication, No. 6, Part 2). Calcutta: IASLIC, 1966.

"Professional Associations." An Annotated Bibliography. In B. M. Gupta et al., ed., *Handbook of Libraries, Archives, and Information Centers in India.* Vol. 10. New Delhi: Aditya Prakashan, 1991, 91–100.

"Professional Associations, Meetings, Literature." In T. S. Raiagopalan, ed., *Year's Work in Indian Librarianship 1987.* Delhi: Indian Library Association, 1988, 198–219.

Ranganathan, S. R. "Andhra Pradesh Library Association." In *Encyclopedia of Library and Information Science.* Vol. 1. New York: Marcel Dekker, 1968, 416.

Rangra, V. K. "Association of Government Librarians & Information Specialists (AGLIS)." In B. M. Gupta et al., eds., *Handbook of Libraries, Archives, and Information Centers in India.* Vol. 10. New Delhi: Aditya Prakashan, 1991, 19–27.

Rao, Raghavendra. "Indian Association of Special Libraries and Information Centers (IASLIC)." In *Encyclopedia of Library and Information Science.* Vol. 11. New York: Marcel Dekker, 1968, 431–433.

Ray, Arun. "Bengal Library Association." In Ramkrishna Saha, ed., *Souvenir.* Calcutta: Bengal Library Association, 1988, 149–152.

Sharma, Jagdish S. "Role of Library Associations for the Betterment of Library Profession." *Indian Librarian* 18 (3) (September 1963), 139–143.

Sharma, R. N. "The Indian Library Association." In *Encyclopaedia of Library and Information Science.* Vol. 38. New York: Marcel Dekker, 1987, 230–233.

Singh, Sewa. "Objectives and Activities of National Library Associations in India: An Evaluation." In S. K. Kapoor et al., eds., *Role of Information Centers in Technology Transfer and Role of State Level and National Library Associations in Library Development in India.* Calcutta: IASLIC, 1980, 117–123.

Vashishth, C. P. "Indian Library Association (ILA)." In B. M. Gupta et al., eds., *Handbook of Libraries, Archives, and Information Centers in India*. Vol. 10. New Delhi: Aditya Prakashan, 1991, 96–108.

❧ 9 ❧

Library and Information
Science Education

HISTORY

Preindependence Period

The present educational system of India is "a product of the British rule and a direct copy of British models,"[1] dating back about two hundred years. In India "library development, with its close ties to education, owes its origin to the British administration. The important libraries of today were established during British rule."[2] There are a variety of educational and research institutions. In 1979 there were 118 universities and 4,460 colleges (excluding preuniversity, intermediate, and junior colleges).[3] In 1998–1999, there were 228 universities[4] and 11,089 colleges.[5]

The history of library education in India began in 1911 in Baroda state. The establishment of a library school in Baroda state was due to the efforts of His Highness the Maharaja Sayajrao III, Gaekwar of Baroda (1862–1939). He was an enlightened ruler, educationalist, and library promoter.[6] He invited "William Alanson Borden (1853–1931), a leading American librarian, who had been a pupil-assistant of Charles Cutter at the Boston Athenaeum and a lecturer-associate of Melvil Dewey at Columbia University's School of Library Economy."[7] Borden was responsible for organizing a free public library system in Baroda state. He envisioned the system in need of trained personnel. He taught the first class in the Baroda Central Library. Describing this first formal training, in 1913 Borden wrote:

I began by selecting a class of ten men and women of exceptional ability and I gave them a thorough training in the theory and practice of librarianship. After they had one year of instruction and another year of practical in the Central Library. I opened a Summer School for town librarians in Baroda City (1913), making the course for five months, and putting the members of original class as instructors. This summer class . . . consists of 25 men whose expenses are paid by the government.[8]

The "Report on Public Instruction" for the year 1910–1911 claimed about the first class that "nowhere in India has there been up to now a single Library class attached to any of the libraries where young men and women could be trained in the most up-to-date requirements of Library economy."[9] An attempt was made in 1912 to introduce a two-year graduate library program at Baroda College, but this program could not be implemented.

Asa Don Dickinson (1876–1960) was another American academic library pioneer in British India who was invited by the University of the Punjab in Lahore (now in Pakistan) for a year during 1915–1916 "to organize its Library on modern American lines." Anis Khurshid wrote:

Some of the developments emanating from British rule significantly differed from the practice then existing in Great Britain itself. For example, the commission of Asa Don Dickinson in 1915 specifically required him to organize the library-training class of Punjab University at Lahore. Such attaining did not exist at all in any British university at that time. The Calcutta University Commission Report (1917–19) on the other hand, stressed the need for appointing of a trained librarian with the status and rank of a professor at Calcutta University. Even this practice was uncommon in British universities where preference for such an appointment was given to those with academic qualifications.[10]

The significant change of American influence at the Punjab University during 1913 occurred due to the appointment of Professor James C. R. Ewing as the vice chancellor of the University of the Punjab (1910–1917). He was an American citizen and had been educated in the United States. As the vice chancellor, he submitted some proposals to the syndicate of the university to allocate "a sum of Rs. 65,000 provided by the government of India for the improvement of the functioning of the University."[11]

Recruitment of "a trained librarian to thoroughly arrange the library and to train a class of young men for such work"[12] was suggested by Ewing. His suggestion was implemented in selecting Dickinson for the position of a temporary university librarian. Dickinson had "received a year's training under Melvil Dewey in the New York State Library. Subsequently, he had 10 years varied experience in library work including 3 years in the Brooklyn Public Library and 3 years in the Washington State College Library."[13] At that time training in librarianship was not available in the British universities. Describing the status of the university librarian in 1915, Anwar wrote, "Dickinson was the first highly educated and professionally trained individual to be appointed as the university librarian in any of the universities in British India. One could extend this exceptional development to most of the British Empire including Great Britain and the British colonies in Asia and Africa."[14] The curriculum introduced by Dickinson covered basic subjects including decimal classification, cataloging rules, list of subject headings, dictionary catalog, and open shelves. The syllabus was enlarged in 1921 by Labhu Ram, a student of Dickinson and the assistant librarian of the University of the Punjab, to include seventy-two lectures instead of the original twenty-five. In 1921 the following subjects were taught: (1) foreign languages; (2) linguistic survey of India; (3) basic selection; (4) law of copyright in England and India; (5) a survey from Tennyson to Bernard Shaw; (6) sources of provincial histories of India; (7) oriental bibliography; (8) milestones of English literatures; (9) library buildings, their designs and equipment; (10) Anglo-Indian literatures; and (11) open access and technical libraries.[15] Dickinson also wrote a library science book, *The Punjab Library Primer* in 1916 in which he described the expansions of Dewey numbers to meet local needs in India as follows: "The Indian librarian will feel the need for further expansions of the 'D.C.' in some fields. . . . The Punjab University Library has in manuscript the elaboration of 290 (Ethnic and other religions) and 495 (Eastern Asiatic languages), which will probably appear in later editions; and has worked out its own expansions of 891.2 (Sanskrit literature) and 954 (History of India)."[16]

The *International Leads* for the summer of 1991 gave the following information about the contribution of Dickinson in library education in India:

Although Dickinson worked in Lahore only for a year, his students and the alumni of his library school established themselves all over India and became leaders in their respective regions, some achieving all India fame. For example, Khan Bahadur K. M. Asadullah was an able student of Dickinson. He worked in the Punjab for some years and then served as the Librarian of the Imperial Library in Calcutta from 1930 to 1947. He made significant contribution to the cause of the library movement in India.[17]

G. C. Bansal and U. K. Tikku, on the beginning of library science education in Punjab wrote, "Outside the USA Punjab University (at Lahore) was the first in the world that introduced a regular training course for librarians at the degree level from as early as 1915."[18] The credit for being the first beginner of library education at the University of the Punjab goes to two American leaders, Dickinson and Ewing. The beginning of library science education in the University of the Punjab was not only the first in India but also "in the East because the other formal library school founded in the East was around 1920 at Boon University in China."[19]

The Andhra Desa Library Association started a library school in 1920. The duration of the course was only for one month. Lectures were delivered by different scholars on various topics in Telugu literature, social work, the history of Andhra, economics, and the library movement. Thus the course was more oriented to the training of social workers than to that of librarians. However, in 1934 the syllabus of the course was modified to include more topics relating to library work.

In 1925 S. R. Ranganathan returned from London, after completing his training in librarianship, to take up the position of librarian of Madras University. He was impressed and inspired by what he observed in England of the potentialities of efficient library service for the public good. He applied the scientific method to solve library problems.[20] He explored his ideas in a series of lectures to an audience of about a thousand teachers who had assembled to attend the conference of the South Indian Teachers Union in 1929. This was followed up by the Madras Library Association starting a new certificate course, an annual summer school of librarianship by Ranganathan. The duration of the course was three months, and subjects of the lectures included laws of library science, classification, cataloging, issue methods, and library routine. This school was taken over by the University of Madras in 1931. In 1937 the three-month training course was upgraded to a one-year full-time postgraduate course, leading to a diploma in library science. Madras University became the first university in India to offer a postgraduate diploma in library science. In 1935 Andhra University started a diploma course.

In 1935 K. M. Asadullah, an able student of Dickinson, started a full-time diploma course in librarianship in the Imperial Library (now the National Library of India), Calcutta. This course was based on the pattern of the Punjab Library School. There was cooperation between the University of the Punjab and the Imperial Library in conducting classes on alternate years (however, the course was offered every year between 1944 and 1946). The course was discontinued after the partition of the subcontinent in 1947.

The Bengal Library Association started a certificate course in librarianship in 1937. The example of the Bengal Library Association was followed by the Bombay Library Association, the Delhi Library Association, the Mysore Library Association, and other library associations in India.

The other university library schools following the example of the Madras Library School were the Banaras Library School, 1941; the Bombay Library School, 1944; the Calcutta Library School, 1946; and the Delhi Library School, 1947. It is evident from the foregoing that in the year of independence (1947), five university library schools offered courses leading to the post–bachelor's degree in library science. The library school at Bombay offered an undergraduate diploma.

Postindependence Period

Following independence, a number of library schools were established in various states. Some are administered by universities or through their affiliated colleges in some states. Delhi was the first to create a separate department of library science; it established the Institute of Library Science in 1958, but it closed down in 1964. Delhi was also the first library school to be under the administrative control of a university. The *Directory of Library and Information Schools in India* "contains information of about 93 schools and other institutions in India, offering training in Library and Information Science at various levels."[21] There are sixty-six schools that offer a bachelor's degree in library and information science, thirty-eight of which offer a master's degree in library and information science, and four of which offer a master of philosophy degree in Library and Information Science. There are nineteen schools that offer a doctoral program in library and information science. There are also three schools offering correspondence courses for a bachelor's in Library and Information Science, and other schools are emerging for this purpose.[22] Today seventy-eight universities offer a bachelor's of library and information science program. Forty universities offer this program through forty-four institutes. Five universities offer a master's of philosophy program, and forty universities have provisions for a doctorate degree.[23]

LEVELS OF LIBRARY EDUCATION

The certificate course is a semiprofessional program. Admission in this program is meant for nongraduates with a high school diploma. The duration of the program is three to six months and is mostly run by part-time faculty. The curriculum includes library administration and organization of library materials. The semiprofessionals with certificates hold junior positions in libraries or join as school or village librarians.

The diploma course in library science was earlier established in many library schools in India. The program lasts one academic year, and the minimum qualification required for admission is a university degree. The graduate diploma course was renamed by some library schools as a bachelor's of library science. The Polytechnics for Women at Ambala, Bangalore, Delhi, Chandigarh, and others offer a two-year diploma course open to high school graduates, which prepares graduates for junior librarian and library assistant positions. The bachelor's degree course leads to the first professional qualification in the field of library science.

The minimum qualification for admission to the master's degree program is a bachelor's degree in library science. Calcutta University experimented with a two-year master's degree program. In a symposium held in September 1986, the head of the Department of Library and Information Science at Osmania University, Hyderabad, decided to introduce the two-year integrated master's program in Library and Information Science. The NEHU was the first university that started this two-year integrated program in 1986. The University of Madras was the next to introduce such a program in 1988. The Institute of Correspondence Education of the University of Madras has also started a master's in library and information science degree program under distance education since 1989.

As a result of computer applications, the University of Mysore took a lead in offering "a one-year diploma course in computer applications to candidates possessing post-master's degree in Library and Information Science."[24]

The master of philosophy in library and information science degree program is offered at some library schools. Delhi was the first to offer the one-year program in 1978. Other schools include Andhra, Tirupati, and Annamalai. The minimum qualification for admission to the Delhi program is a master's degree in library science and a passing entrance examination grade. The Delhi program has three required courses, a dissertation, and one elective.

According to the 1988 statistics, the doctorate in library and information science degree programs have been instituted at twenty schools: Aligarh, Amritsar, Andhra, Banaras, Bombay, Burdwan, Calcutta, Delhi, Gulbarga, Jammu,

Karnataka, Kerala, Madras, Mysore, Nagpur, Patiala, Poona, Punjab, Rajasthan, and Vikram. In 1990 more than twenty-five universities offered Ph.D. programs. The program does not require any course work; it is a research program that enables the student to write a thesis in an area of library and information science under guidance. The minimum qualification for admission to the program is a master's degree in library science. In some universities, such as University of Delhi, the minimum qualification is ordinarily a master's of philosophy degree in library science. The other requirements (e.g., having five years' experience, passing an oral exam) vary from one school to the next. The Ph.D. thesis in evaluated by external examiners. Oral defense is also required for thesis in some schools. Punjab University, Chandigarh, produced "eleven between 1976 and 1986."[25] During the 1980s South Indian universities produced "more than 25" Ph.Ds and in early 1990s "about 50 candidates" were working for doctorates in library and information science in South India.[26] Some of the other schools have registered candidates for the Ph.D. and are working in different areas of research interest (e.g., bibliographic control, classification and cataloging, library legislation, national information systems, manpower, university libraries, library buildings, user studies manuscripts).

There are also programs in the field of documentation, and they are offered by the Indian National Scientific Documentation Center (INSDOC); New Delhi, and the Documentation Research and Training Center (DRTC), Bangalore. Since 1964 the INSDOC in Delhi has offered a two-year program in Documentation and Reprography. Originally called an associateship in documentation, since 1976 the program has been renamed an associateship in information science. The DRTC was established in 1962 at Bangalore. It started a program in documentation, which is equivalent to the master's program in India. The DRTC program, like the INSDOC, is a two-year program. The qualifications for admission to the DRTC program is a bachelor's degree in library science or a master's degree in a subject field with two years' library experience.

Other specialized programs are offered by the Indian Association of Special Libraries and Information Centers (IASLIC) and the National Archives of India. The IASLIC offers a one-year diploma program in special librarianship. The National Archives of India offers a one-year diploma program in archives and related subjects.

CONTENT OF CURRICULUM

The bachelor's of library science courses cover almost all the same subjects originally proposed by S. R. Ranganathan and subsequently recommended by the review committee of the UGC. There are eight or more courses, and all are required. They cover library organization administration, bibliography and book selection reference service, library classification (theory), library classification (practice), library cataloging (theory), and library cataloging (practice). Some schools include some additional subjects. A paper on library development in India (offered by the Andhra School), a project report (offered by the Punjab School), reference

service (practical) (offered by the Poona School), information storage and retrieval (offered by the Banaras School), and indexing and abstracting (practical)
(offered by the Bombay School) are all examples. Four courses in the bachelor's
program were offered in classification and cataloging in all schools. As a result,
flexibility of choosing a variety of courses such as government documents, communications media, research methods, and subject information sources is not provided in the curriculum. Writing about the bachelor of library science curriculum,
Prithvi N. Kaula commented:

As is evident, the scheme of papers (i.e., courses) does not take into consideration developments taking place outside as well as within the country. They do not meet the new functions of the libraries adequately. The emphasis in the scheme of papers should be in
developing adequate and up-to-date library services in institutions.[27]

International library educators Morris Gelfand[28] and Anis Khurshid[29] in their
studies on library education in India also suggested a curriculum change at the
bachelor's level. As a result, some schools have introduced changes in the content
of their curriculum. For example, schools such as Mysore integrated the courses in
theory and practice of cataloging and classification in the curriculum for the bachelor's degree in library science. Shreemati Nathibai Damodar Thackersey (SNDT)
and some other library schools are now offering a course in bibliography and literature of different areas in the humanities, social sciences, and science and technology. In the mid-1980s other changes were made in the content of curriculum for
the bachelor's degree. Information service content was incorporated into the curriculum for the diploma/bachelor's level in the library schools of Bangalore, Delhi,
and some other library schools. Pramod B. Mangla has noted:

With the expansion and development of libraries, information centers/systems in the country, the need to bring in the required emphasis in teaching 'information service' as such in
our curriculum has been well accepted and the curriculum periodically revised and designed
accordingly. An analysis of the curricula of some of our library schools and universities both
at the post-graduate Diploma/Bachelor's degree level and the Master's level indicated that
gradually there has been not only a shift in emphasis towards teaching information service
but also that several new topics of study have been incorporated in the papers dealing with
information service.[30]

The master of library science courses cover eight or nine subjects. However,
there is some variation from school to school. The 1987–1988 curriculum of
Karnatak is given below.[31]

The objectives of the master's degree program in library and information science are as follows:

1. To build up leadership qualities among the candidates
2. To encourage candidates to undertake case studies with a view to impart broader perspectives of the problems involved in the organization and management of the library

3. To acquaint the students with organization and development of the university of subjects and research organization and research methods

The content of courses includes the universe of subject; advanced classification and advanced cataloging (theory); information science; information systems, research and statistical methods; comparative librarianship (focusing on either library in society or choice of public, academic, or special library system to be studied in a comparative setting); advanced classification and advanced cataloging (practical); dissertation, and viva voce; two seminar assignments (one in each term) as well as a tour observation report.

The content of curriculum at the Delhi school in response to new trends and discussions has been revised. Delhi has introduced changes in the content of curriculum in its master's program. It includes courses in information storage and retrieval, computer applications in libraries/information centers, operations research and systems analysis, bibliography and literature, information and literature survey in various subject areas, and information systems and programs.

Several other library schools have introduced courses in information science and other subject areas. Mysore offers courses in information processing and retrieval (theory, practice), choice of system analysis, education for librarianship, information and linguistics, computer applications in libraries, reprography, and library legislation.[32]

The Bombay school differs from other schools in its content of curriculum for the master's program. Its emphasis is on comparative studies in librarianship, research methods and documentation techniques, and current developments in library science. The dissertation is required, and the student must defend its findings orally for the master's program.

Computer applications as a part of library and information science education is now included in the content of the curriculum at different levels of various library schools. In the late 1980s the Department of Library and Information Science at Mysore had introduced a new curriculum for the one-year post-master's library and information science diploma in library automation. The content of courses includes information technology and libraries database systems; programming languages library automation; information storage and retrieval systems; systems analysis and information systems design; practicals: (a) computer programming, (b) information retrieval and SDI, and a project.[33] Mysore's curriculum provides a need in the area of library automation to interested students who would like to have challenging positions in today's changing situation in India.

METHODS OF TEACHING AND EVALUATION

Historical Background: Methods of Teaching

Educators, librarians, library educators, and library science students worldwide were concerned with the problems of methods of teaching and evaluation. In India, for example, the Advisory Committee for Libraries, in its report submitted on

November 12, 1958, recommended that the expert committee, among other things, should consider the problems of "(a) teaching methods; and (b) conduct of examinations."[34] During 1973 the Department of Library Science at the University of Delhi organized an All-India Workshop on the methods of teaching and evaluation in library science. Among the various recommendations made by the workshop, the following were concerning teaching method: "The use of audio-visual aids in the teaching of various aspects of library science should be encouraged. Topics for Project Reports should be selected from the field of library and information science. For Literature Survey, other subjects may also be included with emphasis on the study of literature, sources of information, and bibliographical tools."[35] The Education Commission was appointed by the government of India in July 1964 "to advise the Government on the national pattern of education and on general principles and policies for development of education at all stages and in all aspects."[36] In May 1966 the report was published by the commission. The implications of the report and the Education Commission's recommendations on library education in India have been elaborated by then library educator, Malati Kanbur. Writing about the teaching methods, Kanbur commented:

There is more need for the marked reduction in the amount of formal instructions and a corresponding increase in tutorial work, discussion groups, seminars and independent study in library science courses. The time should be devoted to independent study on some small research project or on solving interesting problems wherein he feels his involvement with the subject. There is also need for change in teaching character of teachers to stimulate curiosity, problem solving ability and originality. Every effort should be made to challenge and stretch the minds of the students by the teachers.[37]

Kanbur also conducted the survey of the library science students on different aspects of library education. The finding of the survey on students' preferences to teaching methods revealed that 64 percent of the students preferred the lecture method, 58 percent practicals, 56 percent discussion, 40 percent tutorials, and 30 percent seminars.[38]

Changes in Teaching Methods

As a result of changes made in the content of curriculum at several levels of education for library and information science in India, workshops, seminars, and a variety of teaching methods now exist. Some of the methods include the lecture method, discussion method, brainstorming case study method, colloquium, practical work, project work, seminar method, tutorials role-playing, audiovisual method, and systems analysis assignments study tour. However, even today the lecture method predominates.

Historical Background: Examination System and Examinations in Librarianship

In the past methods of evaluating university students were based on onetime final examinations at the conclusion of the student program. A similar pattern was in existence in the examinations for degrees in librarianship. Furthermore, the examinations were external in nature. The successful passing of these onetime final examinations resulted in the awarding of a degree. Students who were unsuccessful in passing the examinations did not get the degree. Regarding the examination system, Kanbur reported on the 1964–1966 Education Commission, which stated, "The single reform to bring the desired change in [the] education system is [the] examination system, set syllabus, external examination, cramming habits, [which] all have crippling effects."[39] Kanbur made a survey of the library school students who enrolled during the 1966–1967 academic year in twenty-four universities and found that "the opinion of the majority of the students . . . is that the overall assessment, including their practice hours in the library, tutorials, seminars and discussions, should be preferable to the 'terror' of once [and] for all final examinations."[40]

Analysis of Vikram Library School's Master's of Library Science Examination Results (1971–1987)

Library educators A. Tejomurty and S. Kumar at the Vikram Library School made a statistical study of master's of library science students' performances based on the examination results from 1971 to 1987. Writing about the wastage in professional education, the authors reported, "Out of 116 admitted, 86 students have been awarded M.Lib.Sc. degree. Seventy five students passed in the first attempt, and 11 in subsequent attempts. Thus 29 students could not complete this course."[41] Looking back at the examination procedure, Tejomurty and Kumar commented:

If we look at the examination procedure, there is no provision for any back-paper system. The course has one annual examination of seven written papers, and one dissertation. To pass this examination one has to secure a minimum of 40 percent in each paper, and an aggregate of 50 percent in all the papers combined together. A failure candidate has to appear in all the papers in the next year(s).[42]

On the basis of the foregoing statistical study of student performances at Vikram Library School, the authors concluded that it was very difficult to receive an excellent grade in the Vikram's master's program because of the lack of an internal evaluation and the examination procedure. They observed the need for a change in the examination system and the process of learning.[43]

British educational practices have been influential in India in the past. The British examination system in the United Kingdom was highly criticized by library science students, library educators, and librarians. The problem in gaining the British Library Association's qualifications has been documented by Roy Stokes:

The vast majority of those who go to American library schools will emerge, eventually, with a qualification; this is not true of the British scene. The usual overall pass percentage in the main examinations of the Library Association covering those who have studied by every possible means, is about 40%. The remaining 60% will try again, and occasionally again and again and again, and eventually a fair proportion of these will qualify; but many drop out completely, either out of the profession altogether or simply out of its professional grades.[44]

Observing the library association's examinations, the British library educator D. H. Revill has pointed out:

An examination should test whether the objectives set have been reached, whether the desired terminal behaviors have been attained. Unfortunately, the past examination structure in the British Library Association's examinations with its lack of specific, explicitly stated objectives, cannot do so. This is probably the major reason for continuing and growing student discontent with traditional examinations. . . . They are an inadequate criterion measure.[45]

In India the need for a change in evaluation methods is suggested and anticipated. According to Gerald Bramley's survey:

The position is gradually changing. Indian educationalists realize the pernicious dangers of the examination system (which is a legacy from the British). It is possible to anticipate a movement towards methods more closely aligned to those used in the West, particularly in America, for evaluating a student's ability.[46]

The recommendation made at the Banaras University seminar in 1966 on education for librarianship in India and America suggested that "evaluation of a student should be scattered throughout the year and not only at the annual examination."[47] In this context, Louis Shores, an American library educator, also stated, "Evaluation of students is an important faculty responsibility, and academically this is based on class performance throughout the year and on written or oral examination, and course evaluation by students is considered important."[48] Among the various recommendations made by the workshop on the methods of teaching and evaluation in 1973 in India, the following concerned student evaluations: "The importance of proper evaluation and need for introducing various reforms in the existing methods of evaluation in library and information science was recognised by the workshop."[49]

D. S. Aggarwal, a library educator in India, commented on the U.S. system:

The United States' system of evaluation prescribes for credit system on the basis of the work done by the candidate throughout the year including the weekly assignments, seminars, participation in group discussions and so on, and only a little part of the evaluation work is left for the final examination which, again, is conducted in each of the terms.[50]

It is evident from the foregoing that U.S. methods of evaluating students at the university as well as at the library schools in the past were based on continuous evaluation. As opposed to the British system of the onetime final examination given at the conclusion of the student program, the U.S. system assesses students almost continuously in numerous ways throughout his/her program of study. Furthermore, students are evaluated internally by their instructors at the library schools in the United States. Those who teach also evaluate their students. Examinations are not assessed by the external examiners. Commenting on the Indian system, Aggarwal explained, "External examiners do not find sufficient time and lack the knowledge of the necessary background of the candidate and thus due justice can not be done to the examinee."[51]

In the American Library schools, a variety of methods are used for continuous evaluation of student performance including midterm examination, final examination, term paper or project with an oral report on the term paper or project, oral examination, case study, role-playing, class participation, book report, book review, annotation writing, reference problem, cataloging problem, bibliographic report, book selection projects, and a series of exercises.[52]

The past examination system in India was highly criticized by experts, and as a result the need for a change in the methods of evaluating students became apparent. Other changes in library education in India had also been occurring since the 1970s. For example, a shift to the semester system in some universities took place and new degrees in library and information science were introduced.

Changes in Evaluation Methods

Since the mid-1970s, many universities have developed ways of giving credit for classwork done during the year. K. A. Isaac commented on these changes in evaluation methods:

In several schools sessional marks based on internal assessment are added to the marks of the final examination. Some universities have switched over to the semester system under which two examinations are held, one in November or December and the other in April, and the marks obtained in both along with internal assessment marks determine the final results.[53]

The University of Delhi and North-Eastern Hill University (NEHU) have adopted a semester system and internal assessment methods. In the early 1990s, writing about the evaluation of master's of library and information science students, Krishan Kumar concluded, "Evaluation of students should be done at different stages so that the student knows how well he is doing and the teacher(s) can also modify their approach keeping in view the achievement of the students in terms of the overall objectives of the course."[54]

The 1988 *Directory of Library and Information Schools in India* has revealed the examination and evaluation methods of student performance, which vary from school to school. Some of the methods include final examinations (theory papers), a viva voce test for dissertation, a percentage of marks for internal assessment based on assignments tests and seminars oral examination external examining, and a project report. It is evident from the foregoing that a variety of evaluating methods are now used for students' performance.

STATUS OF FACULTY AND LIBRARY SCHOOLS

In the 1950s the teaching in library schools was generally conducted by part-time instructors, mostly by the librarians from their university libraries. The university librarian became the head of the Department of Library Science. Until the late 1970s many library schools depended solely or mostly on part-time instructors. Some library schools appointed some full-time instructors and they were assisted by part-time instructors. In 1947 S. R. Ranganathan became a full-time instructor at the Delhi Library School. The Aligarh Library School appointed a full-time lecturer in library science in 1956. In the early 1960s ten library schools were able to appoint one or more full-time instructors. These schools include Aligarh, Banaras, Calcutta, Delhi, Kerala, Madras, Nagpur, Punjab, Rajasthan, and Vikram.[55] In 1965 the UGC Review Committee recommended full-time instructors and high qualifications for the appointment of faculty. Progress has been made from part-time faculty to full-time faculty, though slowly.

In the 1980s, based on the recommendations of the UGC, developments in librarianship in India and other countries, and the efforts of library science instructors in the state of Punjab, three library schools—Panjabi at Patiala, Panjab at Chandigarh, and Guru Nanak Dev at Amritsar—received independent status after "a prolonged struggle." The three schools also appointed full-time heads of their independent schools.[56]

The trend is toward a full-time faculty in the library schools. Most schools have now gained an independent status with a full-time head and full-time faculty.

THE FACILITIES

Faculty

There has been an increase in the number of library schools during the past two decades. Due to the increase, there is a problem of finding well-qualified and experienced library science instructors for different levels of programs. Some schools have managed with full-time instructors. The Delhi School in early 1990s was an International Affiliate Institutional member (among other international library schools) of the American Association for Library and Information Science Education (ALISE). The 1992–1993 *Directory Issue of the Association for Library and Information Science* lists nine full-time instructors and one part-time senior programmer for the Delhi School. Among the nine full-time faculty, Krishan Kumar is the head of the Department of Library and Information Science and holds the rank of professor. Three other faculty members also hold full professorship; two are readers (i.e., assistant professors); two are lecturers; and one is a library school librarian with an academic rank. Some of their teaching and research interests include information systems, education for library and information science, international and comparative library and information science, indexing and abstracting, technical writing, statistical research methods, science and technology, intellectual freedom and censorship, academic and public libraries, social science, humanities, networking or cooperation, automation and computerization, computer programming, database design, and management.

Most of the Delhi School faculty members are productive scholars. The published sources[57] reveal their publications of books, chapters in books, and journal articles in different areas of librarianship. Krishan Kumar and Pramod Mangla have also contributed significantly outside the Delhi School. In the past they were presidents of professional organizations. Mangla was vice president of the International Federation of Library Associations and is still active as a special advisor of the IPLA Section for Asia and Oceania.

Some other library school faculty members are also productive scholars and their contributions are well recognized nationally and internationally. They are M. A. Gopinath, former professor, Documentation Research and Training Center, Bangalore, and P.S.G. Kumar, head, Department of Library and Information Science, Nagpur. Furthermore, others, such as K. Navalani, from Patiala, were also Fulbright scholars in the United States.

Equating Qualifications

Some library educators and librarians are interested in practicing library and information science outside of their native country, and for that reason it becomes necessary to equate qualifications in different countries. On the mobility of librarians, Roy Stokes commented, "Our task in the middle of this twentieth century is to create a climate of opinion in which a librarian would consider a move from a library in Washington to a library in Edinburgh or Moscow or Vancouver or Sydney just as reasonable as a move to Seattle."[58]

Mobility of U.S. and British library educators and librarians has occurred in the past three decades. Some British educators, such as D. Batty, R. L. Collison, C. D. Needham, J. Mills, D. J. Foskett, E. P. Dudley, D. Langridge, J. C. Harrison, F. N. Hogg, and W. L. Saunders, were on the faculty of U.S. library schools for a term or longer, depending upon the appointment or immigrant status. Other British educators, such as Norman Horrocks, Michael Buckland, and Blaise Cronin, are continuing their careers in the field of library and information science in America. In the early 1970s the College of Librarianship in Wales had on their faculty a U.S. scholar with a master's of library science degree.

With respect to international employment, Indian qualifications have not always equated with those of the United States or United Kingdom, making mobility for Indian library scholars somewhat difficult. However, now that several Indian universities offer a master's of philosophy and doctorate degree in library and information science, Indo-American and Indo-British cooperation in facilitating scholarly exchanges should follow. Since Indian degrees and knowledge of the field are comparable to their U.S. and UK counterparts, the British Library Association and the International Relations Office of the American Library Association should consider the problem of equating qualifications and suggest possible solutions for implementation. The library profession is a global one, not unlike medicine and engineering. Looking ahead to the future of world librarianship, Richard Krzys and Gaston Litton observed:

Librarianship will have become a profession throughout the world, and its body of knowledge—library science—will by then be composed of the philosophy and theory adequate to the realization of the profession's problems and goals. Not only knowledge . . . but also freedom will be shown through the inner-directed mobility of the librarian of the future . . . no longer will a practitioner feel compelled to work in one city rather, the global librarian will . . . be able to practice librarianship wherever in the world he or she might choose.[59]

At the pre-IFLA conference in New Delhi in August 1992, American and South Asian Library Educators discussed library and information science education. The pre-IFLA conference was organized by the International Relations Committee of the American Library Association. One of the well-known U.S. library educators, Peggy Sullivan, then executive director of the American Library Association, spoke at the conference on international cooperation. Sullivan "stressed the need for changing attitudes of professionals and others toward international cooperation. She suggested exchange of faculty, librarians, students, and researchers between South Asian countries and the United States."[60]

Library and Laboratory

Most library schools are housed in university libraries and lack the minimum physical facilities recommended by the UGC Review Committee in 1965. In his study for standards, Khurshid[61] recommended the desirable standards for library collections, and the collections were below his standards in many universities in India. During 1967, the Department of Library Science at the University of Delhi, which then offered programs leading to post-bachelor's, master's, and doctorate degrees, had two thousand five hundred books in library science and received fifty library science periodicals. During the same year, the Department of Library Science at Gauhati, which offered a program leading to a post-bachelor's degree, had three hundred library science books and received twenty periodicals.[62] The number of these library science collections show the highest and lowest level of library facilities available at the library schools in India during the year 1967. By the late 1970s the number of library science collections have increased at some schools. The Delhi School had about 8,000 books in library science and received 114 periodicals. It has a library science collection librarian similar to most U.S. and British library schools. The Banaras School had six thousand books and received sixty-eight periodicals in library science. At the lowest level there were some newly established library schools which had no separate library science collections library.[63]

In the 1980s some library school librarians are housed within the library schools. The other facilities available at some library schools include audiovisual aids, computer and reprography.

Students and the Admission Requirements

The first professional fifth-year library science degree in India is a bachelor's degree. A bachelor's degree in a subject field is required for admission to the program of bachelor's degree in library science. Prior to the mid-1970s most library schools had admitted students without any library experience. After the mid-1970s prior library experience was required in some library schools for admission into the bachelor's program. Some library schools have a method of "admission tests and/or interviews" for admitting students. Most library schools have also a method of prescribed admission testing for admitting students in the master's program. One to two years of professional library experience is also required for admission to the master's program.[64]

In 1980 Mangla, on women entering the profession of library and information science in India, wrote that "the number of women candidates has been increasing during the past 10-15 years and they now constitute 60-70% of the total in almost all library schools."[65]

Some universities in India have announced their programs for recruitment of students through newspaper advertisements. The salaries of librarians are now improved. The profession of library and information science now has a higher status in society than in the past. These motivations are attracting young men and women in the field of library and information science. However, "attention should be paid to select those who have both the ability to pursue a professional course and are motivated to do service. It has been recommended that the rigorous tests administered to candidates seeking admission to other professional and post graduate studies should also be administered to those seeking admission to library science programs."[66] Scholarships, graduate assistantships, and fellowships like the U.S. and British schools have to be provided to some students in need of financial assistance. The situation in this regard is changing for the better.

Continuing Education of the Faculty

Ranganathan advocated training teachers in library science in the 1960s. He conducted the program for continuing education for teachers of library science once a year at the DRTC in the 1960s. Certain aspects of various teaching methods were included in this program. Library schools from the 1980s to the present time are organizing such continuing education programs for library science faculty and professional personnel, with the financial assistance from the UGC.[67]

The Role of the University Grants Commission and the Indian Association of Teachers of Library Science

The UGC was established in 1953 and a library committee was appointed in 1957. Ranganathan became its chairman and advised it on a variety of subjects relating to libraries and library education. Improvement of library education, among other things, was an important mission of the UGC. To improve and standardize library education, it appointed various committees to seek their suggestions. In the 1950s there were no nationally accepted standards in library education in India, and the UGC made recommendations regarding admission requirements, duration of programs, faculty, teacher-student ratio, and facilities for the bachelor's and master's of library science programs. However, the recommendations were not mandatory. In 1977, a panel on library science was set up by the UGC for improvement of facilities for teaching and research, among other things. The recommendations made by this panel were a "valuable contribution towards the betterment of library science teaching. The Panel is still engaged in exploring the ways and means of improving further library education."[68]

The Indian Association of Teachers of Library and Information Science (IATLIS)

This organization was founded in 1969, and its objectives are to improve the teaching of library science and to energize the teachers of library science through mutual support, evaluation, and cooperative programs. Kaula, then secretary and later president of the IATLIS, wrote, "It held its annual seminar on teaching methods in library science in December 1970. . . . IATLIS conducted a survey of library schools and plans to publish a Library Science Yearbook."[69] In 1988 the IATLIS, through the efforts of H. R. Chopra, A. Tejomurty, and P.S.G. Kumar, brought out the very useful *Directory of Library and Information Schools in India*. In the foreword of this directory, Kaula wrote, "It will . . . help the teachers to understand the growth of Library Science Education in the country during the last 50 years."[70] The directory is useful for comprehensive data of some aspects of library education in India, which are comparable to similar aspects worldwide. Kaula, on the attainment of IATLIS, wrote, "By forming the Indian Association of Teachers of Library Science, India has achieved another distinction in library science by instituting a fellowship for study in library education at DRTC, Bangalore. This has been made possible due to the donation received from a distinguished teacher from the United States."[71]

It is apparent that after the establishment of the UGC, the IATLIS, and efforts made by various other professional organizations and library experts, considerable progress in library education has been made since 1947.

CURRENT ISSUES AND SOLUTIONS

The problems of education for library and information science have been discussed in books, *Festschrifts*, handbooks, national and international conferences, seminars, and workshops since the 1960s. Furthermore, many articles and papers have also been published in the literature of library and information science on most aspects of the field.

Some of the current issues include the following:

1. Employment opportunities
2. Overemphasis on techniques like classification and cataloging
3. Underemphasis on courses on information technology
4. Accreditation
5. Proliferation of library schools, especially at open universities, which leads to a surplus of library and information professionals

Two of these issues are described in the sections that follow.

Employment Opportunities

Since the mid-1970s there has been an increase in the number of library schools offering programs in library and information science. Unlike library schools in the United States, most in India do not offer any placement services for securing professional positions for their graduates. About fifteen hundred B.Lib.Sc./B.L.I.Sc. degree holders, two hundred master's degree holders, and twenty-five associateships are now awarded each year.[72] Up until 1967 the number of graduates who were awarded degrees in India were 5,651. Of these, the Library School of Gujarat reported that 50 percent of its qualified librarians were unemployed; Burdwan and Poona 40 percent; Vikram 30 percent; Aligarh, Nagpur and Shivaji 25 percent; and Baroda and Isabella Thorbun (Lucknow University) Jadavpur, Kerala, 20 percent. Only the library schools of Delhi and Gauhati reported that all its graduates were employed.[73] The vast increase of library science graduates is creating a problem of unemployment in the librarianship profession in India. There is a need for reliable statistics on the demand for library and information professionals from year to year to avoid the problem of unemployment. Increasing student enrollment in the existing programs requires careful consideration.

Accreditation

Accreditation refers to an approval of library schools by an appropriate professional organization. There is no accreditation of library schools by a national professional organization in India, as there is in the United States. The creation of an accrediting mechanism for library education programs leading to the degrees of bachelor's and master's of library science was but one of the UGC Review Committee's (1961–1963) recommendations.[74] Unfortunately, these recommendations did not bring about the desired changes.

Under the present situation, equating degrees is mutually agreed upon by universities. The Interuniversity Board of India, the Association of Indian Universities, the UGC, and the Ministry of Education have also played a role in equating degrees within India as well as the degrees awarded from library schools in foreign countries. Under the present circumstances, it is apparent that it is necessary to explore further questions on accreditation:

1. Is accreditation of library and information science programs necessary in India?
2. If accreditation of library school programs is necessary, which are the most appropriate organizations to be given the responsibility for accreditation?
3. Are there any other alternative methods to accreditation?
4. What process should be followed?
5. Are there elements from the U.S. accreditation model that may be applied to India's programs?
6. If so, is it necessary to invite an American library education expert to serve as a consultant? Are there any benefits from inviting a consultant from the United States?

These questions must get serious consideration before a plan of action is implemented.

CONCLUSION

It is important to anticipate the future demand for library manpower. As recommended by the seminar, "It is high time that proper surveys be made to assess various kinds of job opportunities and the manpower requirements so that the admissions and training program be planned according to the requirements. The State governments be prevailed upon to create more posts of librarians and library workers especially in schools."[75]

Historical and societal differences dictate the variations in the library information science education process from country to country. Equivalence and reciprocity of qualifications may be possible in years to come with international cooperation among employers, library educators, and library associations. Rapid changes in library technology and learning resources are occurring worldwide and have an impact in the content of curriculum. Depending upon their background, candidates in the profession of library and information science should be recruited throughout the world.

APPENDIX 9.1: CHRONOLOGICAL LIST OF UNIVERSITY LIBRARY SCHOOLS' POSTGRADUATE PROGRAMS

Name of the University	City	Diploma/Year of Inception and/or Programs Offered			
		B.Lib.Sc.	M.Lib.Sc.	M.Phil.	Ph.D.
Andhra University	Waltair	1935	1979	yes*	yes

Name of the University	City	Diploma/Year of Inception and/or Programs Offered			
		B.Lib.Sc.	M.Lib.Sc.	M.Phil.	Ph.D.
Madras University	Madras	1937	1977	—	yes
Banaras University	Varanasi	1942	1965	—	1980
Bombay University	Bombay	1944	1968	—	1971
Calcutta University	Calcutta	1945	1975	—	1972
University of Delhi	Delhi	1947	1948	1978	1952
Nagpur University	Nagpur	1956	1984	—	1985
Baroda University	Baroda	1957	1986	—	—
Vikram University	Ujjain	1957	1971	yes	1976
Aligarh University	Aligarh	1958	1971	—	1981
Poona University	Poona	1958	1979	—	1981
Osmania University	Hyderabad	1959	1979	—	yes
Punjab University	Chandigarh	1960	1970	—	1972
Rajasthan University	Jaipur	1961	1974	—	1975
Kerala University	Trivandrum	1961	1979	—	yes
Karnataka University	Dharwar	1962	1971	—	1974
Lucknow University	Lucknow	1962	yes	—	—
S.N.D.T Women's University	Bombay	1961	1978	—	—
Burdwan University	Burdwan	1964	1980	—	yes
Gujarat University	Ahmedabad	1964	1986	—	—
Jadavpur University	Calcutta	1965	yes	—	—
Jiwajl University	Gwalior	1965	1984	—	yes
Mysore University	Mysore	1965	1971	—	1976
Shivaji University	Kolhapur	1965	—	—	—
Gauhati University	Gauhati	1966	yes	—	—
Sanskrit Vishwavidyalan	Varanasi	1967	—	—	—
Marathawad University	Aurangabad	1968	—	—	—

Name of the University	City	Diploma/Year of Inception and/or Programs Offered			
		B.Lib.Sc.	M.Lib.Sc.	M.Phil.	Ph.D.
Kurekshetra University	Kurukshetra	1969	1985	—	yes
Punjabi University	Patiala	1969	yes	—	yes
Bhagalpur University	Bhagalpur	1970	yes	—	—
Bhopal University	Bhopal	1970	1970	—	—
Sagar University	Sagar	1970	yes	—	yes
Ravi Shanker University	Raipur	1971	yes	—	—
Kashmir University	Srinagar	1971	1984	—	yes
Jabalpur University	Jabalpur	1971	—	—	—
Bangalore University	Bangalore	1973	1975	—	yes
Guru Nanak University	Amritsar	1973	1984	—	1988
Madurai University	Madurai	1974	1982	—	yes
S. V. University	Tirupati	1974	yes	yes	yes
Udaipur University	Udaipur	1975	yes	—	—
Sambalpur University	Sambalpur	1976	yes	—	yes
Saurashtra University	Rajkot	1976	1987	—	—
S. K. University	Anatapur	1984	1990	yes	yes
Jammu University	Jammu	yes	yes	—	yes
Patna University	Patna	yes	—	—	—
L. N. M. University	Darbhanga	1976	—	—	—
Calicut University	Calicut	1978	yes	—	yes
Gulbarga University	Gulbarga	1979	1985	yes	1979
Annamalai University	Chidambaram	1979	yes	—	yes
Bhavnagar University	Bhavnagar	1980	1991	—	—
Sardar Patel University	Vallabh-Vidyanagar	1980	1988	1991	—
Mangalore University	Mangalore	1981	—	—	—
A. P. Open University	Hyderabad	1984	—	—	—

Name of the University	City	Diploma/Year of Inception and/or Programs Offered			
		B.Lib.Sc.	M.Lib.Sc.	M.Phil.	Ph.D.
Dr. B. R. Ambedkar-University	Agra	1984	1996	—	yes
Vidya Sagar University	Midnapur	1985	yes	—	—
Jamia Millia Islamia	New Delhi	1985	—	—	—
Guru Ghasidas University	Bilaspur	1985	1995	—	—
South Gujarat University	Surat	1986	—	—	—
Manipur University	Imphal	1986	—	—	—
North-Eastern Hill University	Shillong	—	1986	—	1989
Gujarat Vidyapeeth	Ahmedabad	1988	1986	—	—
Chitrakoot Gramin Vishwavidyalaya	Chitrakoot	1992	—	—	—
North Gujarat University	Patan	1992	—	—	—
Makanlal Chaturvedi-National University of Journalism	Bhopal	1993	1994	—	1995

Note: Several other universities (e.g., Amrawati, IGNOU, Rani Durgawati) also offer a post–bachelor's degree in library science.

*"yes" indicates that these programs are offered.

NOTES

1. K.S. Umapathy, "Education for Librarianship in India," *International Library Review* 9 (1977), 89.

2. Anis Khurshid, "Standards for Library Education in Burma, Ceylon, India and Pakistan," *Herald of Library Science* 9 (4) (October 1970), 335.

3. *Times of India Directory and Yearbook including Who's Who, 1984* (Bombay: Times of India Press, 1984), 197.

4. University Grants Commission (India), *Annual Report, 1998–1999* (New Delhi: University Grants Commission, 1999), 17.

5. Ibid.

6. Murari Lal Nagar, *Foundation of Library Movement in India* (Ludhiana: Indian Library Institute and Bibliographical Center, 1983), 3.

7. Ibid., 2–3.

8. W. A. Borden, "Baroda, India, and Its Libraries," quoted in Anis Khurshid, "Library Education in South Asia," *Libri* 20 (1–2) (1970), 61.

9. *Report on Public Instruction*, quoted in Nagar, *Foundation of Library Movement in India*, 69.

10. Anis Khurshid, "Library Education in South Asia," *Libri* 20 (1–2) (1970), 59–60.

11. Mumtaz Ali Anwar, "Asa Don Dickinson: The Founding Father of Modern Librarianship in British India," *Pakistan Library Bulletin* 21 (2) (June 1990), 13.

12. "Memorandum of the Government of India by the Vice Chancellor," quoted in ibid., 13.

13. Ibid.

14. Ibid., 15.

15. Labhu Ram, "Principal Woolner's Dream, or the Phenomenal Growth of the Punjab University Library, Lahore," quoted in Khurshid, "Library Education in South Asia," 62.

16. "The Punjab Library Primer," quoted in Anwar, "Asa Don Dickinson," 17.

17. "Asa Don Dickinson, American Academic Library Pioneer in British India," *International Leads* 5 (summer 1991), 5.

18. G. C. Bansal and U. K. Tikku, "Library Science Education in Punjab." *International and Library Review* 20 (1983), 395.

19. Abdul Moid, "Library Education in Pakistan," quoted in Anwar, "Asa Don Dickinson," 16.

20. A. Neelameghan, "India, Education for Librarians and Documentalists," in *Encyclopedia of Library and Information Science*, Vol. 11 (New York: Marcel Dekker, 1997), 324.

21. H. R. Chopra, A. Tejomurty, and P.S.G. Kumar, *Directory of Library and Information Schools in India* (Chandigarh: Arun Publishing House, 1988), Preface.

22. Ibid.

23. Jitendra Shrivastava, "Library and Information Science Education in India: Trends, Issues and Implications," In A. N. Raju et al., ed., *Fifty Years of Library and Information Science Education* (Secundrabad: Suchithtritha Graphics, 1997), 5.

24. P. G. Rao and B. R. Babu, "Recent Trends in Education for Library and Information Science in South India," *International Library Review* 22 (1990), 186.

25. Bansal and Tikku, "Library Science Education in Punjab," 400.

26. Rao and Babu, "Recent Trends in Education for Library and Information Science in South India," 184.

27. P. N. Kaula, "Library Science Education," in R. N. Sharma, ed., *Indian Librarianship: Perspectives and Prospects* (New Delhi: Kalyani Publishers, 1981), 196.

28. Morris A. Gelfand, "Survey of University of Delhi Department of Library Science," *Indian Library Association Bulletin* (July–December 1967), 124–125.

29. Anis Khurshid, *Standards of Library Education in Burma, Ceylon, India and Pakistan* (Pittsburgh: University of Pittsburgh, Graduate School of Library and Information Science, 1969), 505–506.

30. P. B. Mangla, "Need for Emphasis on 'Information Service' Course in Curriculum Design with Particular Reference to India," in *Relevance of Ranganathan's Contributions to Library Science*, edited by T. S. Rajagobalan (New Delhi: Vikas Publishing House, 1988), 100.

31. Karnatak University, Post-Graduate Studies in Library and Information Science (M.L.I., Sc.), *Prospectus, 1987–88*, 2, 4, 12.

32. Mysore University, Department of Post-graduate Studies and Research in Library and Information Science—*Restructured M.L.I. Sc. Degree Course*, 1. The co-author (Patel) received the information during his visit as a Fulbright Scholar to the Department of Library and Information Science, Mysore University, January 18–19, 1988.

33. Patel, the co-author, received the notification of approved proposal of a one-year post-M.L.I. Sc. Diploma in library automation during his visit to the Department of Library and Information Science, Mysore University, January 18–19, 1988.

34. India, Ministry of Education, Advisory Committee for Libraries, *Report of the Advisory Committee for Libraries*, rev. ed. (Delhi: Manager of Publications, 1961), 103.

35. "Teaching and Evaluation in Library Science," *University News* 11 (10) (October 1973), 21.

36. Malati M. Kanbur, "Education for Librarianship and Educational System with Special Reference to Education Commission Report," *Herald of Library Science* 7 (4) (October 1968), 256.

37. Malati M. Kanbur, "Education for Librarianship and Educational System with Special Reference, to Education Commission Report (3)," *Herald of Library Science* 8 (2) (April 1969), 114.

38. Malati M. Kanbur, "Education for Librarianship in Indian Universities with Special Reference to Pattern of Entrants—Survey Report," *Annals of Library Science and Documentation* 15 (2) (June 1968), 85.

39. Malati M. Kanbur, *Education for Librarianship with Special Reference to Pattern of Entrants to Library Profession in India* (Delhi: Department of Library Science, University of Delhi, 1968), 86.

40. Kanbur, "Education for Librarianship in Indian Universities—Survey Report," 87.

41. A. Tejomurty and S. Kumar, "Librametric Study of MLIS Results of Vikram University, 1971–87," in *Library and Information Science Education and Teaching Methods* (papers on Ujjain and Gulbarga seminars) (Jaipur: RBSA Publishers, 1991), 95.

42. Ibid., 97.

43. Ibid., 107.

44. Roy Stokes, "In Our Present Differences," *Wilson Library Bulletin* 34 (June 1960), 721.

45. D. H. Revill, "Education for Librarianships Objectives and Their Assessment," *Library Association Record* 71 (April 1969), 108.

46. Gerald Bramley, *A History of Library Education* (London: Clive Bingley, 1969), 119.

47. "Education for Librarianship: Recommendations," *Herald of Library Science* 5 (October 1966), 301.

48. Louis Shores, "Guide to Library Education, Part I: Students." *Drexel Library Quarterly* 3 (January 1967), 59–64.

49. "Teaching and Evaluation in Library Science," 21.

50. D. S. Aggarwal, "Recommendations of the Review Committee on Library Science: An Evaluation," *Herald of Library Science* 6 (April–July 1967), 172.

51. Ibid.

52. Martha Boaz, "Library School Practices in Student Evaluation," Conference on Library School Teaching Methods: Evaluation of Students, in Harold Goldstein, ed., *Library School Teaching Methods: Evaluation of Students* (Champaign: University of Illinois Graduate School of Library Science, 1967), 76.

53. K. A. Isaac, "Methods of Teaching and Evaluation in Library and Information Science Education," in P. B. Mangla, ed., *Library and Information Science Education in India: Papers and Recommendations of an All-India Seminar.* (New Delhi: Macmillan India Limited, 1981), 184.

54. Krishan Kumar, "Evaluation of MLISC Students Using Method of Evaluation by Stage at which Performed," in A. Tejomurty, ed., *Library and Information Science Education and Teaching Methods; Papers of Ujjain and Gulbarga Seminars.* (Jaipur: RBSA Publishers, 1991), 87.

55. P. N. Kaula, "Education for Librarians in India," *Library World* 63 (1962), 225–226.

56. Bansal and Tikku, "Library Science Education in Punjab," 400.

57. *Who's Who among Library and Information Science Teachers in India*, 1988, 16, *India. Who's Who*, 1990–91, 142b–143b.

58. Stokes, "In Our Present Differences," 718.

59. Richard Krzys and Gaston Litton, "Our Professional Destiny: A Global Librarianship," in R. Krzys and G. Litton, *World Librarianship: A Comparative Study* (New York: Marcel Dekker, 1983), 202.

60. R. N. Sharma, "American and South Asian Library Educators Discuss Library and Information Science Education," *Journal of Education for Library and Information Science* 34 (1) (1993), 86.

61. Khurshid, *Standards of Library Education*, 646.

62. Ibid., 600.

63. P. N. Kaula, "Library Science Education," 194.

64. P. B. Mangla, "Library Education in India, Pakistan, and Bangladesh," in *Advances in Librarianship*, vol. 10 (New York: Academic Press, 1980), 201.

65. Ibid.

66. Neelameghan, "India, Education for Librarians and Documentalists," 337.

67. Mangla, "Library Education in India, Pakistan, and Bangladesh," 218.

68. J. S. Sharma, "Librarianship and Library Education in India," in P. K. Gupta and U. Pawan, eds., *Library and Information Science: Current Trends in India: Professor S. N. Srivastava Festschrift* (Jaipur: RBSA Publishers, 1986), 33.

69. Kaula, "Library Science Education," 196.

70. Chopra, Tejomurty, and Kumar, *Directory of Library and Information Schools in India*, foreword.

71. Ibid., 200.

72. Mangla, "Library and Information Science Education in India," in B. M. Gupta et al., eds., *Handbook of Libraries, Archives and Information Centers in India*, vol. 1 (New Delhi: Information Industry Publications, 1984–85), 247.

73. Khurshid, "Library Education in South Asia," 74.

74. India, University Grants Commission, Library Science in Indian Universities, *Report of the Commission Review Committee.* (New Delhi: University Grants Commission, 1965), quoted in Khurshid, "Library Education in South Asia," 68.

75. J. S. Sharma, "Seminar on Problems of Library Science Education in India," *Herald of Library Science* 16 (2–3) (April–July 1977), 233.

SELECTED BIBLIOGRAPHY

Anwar, Mumtaz Ali. "Asa Don Dickinson: The Founding Father of Modern Librarianship in British India." *Pakistan Library Bulletin* 21(2) (June 1990), 12–22.

"Asa Don Dickinson: American Academic Library Pioneer in British India," *International Leads* 5 (Summer 1991), 5.

Bansal, G. C., and U. K. Tikku. "Library Science Education in Punjab." *International Library Review* 20 (1988), 395–403.

Bonn, George S. "State of Library Education in India."*Annals of Library Science and Documentation* 15 (1968), 57–75.

Bramley, Gerald. *A History of Library Education*. London: Clive Bingley, 1969.

Chopra, H. R., A. Tejomurty, and P.S.G. Kumar. *Directory of Library and Information Science Schools in India*. Chandigarh: Arun Publishing House, 1988.

Gopinath, M. A. "Innovative Teaching of Library and Information Science." *Library Science with a Slant to Documentation* 13 (1) (March 1976), 16–23.

Hintz, Carl W. "Education for Librarianship in India." University of Illinois Library School *Occasional Papers* 73 (October 1964), 1–32.

Inamdar, N. B., and Riswadker, M. R. "India," in M. Miles, ed., *International Handbook of Contemporary Developments in Librarianship*. Westport, Conn.: Greenwood Press, 1981, 183–199.

Isaac, K. A. "Need for New Directions in Library Education." *Journal of Library 2nd Information Science* 1 (1) (June 1976), 21–32.

Iyengar, T.K.S. *Education for Librarianship in India*. Chicago: 1967.

Kanbur, Malati M. "Education for Librarianship and Educational System with Special Reference to Education Commission Report." *Herald of Library Science* 7 (4) (October 1968), 249–262; 8 (1) (January 1969), 13–19.

———. "Education for Librarianship and Educational System with Special Reference to Education Commission Report (3)." *Herald of Library Science* 8 (2) (April 1969), 111–121.

———. "Education for Librarianship in Indian Universities with Special Reference to Pattern of Entrants: Survey Report." *Annals of Library Science and Documentation* 15 (2) (June 1968), 76–102.

Kaula, P. N. "Library Science Education." In R. N. Sharma, ed., *Indian Librarianship: Perspectives and Prospects*. New Delhi: Kalyani Publishers, 1981, 183–207.

Khurshid, Anis. "Library Education in South Asia." *Libri* 20 (1–2) (1970), 59–76.

———. *Standards of Library Education in Burma, Ceylon, India and Pakistan*. Pittsburgh: University of Pittsburgh Graduate School of Library and Information Science, 1969.

Kumar, Krishan, and J. L. Sardana. "Research at Doctoral Level in Library and Information Science in Indian Library Schools." *Journal of Library and Information Science* 2 (1977), 119–138.

Mangla, P. B. "Library Education in India, Pakistan, and Bangladesh." in *Advances in Librarianship*. Vol. 10. New York: Academic Press, 1980, 191–240.

———. "Research in Library and Information Science in India." Paper presented at the International Federation of Library Association (IPLA) Conference, Tokyo, 1986 (ED280 478).

Mangla, P. B., ed., *Library and Information Science Education in India: Papers and Recommendations*. New Delhi: Macmillan 1981.

Nagar, Murari Lal. *Foundation of Library Movement in India*. Ludhiana: Indian Library Institute and Bibliographical Center, 1983.

Neelameghan, A. "India, Education for Librarians and Documentalists." In *Encyclopedia of Library and Information Science*. Vol. 11. New York: Marcel Dekker, 1977, 312–349.

Patel, Jashu, et al. "An International Data Collection and Research Program." In John F. Harvey and F. L. Carroll, eds., *Internationalizing Library and Information Science Education: A Handbook of Policies and Procedures in Administration and Curriculum*. Westport, Conn.: Greenwood Press, 1987, 89–104.

Rao, P. G., and B. R. Babu. "Recent Trends in Education for Library and Information Science in South Asia," *International Library Review* 22 (3) (1990), 181–190.

Sharma, C. D. "Library Science Education in United States, Canada, Great Britain and India: Patterns, Equivalences and Illusions." *Herald of Library Science* 10 (3) (July 1971), 222–232.

Sharma, Om Prakash. "The Development of Library Education in India: An Historical Survey." *Library Association Record* 67 (10) (November 1965), 388–394.

Times of India Directory and Yearbook Including Who's Who, 1984. Bombay: Times of India Press, 1984.

Umapathy, K. S. "Education for Librarianship in India." *International Library Review* 9 (1977), 289–301.

❦ 10 ❦

Library Automation

Computerizing Indian libraries has been a rather slow process until recently, largely because of the lack of trained manpower. Since the late 1980s computerization has gained momentum. In the late 1990s the situation has changed completely: more and more library professionals are getting trained in computer application; there are increasing numbers of training programs available for the purpose at different levels; the hardware and software have become more user-friendly; and a wide range of software packages are available suitable for the needs of most libraries.

HISTORY

The automation of routines and information services was initiated in the early 1960s. According to P.S.G. Kumar, "In India, some libraries and information centres made efforts to 'automate' their library routines and information services in the 1960s with punch card unit/sorter and with a couple of second generation general purpose computers that were available at Kanpur and Bombay."[1]

In the early years, the INSDOC and Documentation Research and Training Centre (DRTC), Bangalore, were in the forefront with regard to carrying out experiments in application of computers in the library and information field. According to Ravichandra Rao, the DRTC and INSDOC have been "experimenting with the use of computers in library and information field in India since [the] mid-1960s, with an objective of enhancing the productivity in library operations. Both the centres developed several program packages for catalogue-on-tape, semi-automatic classification (to construct the class numbers), union catalogue, directories, thesaurus construction, information retrieval, SDI service, etc. Apart from these works, both DRTC and INSDOC were teaching the computer applications to library and information field since mid-1960s."[2]

The INSDOC has been a leader in experimentation with computer application in documentation and information work. In 1964 it initially used an IBM 1620 Model I, available at IIT, Kanpur, for processing data in order to compile a union catalog of scientific serials.[3] This was the first experiment on the use of computer for library and information application. The INSDOC processed data for Roster of Technical Translators in India in 1967. Two programs were written for the main part and the indexes.[4]

Haravu and Raizada[5] at the INSDOC performed an experiment to find out the suitability of the IBM 1620 computer for storage and retrieval of data.

The next experiment involved preparing author and subject indexes for the *Indian Science Abstracts*.[6] In 1969 an effort was made to develop a complete and integrated program deck to process data for the "union catalogue for Mysore."[7]

In the early years the DRTC took initiative in using computers for library and information work. Neelameghan[8] published a paper titled "Design of the Document Finding System: General Features" in 1968 in which he described the experiments undertaken at the DRTC on Doc-Finder (a computer used for finding documents).

V. A. Kamath and N. M. Malwad conducted a survey of computer applications in library and information work in India in 1971. They concluded that

There is only *one* library having computerized procedures for procurement; *one* for charging and discharging; *two* for cataloguing; *four* for preparing addition lists; and *one* for preparing union catalogue of periodicals. Among the documentation activities, indexing seems to be more common, though the criteria for indexing are different. There exists *one* computer system for information storage and retrieval, integrating within it a freely faceted scheme of classification such as the Colon scheme of the classification developed by S. R. Ranganathan. Software techniques have been developed in FORTRAN IV, SPS, AUTOCODER and in certain cases COBOL. The programs are meant primarily for the configurations available at the institutions. The libraries generally make use of the spare capacity of available computer facilities which are suitable for the type of work on off-line use.[9]

In the early 1980s P.S.G. Kumar carried out a study covering thirty-seven institutions. He identified seven library routines (book ordering, cataloging, indexing, circulation, serial control, classification and stock taking) and four information activities (CAS, SDI, retrospective searching, and data banks). Kumar concluded:

The experiments conducted at these institutions demonstrated the feasibility of the use of computers in India in library and information work. However, many of these experiments were not brought out into regular operation. After initial experimentation, many of them were abandoned. The reasons were numerous—lack of financial resources, no proper support from authorities, change in personnel, etc. None of these experiments tried to study

economics of computerization. Many did not bother about the measurement and evaluation of the computerized services as compared to manual systems. Almost all the experiments centered around solving simple problems, using in-house hardware and simple
soft-ware packages. Twenty-one out of the thirty-seven institutions have computerized
only one operation. Six of them have computerized a couple of operations. Nine out of the
thirty-seven have computerized 3–8 library operations.[10]

In the early 1980s, libraries of the Bhabha Atomic Research Center/Technical
Information Center (BARC/TIC); the Indian Institute of Technology (ITT); the
Tata Institute of Fundamental Research (TIFR), Mumbai; the Indian Statistical
Institute (ISI), Calcutta; and the Indian Space Research Organization (ISRO),
Bangalore had access to second generation computers.[11]

In 1983 Ravichandra Rao wrote, "Although the world trend in 1980s is towards
the use of on-line systems, either using mini-computers or micro-processors, the
computer-based information systems in India are still in their infancy stage.
Though some information activities and a few library functions have been computerized in different information centres or special libraries (largely attached to
scientific and technical organizations), there is definitely no integrated computer-based information system, even at the local level."[12]

One of the important developments in recent years in India was the implementation

of online retrieval system at the National Aeronautical Laboratory (NAL). In this system,
the databases of the European Space Agency (ESA)/IRS were accessed (through Euronet,
via satellite link between Bombay and Rome, and through a dedicated cable between
Bangalore and Bombay). NAL in Bangalore was linked with the main computer of ESA, situated in Frascati, Italy. INTELSAT provided the vital link in this chain of telecommunication. The ESA/IRS offered more than 70 files of information, primarily science-related.
This project initially cost about Rs. 37 lakhs and the operational cost was about Rs.
1,000/per query. Because of its high operational cost, this project was terminated in April
1988.[13]

This was an experiment that failed because the conditions necessary for its success
did not exist. The cost of technology was too high and the number of users/queries
was far below the optimum level. The process involved lacked foresight, imagination and experience necessary for the successful implementation of such a program. Hardly any marketing of the service had been done.

Since late 1980s computerization of libraries in India has picked up for the following reasons:

1. The policy of the government of India has been to encourage computerization as an important step toward modernizing institutions.
2. The increasing availability of commercial library-specific software packages has allowed
libraries a wider choice meeting its software needs.
3. The increasing use of the CDS/ISIS package has led to the cultivation of a computer culture.

4. The increasing organization of training programs has led to the availability of trained manpower, essential for any meaningful computerization program.
5. Local, regional, and national library and information computerized networks have been established.
6. There has been increasing availability and use of national and international databases.
7. There has been increasing availability and use of newer information technologies (such as CD-ROMs, e-mails, etc.).

Up to the 1980s university libraries were little affected by information technology except in the field of reprography. Under the INFLIBNET program, the UGC started funding university libraries in 1991 to promote automation activities. By March 1998[14] eighty-seven university libraries had been funded for creating core facilities for information access. Thus by the final decade of the twentieth century university libraries were greatly affected by the rapid changes taking place in information technology.

As part of an effort toward globalization, the government of India has made it national policy to take steps to encourage computerization and modernization of its institutions.

In India the Videsh Sanchar Nigam Ltd. (VSNL), an agency of the government, threw open the gates to the Internet to the general public through Gateway Internet Access Service (GIAS).[15] To use this service, one needs to have a minimum of 486 SX PC with 25 MHZ processor speed, 8 MB RAM, 8 MB hard disk space and a modem with 32 bps data transfer capacity. The facilities that VSNL offers include e-mail, telenet, and file transfer protocol (FTP). E-mail enables one to send messages to the users on terminals located elsewhere. FTP allows transfer of files. Telenet enables one to login to a remote computer hooked to the Internet (a network of networks). The facilities offered by VSNL have popularized Internet use among the public.

A new revolution in the searching of databases is taking place in India. Internet connection is being offered by VSNL to educational institutions at a nominal cost. The Internet connection allows access to worldwide information services; Internet resources can be used as a tool for acquiring, cataloging, indexing, storing, retrieving, and disseminating information (through use of different systems such as e-mail, bulletin boards, electronic journals and electronic publications, and FTP); and the Internet can be used for providing reference and referral services. This has encouraged libraries to use the Internet.

On October 24, 1997, the government of India announced an Internet policy that provided for the end of the VSNL monopoly.[16] This is likely to encourage further use of e-mail and the Internet.

Recently, the National Association of Software and Service Companies (NASSCOM) inaugurated video e-mail facility. For Rs. 15, one can transmit video images and the voices for a three-minute duration through public booths. Such facilities are being made available even in rural areas. Thus rural public libraries can take advantage of such a facility, which is quite cheap as compared to telephone charges for long distance calls.

In the 1990s, as a result of the availability of reasonably low-priced technology, and also changes in the attitudes of librarians and authorities, automation has become a possibility even for small libraries. There is no doubt that the encouraging policies of the national government are helping foster change.

STATUS IN THE EARLY 1980s

According to Kumar, "Computerization in the field of library and information work in India started in 1964 with INSDOC's initiative to computerize the compilation of a union catalogue." He further adds that the Reactor Research Centre, Madras; the Tata Institute of Fundamental Research, Bombay; and the Bhabha Atomic Research Centre, Trombay, "have not only taken lead in introducing computerization at the earliest, but have also tried to evolve a comprehensive computerized system."[17]

Kumar collected data in early 1980s. He listed nine institutions in the descending order of the total number of computerized operations.[18] These data appear in Table 10.1.

The ITT library, Madras; the Defence Scientific Information & Documentation Centre, Delhi; the Indian Standards Institution, Delhi; the Structural Engineering Research Centre, Roorkee; the Indian Institute of Petroleum, Dehra Dun;

Table 10.1
Institutions Using Computers in the Early 1990s for Three or More Operations

Institution	Number of Operations Computerized
Reactor Research Centre, Kalpakkam	8
Tata Institute of Fundamental Research Library, Bombay	7
Bhabha Atomic Research Centre, Trombay Technical	6
Library of IDL Chemicals Ltd., Hyderabad	5
Bharat Heavy Electrical Ltd., Hyderabad	5
INSDOC, New Delhi	4
Physical Research Laboratory Library, Ahmedabad	4
National Aeronautical Laboratory Library, Bangalore	4
Documentation Research and Training Centre, Bangalore	3
IIT Library, Kanpur	3

and the Central Food Technological Research Institute, Mysore, had computerized two operations each. Twenty-one of the libraries/information centers had computerized one operation: the ITT library, Delhi; the Hindustan Aeronautics Ltd., Bangalore; the Central Mechanical Engineering Research Institute, Durgapur; the Information Planning & Analysis Group of Electronics Commission, New Delhi; the National Informatics Centre, New Delhi; the Institute of Armament Technology, Pune; the Indian Statistical Institute, Calcutta; the Naval Physical and Oceanographic Laboratory, Cochin; the Indian Institute of Management, Calcutta; the Ahmedabad Textile Industries Research Institute, Ahmedabad; the Central Mine Planning and Design Institute, Ranchi; the Central Leather Research Institute, Chennai; the Central Machine Tools Institute, Bangalore; the Central Drug Research Institute, Lucknow; the Regional Research Laboratory, Hyderabad; the Bharat Heavy Electricals, Delhi; the Computronics India, Mumbai; the Indian Council of Agricultural Research, New Delhi; the University of Delhi, Delhi; the Indian Institute of Petroleum, Dehra Dun; the Punjab Agricultural University, Ludhiana; and the Indian Institute of Science, Bangalore (sponsored by the University Grants Commission).

PRESENT SCENE

Biradar conducted a survey in 1994–1995 to evaluate technological infrastructure of government-funded academic and research libraries. He concluded that "of the total 1,213 government funded academic libraries in the institutions, 339 libraries responded; among them 64 per cent have PCs, 16 per cent have LAN, 9 per cent have UNIX systems, 46 per cent have library automation packages, 23 per cent have CD-ROM drive, 2 per cent have CD-NET, 11 per cent have online facility, 45 per cent have microfiche reader/printers and 23 per cent of them are members of a library network."[19] The infrastructure in academic libraries is improving slowly. These are encouraging signs.

National Documentation Centers

The Indian National Scientific Documentation Centre (INSDOC) is a premier S&T information organization in the country, serving the information needs of the scientists and technologists. It has played a pioneering role in initiating computerization and has made significant contributions in the areas of library automation, database creation, and computer networking.

The functions and services provided by the INSDOC have been largely computerized. A majority of the staff have been trained in handling computers for different purposes.

The INSDOC has access to a large number of international and indigenous databases. Bibliographies are prepared on specific requests on a particular subject using online search facilities.

The INSDOC offers ten indigenous databases ported on its online host system for public access. These are:

1. Polymer Science Literature Database
2. Material Science Bibliographic Database
3. Medicinal and Aromatic Plants Abstracts Database
4. Indian Patents Database
5. Experts Database
6. Database of Standards
7. INSDOC's Serials Contents on Multimedia Database
8. National Union Catalogue of Scientific Serials in India (NUCSSI) Database
9. Metallurgy Database
10. National Science Library Catalogue

The above databases are also available offline.

The INSDOC (New Delhi) has recently brought out the National Union Catalogue of Scientific Serials in India (NUCSSI) database on CD-ROM, which covers holdings information of over four hundred major libraries in India. It is current through 1996.[20]

The INSDOC brings out *Indian Science Abstracts* (ISA) as a bimonthly. From 1990 the ISA is available in electronic form. The *Indian Science Citation Index* is available in machine-readable form from 1990 onward.

The INSDOC has established the Scientific and Industrial Research Network (SIRNET), linking up of S&T institutions throughout the country. Using SIRNET one can send and receive e-mail. It is capable of taking document supply orders and receiving literature search or contents information of select journal output on e-mail. There are now 107 nodes throughout the country.

The INSDOC conducts a number of short-term training courses in computer applications to library and information science activities. In 1993–1994, eight such causes were organized. This has given impetus to computer application in libraries.

The National Social Science Documentation Centre (NASSDOC), New Delhi, installed a computer facility in 1985. It is a member of DELNET. It has facilities for e-mail, CD-ROM searching, and the Internet. The center has acquired a number of databases on CD-ROM in the area of social sciences and allied subjects. It has also created a number of databases in machine-readable form. Some of these include an area studies bibliography, current contents of Indian social science periodicals, conference alert, database of ICSSR research project reports, directory of social science research and training institutions in India, list of social science periodicals, and union catalog of social science periodicals.

The DESIDOC has developed a library automation software called the Defence Libraries Management System (DELMS) in-house. It has computerized the library acquisition, circulation control and serials control. A database of the holdings of Defense Science Laboratory has been created. It has also created a centralized database of the holdings of the libraries and technical information centers of the DRDO. It uses the latest information technology and offers e-mail, online access to a large number of databases, Internet, CD-ROM database search, and so on. From time to time, it organizes training programs in the application of information technology.

National Libraries

A computer center was set up in December 1987[21] at the National Library, Calcutta. The library uses MINISIS for bibliographical control of library operations, and CDS/ISIS is being used to create databases for special areas or subjects. The library developed a standardized chart of diacritics for automated bibliographic services in Indian languages. The computerization program is moving slowly.

The catalog of the National Science Library is available online and covers both monographs and serials. The National Science Library acquires annually more than five hundred periodicals in electronic form on CD-ROMs. The library assists CSIR laboratories in the acquisition of foreign scientific and technical periodicals under the CAP project. A database of serials received under the CAP project has been created. A database of current journals available in the library has also been created.

The National Medical Library (NML) uses Libsys software for cataloging of books, acquisition of books, serials control, information storage and retrieval. The library has applied CDS/ISIS for indexing services. The NML serves as a national focal point of the HELLIS Network (a regional network of Health Literature Library and Information Service in Southeast Asia) and uses MEDLINE and POPLINE databases on CD-ROM for literature search service.

The Indian Agricultural Research Institute (IARI) library has e-mail, Internet access, and CD Net. It has a good collection of CD-ROM databases. Users are allowed to search these databases themselves. The library has created a database of books, special research bulletins, theses, and so on. It has a facility for OPAC.

University Libraries

A survey of university libraries was conducted in 1994–1995. It was found that "out of the 156 universities, 72 universities have responded and 60 per cent of them have PCs, 7 per cent have LAN, 6 per cent have UNIX, 43 per cent have library automation packages, 17 per cent have CD-ROM drives, 3 per cent have CD-Net, 1 per cent have online facility, 42 per cent have microfiche reader-printers and 64 per cent of them are members of library networks. They subscribe to 34 CD-ROM databases."[22]

University libraries are now giving their attention to creating databases. As of March 1998, twenty university libraries had more than thirty thousand records, seven between fifteen thousand and thirty thousand, three between three thousand and fifteen thousand, and ten had fewer than five thousand records.[23]

University libraries in the United States and United Kingdom have been in the forefront of library automation. However, university libraries in India have been lagging behind with a few notable exceptions:

The University of Hyderabad library, NEHU library, Jawaharlal Nehru University library, and Panjab University library, for instance, have been quite active in this regard.

The Indira Gandhi Memorial Library, University of Hyderabad, started automation in 1989. Now it has sixteen PCs, four multimedia systems, seven drive CD-ROM net, flatbed and handheld scanners, and so on. The entire book collection is in machine-readable form. The library is connected to Campus Network. Thus the users from various points on the campus can access the library catalog. The library has computerized all its in-house operations. For OPAC, six PCs have been provided for users. The introduction of bar codes has strengthened the circulation counter. The library has e-mail and Internet facilities and has access to the Institute of Physics electronic journal online, World Book literature, and so forth. The library uses INET connectively to access INFLIBNET databases.[24]

North-Eastern Hill University Library (Shillong) introduced computerization in 1989. The library has facilities for e-mail, the Internet, CD-ROM searches, fax, and CD-Net. Fourteen CD-ROM databases are available. It subscribes to OCLC (online union catalog). Sections of the library have been connected through local area network (LAN). The departments and centers of studies of the university can access through a network, library bibliographic databases from their departments and centers. Over fifty thousand records of the library collection have been created as a database for computer access.

The Jawaharlal Nehru University Library, New Delhi, has created bibliographic records of books and articles from periodicals in social sciences, the humanities, and science and technology. It has facilities for e-mail.

Panjab University Library has a computer network, CD-ROM server, Internet, fax, and e-mail facilities.

College Libraries

The UGC has given grants to selected colleges for computerization. In 1996–1997, 168 colleges were provided Rs. 1.25 lakh each for purchase of two PC/XT, one printer, one AC and one servo voltage stabilizer. On the whole, college libraries have been neglected compared with university libraries.

A number of college libraries of the University of Delhi have initiated application of computer. These include the Hindu College Library, the Sri Ram College of Commerce Library, the Dayal Singh College Library (evening), the College of Business Studies, and the University Medical College.

Specialized colleges in the fields of engineering, agriculture, and medicine, for example, are far ahead of other colleges in the matter of computerization. Visvesvaraya Regional College of Engineering (NAGPUR) has computerized its library. It has created an OPAC (Online Public Access Catalog), it provides

CD-ROM search, and its circulation has been computerized. The College of Business Studies, Delhi, has computerized its acquisition and cataloging functions.

The Kasturba Medical College Library, Manipal, has computerized its serials control and provided computerized SDI to its teachers. It has thirty CD-ROM disks and provides CD-ROM database searches. The ABSM College of Dental Sciences Library, Mangalore, has computerized its catalog, has local area network facility, and provides CD-ROM database searches. These are but a few examples.

School Libraries

Leading public schools have initiated computerization of their libraries. Delhi Public School, R. K. Puram, New Delhi, has computerized circulation and catalogue. Overdue notices, list of daily issue, and subject lists have been computerized. Internet access is also available for students and teachers.

Special Libraries

The main players in the area of library automation in recent years in India have been the special libraries. They have been in the forefront of library automation. There are several factors that have favored the adoption of new technologies in these libraries. According to Haravu,

although most of these are publicly funded, they function relatively autonomously and so decision making is easier. Secondly, special libraries are under pressure to deliver more efficient services and to provide better and wider access to information. The easy and wide availability of personal computers has undoubtedly contributed to special libraries being able to automate their libraries and to their building of specialized databases. The one factor that has probably made the greatest contribution to automation in special libraries in India is the free availability of Unesco's Micro CDS/ISIS and the relative ease with which it is possible to build specialized databases using CDS/ISIS.[25]

Libraries attached to R&D institutions under the Council of Scientific and Industrial Research (CSIR), the Indian Council for Medical Research, the Indian Council for Agricultural Research (ICAR), and the Defence Research and Development Organization (DRDO) have been quite active in computer application. In addition, libraries belonging to private and public sector industrial R&D organizations such as Bharat Heavy Electricals Limited (BHEL) and Steel Authority of India (SAIL) have made good progress.

The Library of ICRA, Ltd., uses software such as Oracle, Netscape Communication, MS Internet Explorer, MS Office, and Lotus Smartsuite. It has generated five databases, namely, Clinele (a financial database of companies with six thousand records), Prowess (an industrial information database about prospects, government plans, etc. with six thousand records), VANS (a database of articles in full texts from leading financial newspapers and also business magazines from January 1995 onward with twenty thousand records), annual reports (three thousand to four thousand records). It also has facility for CD-ROM database searches and the Internet.

The Library of the Indian Institute of Health Management Research, Jaipur, is fully computerized (acquisition, cataloging, circulation, and serial control). It uses the LibSys software package. A CD-ROM workstation, an audiovisual unit, an e-mail system connected with ERNET and GEMS-400 network and micro-earth station (U-SAT 4), establishing direct computer communication facility with NICNET, have been set up in the library. The library provides access to international databases such as Popline-CD, Health Plan–CD, MEDLINE, AIDSLINE, AIDS DRUGS, and others. Efforts are under way to set up an electronic library.

There are four Indian Institutes of Management at Ahmedabad, Bangalore, Calcutta, and Lucknow whose libraries are well equipped with computer hardware and software, which are used for various library operations. The libraries are working with PC-based, single users and stand-alone computer systems and software. Although their computer systems and library software are not suitable for resource sharing and networking, they are taking steps to rectify this. The Indian Institute of Management Library, Calcutta, has installed an INTEL 8046 system with three terminals in the LAN environment and it has also acquired MAITRAYEE, a software package for the purpose.

Public Libraries

Public libraries are lagging behind in information technology. Photocopy machines are common on public libraries. Some public libraries have initiated computer applications, but otherwise the scene is bleak. The Delhi Public Library has initiated computerization.

SOFTWARE

Libraries are using a wide variety of library-specific software applications. Many are compatible on IBM PC/XT/AT. The CDS/ISIS software developed by UNESCO predominates. This package is available at a nominal cost to nonprofit organizations. Commercial packages, despite their higher costs, are being increasingly used by libraries. LibSys is a good example of a widely used commercial package. There are some in-house-created software applications being used in libraries. The IIT library, Kanpur, for example, use iit KLAS.

Some of the library-specific software packages being used in Indian libraries appear in Table 10.2.

CDS/ISIS

Computerized Documentation Service/Integrated Set of Information Systems (CDS/ISIS) was developed by UNESCO. The CDS/ISIS is a software package. The latest version is 3.0, which provides facility for LAN. It is being promoted by

Table 10.2
Library Specific Application Software Packages in Use

Organization/Manufacturer	Package
Amita Consultants, Bombay	NILIS
Blitz Adio-Visuals, Pune	Libary Management Software
Computer Maintenance Corporation Limited	MAITRAYEE
Datamatics Consultants Pvt Ltd., Bombay	Library Management
Datapro Consultancy Services, Pune	LIBMAN
Defence Science Information and Documentation Centre, Delhi	DELMS and Sanjay
ET&T	SOFT LIB
Frontier Information Technologies Pvt Ltd, Secundrabad	LIBRIS
Golden Age Software Technologies, Bombay	GOLDEN LIBRA
IIT Library, Kanpur	iit KLAS
Hindustan Computers Ltd, Bangalore	UNILIB
IVY Systems Ltd, New Delhi	LIBRA
Kasbah Systems Software, Madras	LIBMAN
LibSys Corporation Pvt Ltd, New Delhi	LibSys
M N Dastur & Co. Ltd.	Libin Fo
MIPS India Ltd	Library Management Software
Minifax Electronics Systems Pvt Ltd, Bombay	ARCHIVES (1, 2, 3)
National Informatics Centre, New Delhi	BASIS plus, TECH LIB plus
National Institute of Science, Technology & Development Studies, New Delhi	Trishna
Nirmal Institute of Computer Expertise, Tiruchirapalli	NIRMALS
Ober Information System, Calcutta	ACQAS, ASCAT, ASCIR, SERAS, ASIRE
Pragathi Computers Pvt Ltd, Madras	Integrated Library Management Software
RACSMA, Bangalore	Raisma Library Management

Table 10.2 continued

Softlink India, N. Delhi	OASIS
Soft-AID, Pune	Librarian, Ver. 3.0
Systems Data Controls Pvt. Ltd., Bombay	Library Manager
Tata Unisys, Noida	TULIP
U&I Software Pvt Ltd., Bangalore	Library Management System
UNESCO (Distributed by National Information System for Science and Technology, New Delhi)	CDS/ISIS
Uptron-India Ltd., New Delhi	SALIM
Wipro Information Technology Ltd., Secunderabad	WILISYS

UNESCO and distributed in India by the NISSAT, the DSIR, the government of India, and New Delhi at a nominal cost for not-for-profit organizations.

CDS/ISIS has played an important role in computerization of libraries in India. As of September 31, 1992, there were 775 installations of a mini-micro-version of CDS/ISIS. Today the number of installations has increased to one thousand, two hundred. This package was being "supplied free of cost by NISSAT to non-profit making organizations, so this was the most prominent reason for its acquisition by a large number of libraries."[26] This highly rated package is used mainly for information storage and retrieval.

It is basically a bibliographic database creation software package. It enables one to create a good bibliographic database and to retrieve information on almost all fields. It is a menu-driven generalized information storage and retrieval system particularly meant for the computerized management of structured textual databases. Being generalized in nature, it can handle different types of databases. It can also handle Indian-language materials with the help of a GIST card. It possesses the facility of accepting interface programs written in CDS/ISIS Pascal. Doing library automation with CDS/ISIS is not possible because this requires a real library automation software package.

In one survey[27] of nineteen libraries using CDS/ISIS, it was found that it is being used for bibliographic information storage and retrieval system (eighteen libraries), serials acquisition and control system (five libraries), a monographic (nonserial documents) acquisition system (two libraries), a document circulation system (one library), personnel information management system (one library), and a financial management system (one library).

The Delhi Library Network (DELNET) has recommended that its members design their databases in CDS/ISIS.

The products being produced using CDS/ISIS include:

Bibliographies
Indexes
Current awareness services
Abstracts bulletin
OPAC
SDI
Lists of various kinds (lists of vendors, list of participants to a conference/seminar etc.)

A selected list of libraries using CDS/ISIS include:

Central War Commission, New Delhi
Dayal Singh College (Evening), New Delhi
Development Library-cum-Resource Centre and Archives, YMCA, New Delhi
India International Centre, New Delhi
Indian Institute of Public Administration, Delhi
Indian Institute of Technology, New Delhi
Institute of Defence Studies and Analysis, New Delhi
Indian Statistical Institute, New Delhi
Jawaharlal Nehru University, New Delhi
National Institute of Educational Planning and Administration, New Delhi
National Institute for Entrepreneurship and Small Business Development, Hyderabad
National Institute of Fashion Technology, New Delhi
National Institute of Immunology, New Delhi
National Institute of Science, Technology, and Development Studies, New Delhi
National Science Library, New Delhi
National Social Science Documentation Centre, New Delhi
Planning Commission, New Delhi
Tata Consultancy Services, New Delhi
Tata Energy Research Institute, New Delhi

In libraries where CDS/ISIS is used, there were very often initial difficulties in designing databases because of difficult-to-understand instructions in the manual. Unfortunately, most often libraries have not used controlled vocabulary, leading to problems.

According to Bhargava and colleagues,[28] the package is not capable of handling numerical operations like the calculations of overdue documents, budgetary allocations, and the expenditure on acquisition. It is not suitable for interconnecting two or more databases for a single application (e.g., linking an acquisition system with the online catalog and circulation systems), and it does not update inverted files automatically (e.g., whenever a change is made in the database). Moreover, the purchase price should be a consideration but not a major factor in the choice of a software.

A Hindi version of CDS/ISIS, version 2.3 named TRISHNA, has been developed by the NISTADS with the collaboration of the NISSAT. The DESIDOC has developed a library software package named SANJAY that uses CDS/ISIS Pascal interface.

The Columbia Library System

The Columbia Library System was developed by Columbia Computing Services of Canada. It is not easily available. Shastri Indo-Canadian Institute Library, New Delhi is using it. They are using it for information storage and retrieval.

DELMS

DELMS (Defence Library Management System) has been developed by the DESIDOC for defense libraries in India. This software can perform all library activities. It is available free of cost to libraries attached to the DRDO. The Solid State Physics Laboratory, Delhi, is using DELMS for bibliographic information storage and retrieval, circulation control, serials acquisition, and control. The products are indexes, bibliographies, and CAS.

iit-KLAS

iit-KLAS, a library software program, has been designed and developed at IIT Kanpur by a team of library professionals and software experts from the Central Library and Department of Computer Science and Engineering. This software has been in use at the IIT Kanpur, Central Library, for over four years. The software has four modules (acquisitions, cataloging, circulation and serials control modules). In addition, an online academic information center (AIC) serves as a window through which members search and view information generated by other modules. The AIC features user services such as online catalog search, current contents search, new arrivals, journal subscriptions, journal holdings, circulation queries, current contents profile entry, and book indent queries. The AIC is available not only over the campus local area network but also on the ERNET Wide Area Network.

iit-KLAS has been supplied to several institutions and has proved to be quite successful in terms of its performance and reliability. It is easy to use and offers comprehensive functionality. It is not tied to any computer make or model but can be run on a range of host computers, from desktop micros to mainframes.

ILMS

ILMS (Integrated Library Management Software) has been developed jointly by the DESIDOC and INFLIBNET. The software has been designed to work under DOS and Unix environments. Cataloging and circulation modules have been completed and installed in libraries. Acquisition and serial control modules are under development.

LIBRIS

LIBRIS software was produced by Frontier Software Technology, Hyderabad. DELNET uses LIBRIS for developing the union catalog of books, but it has not proved successful, due to lack of after sales technical support. Also, it did not fully meet the requirements of library professionals.

LibSys

LibSys is a library-specific software application used by over 125[29] libraries, including university, special, and government libraries. It is a comprehensive and integrated library software package that supports various activities such as acquisition, cataloging, circulation, indexing and abstracting of articles, OPAC, and so on. In addition, it can be used for providing information services and products, such as current awareness service, SDI, and compilation of indexes and bibliographies.

LibSys is a menu-driven and multiuser system and is user-friendly. Library staff can start using it without any prerequisite programming knowledge or computer skill.

The installation procedure is easy enough. It allows user-defined security and minimum possible data entry and provides database recovery procedure and help facility at every stage. It also has a powerful editing facility and supports networking of libraries.

LibSys can work on the following kinds of machines/computer systems:

UNIX
XENIX
DOS
LAN (Novell)
Windows (single user)
Windows (multiuser)

LibSys does have certain shortcomings, however. It does not support the Colon classification system. There is no provision for thesaurus construction.

Customer support is poor, as is R&D support of the company. Due to customization, there is a lack of standardization of functions, processes, and various outputs in libraries. A source code is not provided by the company to its users. Thus users are completely dependent on the company and they are forced to sign an annual maintenance contract with the company. Finally, its increasing popularity has led to the software's rising costs.

LibSys is considered quite a good system by its users. It is increasingly being adopted by Indian libraries. Many libraries previously used other software programs (developed in-house or purchased from the companies), which have now switched to LibSys. There are also many libraries that initially used CDS/ISIS and that have now shifted to LibSys. These include the British Council Library, New Delhi, the Indian Agricultural Research Institute Library, New Delhi, the Indian Institute of Technology Library, Kharagpur, the National Chemical Laboratory Library, Pune, and the Tata Energy Research Institute Library, New Delhi.

MAITRAYEE

MAITRAYEE[30] is an integrated software package developed by the Computer Maintenance Corporation Limited. It is meant for library automation and networking and operates in a multiuser environment. As it is based on INGRES, it proves costly for network participants who are required to buy the INGRES library. This software is being used in CALIBNET (Calcutta Libraries Network) for computerization and networking of libraries of Calcutta. The Indian Institute of Management (Mumbai) also uses it and has also installed the INTEL 80486 system (Micro Computer System) in the LAN environment.

MINISIS

MINISIS was developed by the International Development Research Centre of Canada for information storage and retrieval. It is a software suitable for bibliographic, library information management, and textual database applications. It operates on mini- and supermini-computers. It has been developed to run on the HP 3000 family of computer systems.

The following are some of the libraries using MINISIS: the Central Secretariat Library, New Delhi; the Indira Gandhi National Centre for Arts Library, New Delhi; the Centre for Development of Instructional Technology (CENDIT) Library, New Delhi; the Asia Pacific Centre for Technology Transfer (APCTT) Library, Bangalore; the Central Water Commission Library, New Delhi; the Centre for Biomedical Information Library, NIC, New Delhi; the Jawaharlal Nehru University Library, New Delhi; the Prime Minister's Secretariat Library, New Delhi; and the National Council of Applied Economic Research (NCAER) Library, New Delhi.

The Jawaharlal Nehru University Library and the Central Water Commission Library adopted MINISIS as it was available free of cost. The training facility was also free of cost. The former uses it only for bibliographic information storage and retrieval, whereas the latter uses it for information storage and retrieval, acquisition system, membership information, serial control system, SDI, and CAS. The National Council of Applied Economic Research, New Delhi, brings out the indexing journal Artha Suchi, using an IBM HP-3000 computer and MINISIS software.

SANJAY

SANJAY was developed by the DESIDOC[31] initially for DST Library. It interfaces thirty-five Pascal programs with micro-CDS/ISIS. It operates in a multiuser environment. The Documentation Centre of the National Institute of Immunology, New Delhi, has been using SANJAY since 1992. It uses this software for acquisition, information storage and retrieval, membership, circulation, serials acquisition and control. The library has been providing CAS and bibliographies.

TECHLIBplus

National Informatics Centre is a reseller in India of BASICplus with TECHLIBplus, software products from Information Dimensions Inc. BASICplus is an electronic document management system (covers full-text retrieval, thesaurus, etc.). TECHLIBplus is a comprehensive library automation package (OPAC, cataloging, acquisition, serials control, circulation, MARC support).

HARDWARE

Most of the libraries have PC AT (286 and above). Most of the computerizing libraries possess their own computer systems. As a consequence, they are able to use these systems for library application without any restrictions. Of course, in some cases they use only the parent organization's computer facilities. In certain cases, the library may have its own computer system and also have access to the parent body's computer facilities. The Library of the National Physical Laboratory has PCs and access to the parent body's main frame computer.

TRAINING

To enable librarians to initiate computerization in their libraries, training courses are organized by various organizations.

The National Information System for Science and Technology (NISSAT) has played a very important role in promoting computer culture in library and information environment in India. It has supported financially different national level associations and institutions to organize workshops for training manpower in computer application. It has also distributed CDS/ISIS at a nominal cost to nonprofit organizations.

National associations like the Indian Library Association, the IASLIC, and the AGLIS have played an important part in organizing training courses, workshops, seminars, and so on on computer application. In one year alone, the Indian Library Association organized eleven workshops for training manpower in computer application.[32]

The INSDOC is a premier S&T information organization in India, serving the needs of the scientific community. To train manpower, it organizes computer-based training programs every year. These consist of short-term training courses (varying from two days to five weeks) and attachment training programs. The training content and schedule for attachment training programs are "specifically designed for each participant individual or group of trainees taking into account the professional background and needs."[33] The duration may vary between one week and six months. Between 1996 and 1997, nine short-term training courses were conducted on different topics.

The INFLIBNET, in collaboration with other organizations, has conducted a number of training courses on applications of computers to library and information services, which run for three to four weeks. The first course was organized in November–December 1992. So far fourteen training courses have been conducted for operational library staff.

The INFLIBNET program provides on-site training to operational staff working in participating libraries. Teams of technical staff visit the participating libraries for giving "necessary assistance in the installation of Unix-based library management software (ILMS), database creation activities, remote access, e-mail, online, use of GIST card and bar code etc."[34] Already INFLIBNET staff has assisted twelve universities for providing on-site training.

The INFLIBNET organized three workshops, in collaboration with other organizations in February 1994 and February 1995. These workshops, organized for library executives on management of modernized libraries, lasted for two weeks each.

The library under the Centre of Distance Education, University of Hyderabad, started in 1998 a postgraduate diploma in library automation and networking. This two-semester specialized course is the first of its kind. The experiment shall be watched with interest.

CONVENTIONS

The INFLIBNET organizes on an annual basis the National Convention for Automation of Libraries in Education and Research (Caliber). The first convention was held in 1994 at Ahmedabad; the theme was library automation. The themes of the 1995, 1996, 1997 and 1998 conventions were information access through networks, library database management, information technology applications in academic libraries, and information management in academic and research libraries, respectively.

REPROGRAPHICS

Since the late 1980s, reprographic facilities have gained momentum due to the following reasons:

1. Availability of state-of-the-art document reproduction systems (such as paper photo-copiers and microfilm copiers)
2. Funding by grant-giving bodies such as UGC
3. Increasing commercialization of document reproduction (paper photocopiers) services.

On college and university campuses, such services are well established.

With respect to reprographics, "the main handicap is that technology is developing at such a rapid pace that machines installed today become obsolete in a couple of years. Their replacement and maintenance pose big problems to the institutions due to rising costs and the budgets not keeping pace with inflationary trends."[35] As a consequence, libraries are encouraging private vendors to install their machines on the campus or even within the library.

REPRODUCTION OF CATALOG CARDS

There are a variety of methods being used for reproduction of catalog cards. These include use of automatic typewriters (under such trade names as Flexowriter and Justowriter, e.g., and the product is in the form of punched tape, usually paper), wax-stencil duplication (e.g., flat-bed machines), xerography, offset printing, letterpress printing and computer printout.

Small flat-bed duplicators used for duplicating catalog cards are becoming quite popular. These are hand-driven, cheap, and give good results. There is no need for special training; anyone can handle them easily. Such types of duplicators are being manufactured in India.

One such machine is the Card-O-Print card duplicator, manufactured by Donewell Rotaries, New Delhi. A wax-stencil master is cut by means of a typewriter. The cut stencil and a card are placed in the machine. The cover of the machine is moved once for each printout. Such a machine can be used for small printing jobs like catalog cards, labels, invitations, name slips, and so on.

The INFLIBNET program has developed the Application Interface Program for generating catalog cards on CDS/ISIS. The program generates catalog cards of various types (main and added entries) as per AACR2 format from data in ISO-2709 format having standard tags from CCF.[36]

MACHINES FOR VARIOUS LIBRARY PURPOSES

There are a variety of machines available on the market for many library purposes. These include:

Book-insect killing machine (electric), which is used for spraying powerful vapors and fumes to kill insects and their eggs

Dust cleaner

Electric stylus, which is used for writing permanently the name of the book, its call number, and other information on the binding of a book

Letter embossing machine, which is used for embossing letters, names, and so on on self-adhesive tape

Library laminating machine, which is used for laminating newspapers, articles, old important papers, library cards/tickets, and so on

Multipurpose paper cutting-stitching machine, which is used for stapling, cutting and trimming.

The above machines are manufactured in India, as are the materials used with them. These machines are being used increasingly in Indian libraries, and a wide choice of products is available.

INDIGENOUS DATABASES

There is a dearth of indigenous databases, and international databases provide meager coverage of Indian contributions. Thus there is a need for indigenous databases in different fields. According to Gredby and Hopkinson, "India has for long had databases set up by specialist libraries and documentation centers rather than by national, public and academic libraries."[37] Thus national institutions/organizations should do this job seriously. Public and academic libraries should undertake the designing of databases on a large scale so as to improve access to information sources.

STANDARD FOR BIBLIOGRAPHIC DESCRIPTION

The Bureau of Indian Standards[38] has formulated IS:11370-1985 for exchanging the bibliographic records in machine-readable form. This standard defines the structure of the communication format and presents guidelines for the exchange of bibliographic records of any kind of documents. This standard is being used widely. Indian MARC is very closely based on UK MARC, 1985.

COMMERCIAL AGENCIES

Commercial agencies are coming forward in the field of information handling. Informatics (India) Private Limited is located in Bangalore and was the first to introduce CD-ROM technology in India. It helps install a system in a library and provides online access to five hundred databases through global data networks. The company builds databases and also provides training.

Softlink India, New Delhi, provides the following services:

1. Free consultation, preparation of project proposal, and project implementation
2. Data entry of library collection
3. Total library automation and/or library computerization, on a turnkey basis
4. Training and support services for OASIS, a library automation software package

Programme Management Division (PMD) of the INSDOC identifies agencies for undertaking projects sponsored by them. The division "prepares the proposals for submission to external agencies for undertaking their projects, negotiates with them and pursues the proposals till the final sanction. Once the proposal is approved by the sponsoring agency, PMD identifies the team members of INSDOC and monitors the progress of the projects."[39]

The INSDOC has undertaken many projects. One such project was about setting up a resource sharing network system for Chennai given by the MALIBNET Society. It has implemented a turnkey project for establishing nodes under the Scientific and Industrial Research Network (SIRNET) for connecting the offices of the Central Pollution Control Board, the State Pollution Control Boards, and the Ministry of Environment and Forests to achieve communication facilities. Communication facilities refer to the telephone lines, fax, and library and information network.

INFLIBNET

The INFLIBNET program of the UGC was initiated with its headquarters at Ahmedabad in 1991. Under this program, the Information and Library Network Centre (INFLIBNET) has been established at Ahmedabad. The center has become the Interuniversity Centre. The INFLIBNET has been registered as an autonomous society at Ahmedabad in May 1996 with countrywide jurisdiction. Its program is a project of the Inter University Consortium for Astronomy and Astrophysics (IUCAA). It is a cooperative venture in resource development, sharing, and utilization. Its main aims are:[40]

1. To establish a national network of libraries and information centers in universities, colleges, institutes of higher learning and R&D institutions in India
2. To modernize libraries and information centers
3. To establish a mechanism for information transfer and access to support scholarship, learning, and academic pursuits
4. To facilitate resources development, sharing, and utilization

During the last few years, the UGC has provided funds under the INFLIBNET program to university libraries for the purpose of (a) procuring computer hardware and software, (b) establishing of the communication facilities, and (c) converting retrospective data in machine-readable form.

Fifty-four university libraries had been funded until March 1996. The UGC provided a special grant of Rs. 1 lakh for establishing a core facility for providing access to information in those university libraries, which had not received funding for the establishment of computerization and networking facilities. This amount was provided on the condition that the concerned university shall "bear the expenses towards providing a telephone in library, subscribe to data networks and take care of recurring expenditure."[41]

Fifteen universities were funded during the 1996–1997 year for computerization and automation of their libraries. Also, the UGC provided a special grant of
Rs. 1 lakh to all those universities that did not get a normal grant, which is given
for automating libraries and maintenance, under the INFLIBNET program by the
end of 1996–1997. Special grant was given to establish core facilities for information access. The UGC has funded eighteen universities under the INFLIBNET
program during 1997–1998.

All these university libraries have been given Rs. 6.5 lakhs like the previous 69, as one time
grant for the purchase of computers, network related equipment, subscribing to telephone
lines, and preparing the sites, etc. These universities will also be supported for the first five
years with a recurring grant to meet the salary of 'Information Scientist', data entry work,
telephone charges, consumables and maintenance charges. Libraries funded under this programme will have to sign Memorandum of Understanding, follow the guidelines with respect to data base creation and automation of libraries given by the INFLIBNET. These
libraries will also be provided with Integrated Library Management Software being developed by INFLIBNET. All the participating libraries are expected to contribute the data to
the union databases being created at the Centre and share the resources."[42]

The INFLIBNET center has created a national database of two thousand experts
in various disciplines in science, technology, humanities, social sciences, and so
forth.

NETWORKING

Realizing the importance of sharing data, two kinds of networks have been
launched: general purpose and specific purpose networks.

General Purpose Networks

General purpose networks can be used to access e-mail, the Internet, the
INFLIBNET union catalog online, and other national or international databases.
Some of the leading networks, such as ERNET, NICNET, I-NET, GIAS, SIRNET
and INDONET, have already been mentioned.

Government data networks include ERNET (Education and Research Network), NICNET, I-NET, and GIAS (Gateway Internet Access Service) of VSNL.

ERNET is operated by the ERNET Project of the Department of Electronics,
government of India. Using ERNET, one can send and receive e-mail from any
part of the world. One can also access foreign databases online via the Internet.

NICNET is a network of the National Informatics Centre, under the Planning
Commission. It provides e-mail to academic institutions under the RENNIC project. There is no INTERNET access.

I-NET is a network of the Department of Telecommunications. It does not provide e-mail on its own, but does provide a means of transferring data to the other
end. The INFLIBNET recommends university libraries to subscribe to I-NET. A

library having an I-NET account can access[43] (1) the INFLIBNET Union Catalogue; (2) the nearest ERNET node without using normal STD, which reduces considerably telecommunication charges; and (3) the Internet (text only, no graphics) in a cost effective way (one has to subscribe to GIAS in addition).

GIAS charges a registration fee of Rs. 500. The subscription rate for an institution is Rs. 5,000 per year for five hundred hours. By subscribing to GIAS, one can have access to both e-mail and the Internet; information will be presented in a textual form only. However, by paying a subscription of Rs. 15,000, one can access information in both text and graphic forms.

SIRNET (the Scientific and Industrial Research Network) of the INSDOC/CSIR links S&T establishments of CSIR. It provides e-mail facility among the laboratories and also access to indigenous databases of the INSDOC.

The INDONET is a computer communication network of the Computer Maintenance Corporation.[44] It provides facilities for distributed data processing, software export, and making computer power available to people. It provides services like e-mail, file transfer, software library service, and access to networks abroad.

Specific Purpose Networks (Library Networks)

Due to escalating costs of documents and perpetual budget cuts, Indian libraries are facing acute resource crunch problems. The solution lies in resource sharing, and toward that end a number of networks have been launched at various levels.

Due to the support provided by the NISSAT, a number of metropolitan city library networks have been created for resource sharing. These include ADINET (for Ahmedabad), BALNET (for Bangalore), BONET (for Mumbai), CALIBNET (for Calcutta), DELNET (for Delhi), MALIBNET (for Chennai), MYLIBNET (for Mysore), and PUNENET (for Pune).

The INFLIBNET took the initiative to start ADINET (Ahmedabad Libraries Network), a city network sponsored by the NISSAT/DSIR for initially linking libraries of about thirty-two important institutions in Ahmedabad. It was formally inaugurated on March 25, 1995, and it has since been registered as a society. This network is being used as a test-bed for the INFLIBNET.[45]

BALNET (Bangalore Library Network) was inaugurated on June 26, 1995. It is a nonprofit-making body, which works on sharing the responsibilities by participation.

CALIBNET (Calcutta Library Network) was conceived in 1986 as a network for the Calcutta metropolitan area. It is largely government funded. The NISSAT provided a grant to initiate the network. Its members comprise thirty-eight libraries.

The Delhi Library Network has been in operation since January 1988 and was registered as a society in July 1992, sponsored by the NISSAT, Department of Scientific and Industrial Research, government of India. It is being promoted by the National Informatics Centre, Planning Commission, government of India, and the India International Centre, New Delhi.

Its main objects are "to promote sharing of resources among the libraries by developing a network of libraries, by collecting, storing and disseminating information and by offering computerised services to the users to coordinate efforts for suitable collection development and reducing unnecessary duplication wherever possible."[46] Thirty-one institutions are institutional members; three are associate institutional members. In addition to use by the institutional and associate institutional members, e-mail is also used by nine other institutions.

The admission fee is Rs. 5,000, institutional membership Rs. 5,000 per year. Associate institutional membership is Rs. 10,000 per year and subscription to e-mail is Rs. 5,000 per year.

DELNET provides the following facilities:[47]

1. Maintains an online union catalog of books available in its member libraries. On October 1, 1994, the union catalog had 91,957 bibliographic records with 105,819 locations data.

2. Provides e-mail to its members, which was developed by the Department of Electronics, government of India. Forty-three libraries use DELNET e-mail. The member libraries have access to ERNET users and also to Internet users. The members can also use RENNIC mail facility of National Informatics Centre, which allows them e-mail access with facilities to search national and international databases.

3. Provides access to its members to different databases maintained by National Informatics Centre of the Planning Commission. DELNET also provides access to international databases through DIALOG.

4. Maintains a union list of current serials available in Delhi libraries with the support of the NISSAT and cooperation of the Jawaharlal Nehru University Library.

5. Offers retroconversion facilities to the libraries through specialized agencies and also facilitates the use of modern tools such as CD-ROMs and online facilities for retroconversion purposes.

6. Promotes interlibrary loans through the use of online union catalog, e-mail, and courier service.

7. Conducts training programs in the use of CDS/ISIS and e-mail.

8. Maintains a referral center that provides reference facilities to participating libraries. The referral center also looks after the access to the central database and monitors access to international databases like Blaise-line.

9. Organizes national workshops and meets.

10. Helps the participating libraries in the creation of bibliographic databases.

11. Provides technical assistance in the computerization of libraries and gives advice on hardware requirements.

12. Organizes lectures by networking specialists.

DELNET publishes a newsletter to spread awareness about library networking in India. It provides information about advances, achievements, and needs of libraries and their services.

It is making steady progress. It has been claimed that "DELNET helped its member libraries in saving nearly Rs. one crore in foreign exchange by rationalisation of subscriptions to foreign periodicals in Delhi libraries during 1991–1994."[48]

There is no doubt that DELNET is beginning to play a major role in the creation, storage, dissemination, and exchange of information in Delhi.

MALIBNET (the Madras Library Network) was registered as a society in Chennai in February 1993. MALIBNET was inaugurated in June 1993. A main computer system has been acquired, installed, and made operational with no direct funding from the government. Five institutions (Anna University, IIT (Madras), CLRI, Madras University, and Mat Science) have already been linked.

MAJOR PROBLEMS

Major problems faced in automating the libraries may be grouped into these categories:[49]

1. Enough manpower having necessary computer skills is not available
2. Nonavailability of suitable and adequate IT infrastructure
3. Design, development, and maintenance of machine-readable catalogs with certain standards. A major problem is regarding how to create a machine-readable catalog of in-house collections.
4. Lack of proper AMC services and consultancy services, especially in those libraries located in remote places
5. Lack of proper infrastructure—space, continuous power supply, telecommunication facility, and so on
6. Limited budgets and increasing costs of systems.

These problems also exist in other types of libraries. Academic libraries may claim at least one advantage in that they generally have an on-campus computer department or center that can provide advice and even some support services.

SUGGESTIONS

Ravichandra Rao[50] has suggested that to accelerate the development of automation in India, further attempts must be made to:

1. Organise a series of intensive courses on computer applications to library and information works, for different levels of people.
2. Introduce three compulsory papers on programming and system analysis, library automation, and information retrieval.
3. Encourage students (at the MLibSC and MPhil levels) to write dissertations in the area of library automation and information retrieval.
4. Conduct cooperative projects at the regional levels to develop software exclusively for library automation and information retrieval.
5. Publish Indian Science Abstracts (ISA), Indian National Bibliography and other bibliographical publications in machine-readable form.

6. Use microcomputers for experimental work and instructions at schools of library and information science.

These suggestions are useful ones. Some of these have been implemented and others are being processed.

FUTURE

"In the light of the emergence of the NISSAT programme and India's participation activities in world science information programs, automation activities in India seem to be very promising and it is hoped that there will be considerable development in this area in the near future."[51] This remark is apt.

Library automation seems to be inevitable. The library scene is fast changing and automation activities are picking up. There is increasing awareness of information technology and its application among librarians. There is increasing funding support from agencies such as the UGC, the INFLIBNET, the NISSAT, and other similar organizations. Many metropolitan networks have emerged, which have provided impetus to automation activities in their respective regions. E-mail, CD-ROMs, LAN, machine-readable catalogs, and so forth are being increasingly used for resource sharing now that librarians have realized that resource sharing is a solution to overcoming the problem of scarce resources. Initially library automation meant computerization of housekeeping operations only. Now, when we use the term *library automation*, it covers housekeeping jobs, reader's services (including information services based on CD-ROM databases, e-mail, etc.), management support activities, and even networking.

According to Ravinchandra Rao, "In the immediate future, most of the academic libraries in India will have a number of both bibliographical and full text CD-ROM databases, and Internet-users can access local, regional, national and international sources; such sources also will be used/accessed by librarians to answer a variety of reference queries. In such an environment, academic librarians must be familiar with the Internet and its operations, availability of sources in Internet, operation of online databases—bibliographic, fulltext, CD-ROM, public access catalogue, and spreadsheet, DTP, etc."[52] This prediction also holds true for other types of libraries. However, by and large school libraries and public libraries are likely to lag behind. The automation program in these libraries will pick up slowly.

CONCLUSION

Special libraries and documentation and information centers were the first to introduce automation. University and college libraries were late starters.

Automation activities in academic libraries in India slowly picked up with the support from INFLIBNET, UGC, NISSAT and other similar agencies combined with increased awareness of IT and its applications among librarians. Academic librarians in India are beginning to use E-mail, CD-ROM, LAN, machine-readable catalog, etc for resource sharing. This change in academic libraries is due to rapidly changing telecommunication and technological environment, a desire for progress and declining resources. Perhaps the key to change is the willingness to share resources and to work together to bring a "change."[53]

Libraries attached to leading public schools have initiated the process of automation. Other kinds of schools have a long way to go before automation becomes a reality. Public libraries are also lagging behind.

A number of metropolitan networks have been formed, which member libraries are using for accessing local, national, and international databases. There is a long way to go before comprehensive indigenous databases become available. A start has been made, but the next few years are crucial in this regard. Use of local networks involves some problems. Often, local libraries have problems due to lack of software or hardware compatibility.

Today many libraries have access to the Internet, thus enabling users to have access to a wide range of sources of information, including international, national, regional and local databases. More and more libraries desire both bibliographical and full-text databases on CD-ROM, which allow librarians to provide answers to a variety of reference questions.

It was observed that "there was a trend towards commercially available library specific application software packages as they needed no more than a clerical skill for data entry. The trend may be attributed to two reasons: lack of initiative and lack of proper training. Some libraries had initially started their computerization programmes with the use of CDS/ISIS and later shifted to some commercial package, while a few other libraries were planning to do so in near future."[54] This observation is significant because a commercially available software, LibSys, is becoming quite popular.

NOTES

1. P.S.G. Kumar, *Computerization of Indian Libraries* (Delhi: B. R. Publishing, 1987), 47.

2. I. K. Ravichandra Rao, *Library Automation*, 2d ed. (New Delhi: Wiley Eastern, 1990), iii.

3. A. S. Raizada et al., "Union Catalogue Processing by Digital Computers," *Annals of Library Science & Documentation* 11 (4) (1964), 54–76; A. S. Raizada, "Computerized Compilation of Union Catalogue," *Annals of Library Science & Documentation* 16 (1969), 88–91.

4. A. S. Raizada, et al., "Directory Compilation by Computers," *Annals of Library Science & Documentation* 14 (2) (June 1967), 89–101.

5. L. J. Haravu and A. S. Raizada, "Computerized Data Retrieval: An Experiment with IBM 1620," *Annals of Library Science & Documentation* 14 (2) (June 1967), 76–78.

6. L. J. Haravu and S. N. Sur, "Author Index to ISA," *Annals of Library Science & Documentation* 14 (2) (March 1967), 9–19; A. S. Raizada et al., "Keyword Index to Indian Science Abstracts," *Annals of Library Science & Documentation* 14 (2) (March 1967), 20–33.

7. A. S. Raizada et al., "Union Catalogue Processing," *Annals of Library Science & Documentation* 16 (2) (1969), 88–92.

8. A. Neelameghan, "Design of the Document Finding System: General Features," *Annals of Library Science & Documentation* 5 (4) (December 1968), 303.

9. V. A. Kamath and N. M. Malwad, "Computerized Information Storage and Retrieval System in India with Special Reference to the Activities of Bhabha Atomic Research Centre." *Proceedings of ISLIC International Conference on Information Science*, vol. 1 (Tel Aviv, ISLIC 1971), 77–89.

10. Kumar, Computerization in Indian Libraries, 275.

11. I. K. Ravichandra Rao, "Application of Computer Technology to Library and Information Services in India," in P. B. Mangla et al., ed., *Fifty Years of Librarianship in India: Past, Present and Future* (Delhi: ILA, 1983), 430.

12. Ibid., 429–430.

13. Rao, *Library Automation*, 6.

14. INFLIBNET Newsletter 4 (1) (January–March 1998), 3.

15. Sandeep Sharma, "Internet—An Emerging Society," *Hipa News Letter*, 5 (3) (1996), 10.

16. N. Vittal, "Information Technology, and Library Networking: The Challenges Ahead" (First DELNET Lecture, New Delhi, 1998), (mimeograph), 5.

17. Kumar, *Computerization of Indian Libraries*, 301.

18. Ibid., 275.

19. S. K. Biradar, "A Report on Organization Study and Market Research for Evaluation of Technological Infrastructure of Government, Academic and Research Libraries for Dissemination of Information to Users." This report was submitted to the Kousali Institute of Management Studies, Dharwad, as a part of an M.B.A. program in 1994–1995. Quoted in I. K. Ravichandra Rao, "Automation of Academic Libraries in India," in *Information Technology Applications in Academic Libraries*, edited by A. L. Moorthy and P. B. Mangla (Ahmedabad: Information and Library Network Centre), 1.

20. *IASLIC Newsletter* (May 1997), 3.

21. D. N. Banerjee, "India's National Library," *Herald of Library Science* 33 (3–4) (July–October 1994), 234.

22. I. K. Ravichandra Rao, "Automation of Academic Libraries in India," in A. L. Moorthy and P. B. Mangla, eds., *Information Technology Applications in Academic Libraries* (Ahmedabad: Information and Library Network Centre, 1997), 1.

23. *INFLIBNET Newsletter* 4 (1) (January–March 1998), 2.

24. Ibid., 5–6.

25. L. J. Haravu, "Library Automation and Networking in India: An Overview of Recent Developments," in C. P. Vashishth, et al., ed., *New Horizons in Library and Information Science* (Madras: T. R. Publications, 1994), 500.

26. Manoj K. Joshi, "Use of CDS/ISIS in Libraries of Delhi: An Analysis," *ILA Bulletin* 28 (3–4) (October–March 1993), 98.

27. Ibid.

28. J. K. Bhargava et al., "Sanjay: An Indian Library Automated Package Based on CDS/ISIS," *Program* 27 (1) (1993), 31–66.

29. "LIBSYS: An Integrated Library Management Software Package." *NISSAT Newsletter* 8 (3) (1989), 9–14.

30. P. Tagore et al., "MAITRAYEE Library Computerisation and Networking Software," *NISSAT Newsletter* 10 (3) (1991), 7–9, 15.

31. DESIDOC Software System Team, "Sanjay: Augmented CDS/ISIS package for library automation," *NISSAT Newsletter*, 10 (3) (1991), 3–6.

32. C. P. Vashishth, et al., ed., *Computerization and Library Network* (Delhi: Indian Library Association, 1991), vii.

33. *Training Course Calendar* (April 1996–March 1997) (N. Delhi: INSDOC, 1996), 3.

34. V. S. Cholin, and K. Prakash, "Status of Computerisation and Networking of University Libraries in India," *CALIBER 97* (1997), 7.

35. Krishan Kumar and N. Datta, "Reprographic Services in Delhi University Library: A Case Study," CLIS *Observer* 3 (1–2) (June–April 1986), 9.

36. *INFLIBNET Newsletter*, 1 (3) (October 1995), 1.

37. Ellen Gredby and Alan Hopkinson, *Exchanging Bibliographic Data: MARC and Other Informational Formats* (Ottawa: Canadian Library Association, 1990), 117.

38. Bureau of Indian Standards. IS: 11370-1985. *Guidelines for the Data Elements and Record Format for Computer-based Bibliographic Databases for Bibliographic Description of Different Kinds of Documents* (New Delhi: Bureau of Indian Standards, 1985).

39. *Annual Report, 1993–94* (New Delhi: INSDOC), 37.

40. Pramod Kumar, "From Director's Desk," *INFLIBNET Newsletter* 1 (1) (April 1995), 1.

41. V. S. Cholin and K. Prakash, "Status of Computerisation and Networking of University Libraries in India," 7.

42. "New Varsities under INFLIBNET," *University News* 36 (38) (September 21, 1998), 21.

43. S. M. Salgar, "Network Services for Libraries," *CALIBER-97* (1997), 79.

44. V. Jain and A. K. Rai, "Education and Research Networks in India: A Brief Note," *CALIBER-97* (1997), 92.

45. *INILIBNET Newsletter* 1 (1) (April 1995), 3.

46. *Delnet* (New Delhi: Delhi Library Network, 1994), (brochure), 2.

47. Ibid., 2–5.

48. Ibid., 3.

49. Rao, "Automation of Academic Libraries in India," 1.

50. Rao, *Library Automation*, 7.

51. Ibid.

52. Rao, "Automation of Academic Libraries in India," 4.

53. Ibid.

54. Joshi, "Use of CDS/ISIS in Libraries of Delhi; An Analysis," 103.

SELECTED BIBLIOGRAPHY

Haravu, L. J. "Library Automation and Networking in India: An Overview of Recent Developments." in C.P. Vashishth et al., ed., *New Horizons in Library and Information Science* (Madras: T. R. Publications 1994), 499–514.

Kamath, V. A., and N. M. Malwad. "Computerized Information Storage and Retrieval System in India with Special Reference to the Activities of Bhabha Atomic Research Centre." *Proceedings of ISLIC International Conference on Information Science*, vol. 1 (Tel Aviv 1971), 77–89.

Kumar, P.S.G. *Computerization of Indian Libraries* (Delhi: B. R. Publishing 1987).

Moorthy, A. L. , and P. B. Mangla, ed. *Information Technology Applications in Academic Libraries in India with Emphasis on Network Services and Information Sharing* (Ahmedabad: Information and Library Network Centre, 1997).

Ravichandra Rao, I. K. "Application of Computer Technology to Library and Information Services in India." In P. B. Mangla et al., ed., *Fifty Years of Librarianship in India: Past, Present and Future* (Delhi: Indian Library Association 1983), 429–450.

———. "Automation of Academic Libraries in India." in A. L. Moorthy and P. B. Mangla, ed., *Information Technology Applications in Academic Libraries* (Ahmedabad: Information and Library Network Centre, 1977).

———. *Library Automation*, 2d ed. (New Delhi: Wiley Eastern, 1999).

Vashishth, C. P. et al., ed., *Computerization and Library Network* (Delhi: Indian Library Association, 1991).

Index

About the Authors

JASHU PATEL is Professor of Library Science and Communication Media at Chicago State University. He holds an M.L.S. and a Ph.D. in Library and Information Science from the University of Pittsburgh. He was a senior Fulbright Scholar that took him to seventeen universities in India and Nepal. He has published several articles on librarianship, as well as chapters in books.

KRISHAN KUMAR was formerly Head of Department of Library and Information Science, University of Delhi. He has been chairman of the editorial board of the *Journal of Library and Information Science*, and editor of the *Library Herald*. He is a past-president of both the Indian Library Association and the Indian Association of Teachers of Library and Information Science. He is the author of numerous articles and several books.